CW00670264

Effective Client Management in Professional Services

This book is dedicated to my wife, Daphne, for her unswerving support.

Effective Client Management in Professional Services

How to Build Successful Client Relationships

JACK BERKOVI

Routledge
Taylor & Francis Group

LONDON AND NEW YORK

First published in paperback 2024

First published 2014 by Gower Publishing

Published 2016 by Routledge
4 Park Square, Milton Park, Abingdon, Oxon OX14 4RN

and by Routledge
605 Third Avenue, New York, NY 10158

Routledge is an imprint of the Taylor & Francis Group, an informa business

Copyright © Jack Berkovi 2014, 2016, 2024

The right of Jack Berkovi to be identified as author of this work has been asserted in accordance with sections 77 and 78 of the Copyright, Designs and Patents Act 1988.

All rights reserved. No part of this book may be reprinted or reproduced or utilised in any form or by any electronic, mechanical, or other means, now known or hereafter invented, including photocopying and recording, or in any information storage or retrieval system, without permission in writing from the publishers.

Trademark notice: Product or corporate names may be trademarks or registered trademarks, and are used only for identification and explanation without intent to infringe.

Publisher's Note
The publisher has gone to great lengths to ensure the quality of this reprint but points out that some imperfections in the original copies may be apparent.

British Library Cataloguing in Publication Data
A catalogue record for this book is available from the British Library

Library of Congress Cataloging-in-Publication Data
Berkovi, Jack.
   Effective client management in professional services : how to build successful client relationships / by Jack Berkovi.
      pages cm
   Includes bibliographical references and index.
   ISBN 978-1-4094-3789-5 (hardback) -- ISBN 978-1-4094-3790-1 (ebook) -- ISBN (invalid) 978-1-4724-0798-6 (epub) 1. Customer services. 2. Service industries--Marketing. 3. Professions--Marketing. I. Title.
   HF5415.5.B465 2014
   658.8'12--dc23

                                                                2014020509

ISBN: 978-1-4094-3789-5 (hbk)
ISBN: 978-1-03-283694-2 (pbk)
ISBN: 978-1-315-57890-3 (ebk)

DOI: 10.4324/9781315578903

Contents

List of Figures

List of Tables

List of Interviewees

These were conducted during the period July 2013–March 2014.

Scott Barnes, CEO, Grant Thornton UK LLP

Sue Best, Marketing Director, ICAEW

Vikki Bingham, Head of Client and Business Development, GVA

Anne Blackie, Head of Bids & Client Care, Grant Thornton UK LLP

Richard Chaplin, Founder, Managing Partners' Forum

Douglas Commaille, Founder, DCLW Consulting

Darren Cox, Global Key Account Manager, Grant Thornton International

Richard Crook, Head of BD, UK/Europe, Savills

Dana Denis-Smith, Founder, Obelisk Legal Support

Dr Charles Doyle, Group Chief Marketing Officer & Global Head of Research, JLL

Nicola Duke, Head of Client Care, Mills & Reeve

Allan Evans, Global Head of Client Service, BDO LLP

Louise Field, Head of Client Service & Insight, Bird & Bird

Philip Gardner, Head of Client Service, Knight Frank

Mark Jeffries, Senior Partner, Mills & Reeve

Rolland Keane, Marketing & Development Director, Penningtons Manches LLP

David Kerr, CEO, Bird & Bird

Sir Nigel Knowles, Global CEO & Managing Partner, DLA Piper

Christian Marroni, Head of Global Media Relations, Freshfields Bruckhaus Deringer LLP

Claire Mason, MD and Founder, Man Bites Dog

Diane Nagy, Head of EMEA CRM, DTZ

Ashley Nicholls, Founder, The Recruitment Site

Jean Stephens, CEO, RSM International

Keith Wells, Director, Redstone Consultants

Interview subjects (Chapters in brackets):

An engaged team, Claire Mason (1)

New CEO simplifies the organisation to improve Client focus, Scott Barnes (1)

Challenges faced in hiring the right talent, Ashley Nicholls (2)

A sector-focused development strategy, Mark Jeffries (3)

How Bird & Bird internationalised its business, David Kerr (3)

How RSM manages its global network, Jean Stephens (3)

Managing global key accounts, Darren Cox (3)

Client focus programmes at Mills & Reeve, Nicola Duke (4)

Client satisfaction programme at Savills, Richard Crook (4)

A passion for Client care, Allan Evans (5)

The challenges of managing a global brand, Bradley Neill (6)

List of Case Studies

Jack Berkovi has produced a first class book on effective Client management with specific reference to professional services firms. The book is very well structured and easy to read, with clever use of pertinent case studies to amplify the points raised. In addition, the author has provided review questions at the end of each chapter as a way of helping the reader consolidate his/her knowledge. Finally, I believe that the book is a must read for partners and senior directors of such firms as it delivers a valuable framework for appreciating effective Client management.

Georges Selim, Emeritus Professor and
former Head of the Faculty of Management, Cass Business School, UK

High quality practical guidance based on the insight gained through career-long reflection and learning is a rare resource. Jack Berkovi provides a structured approach to the processes essential for a properly managed function and this alone makes this a valuable publication. Even more importantly he adds genuine insight into the cultural and 'soft' issues that effective managers need to understand.

Rob Melville, Cass Business School, UK

This is a comprehensive handbook for anyone interested or engaged in this important area. Easy to read and intensely practical. It provides solid advice on what to do, supplemented with case studies which bring the theory to life. The Thought Starters, check lists and review questions are particularly helpful.

Jonathan Geldart, Executive Director – Markets Development (China),
Grant Thornton International Ltd.

This is a timely, practical, and comprehensive guide for professional service providers, reminding us all that our overriding obsession should be with understanding our Clients, meeting their needs, caring about their success, and exceeding their expectations.

Richard Susskind, OBE, author of *Tomorrow's Lawyers*

In an increasingly disrupted and competitive market, keeping their promises to Clients can be a significant enterprise risk for professional firms. Through exploration of his Client Management Model™ Jack Berkovi provides a comprehensive blue print for firms to audit, then sharpen their Client care activities, to achieve improved and sustainable revenue streams from key Clients.

Paul Lemon, CEO, Managing Partners' Forum and
Professional Marketing Forum

About the Author

Jack Berkovi is an international marketing and business development specialist with most recent experience in professional services. Armed with a BSc (Hons) degree in Mechanical Engineering from City University, London, he soon became proficient in the identification and solution of business problems. Following management and marketing roles with US multinationals Procter & Gamble and 3M, he joined global industrial consumables Norton Company. He led a Customer service team before moving into product management with key account management of British Steel, Ford and Unipart. His international career took him to Luxembourg in 1982, reporting as Business Manager to a Norton VP for developing global and European industrial consumables businesses. In 1985 he completed a Business Study Program in Japan, representing Luxembourg and Norton. He returned to the UK to join Time/system, a time management company of International Thompson, where he became Managing Director. His key Clients included Airbus Industrie, BP International, Guinness, Hitachi and Standard Chartered Bank.

Following his natural curiosity and passion for helping Clients, in 1988 Jack moved into marketing consultancy as Operations Director with Marketing Improvements Group, London. During this period, he completed an MA in European Marketing Management at Brunel University; his dissertation focused on marketing of UK-based professional services in France. This led to him being engaged by accountants, chartered surveyors and lawyers to improve their business processes. Among many assignments, he conducted marketing strategy, key account management and development programmes for Clients in

Australia, Europe and the USA. These included: Australian National Industries, Balfour Beatty, BOC, De La Rue, Foseco, Henkel, Hewlett Packard, Jones Lang LaSalle, Kimberly-Clark, the Patent Office, PricewaterhouseCoopers, Savills, Strutt & Parker, Tarmac, Titmuss Sainer Dechert and United Business Media.

MIG joined accountants RSM Robson Rhodes in 1999, where Jack became Head of Marketing for their technology, media and telecommunications sector; he then managed their corporate campaigns and business development. He led a major survey into corporate fraud, endorsed by the UK Home Office, and developed a diagnostic tool PCRIME to enable companies to evaluate their preparedness to combat fraud. This work was endorsed by UNCITRAL, a branch of the United Nations at a time when he acted as marketing adviser to the UK's North East Fraud Forum. Another initiative led RSM Robson Rhodes to be awarded Auditor of the Year for two consecutive years. After its merger with business advisers Grant Thornton UK in 2007, Jack was appointed Senior Manager, Corporate Campaigns, following which the firm achieved Auditor of the Year for two successive years. He then became Head of Brand and Client Care. During his stewardship, levels of Client satisfaction and unprompted brand recognition both increased.

Jack is married with two children, six grandchildren and lives in London. In 1979 he joined the Chartered Institute of Marketing; in 2008 he became a Freeman of the City of London, having joined the Marketors livery company. His wide range of interests include: bridge, charity fundraising, chess, reading and theatre. He is also a games inventor and modern jazz pianist.

Jack is now engaged in marketing and business development consultancy and is Director of a recruitment company. He also acts as Relationship Manager for the international Managing Partners' and Professional Marketing Forums, which assisted with the *Client Care Survey* featured in this book.

Preface

The rationale for this book centres around putting the Client first, everywhere, in the activities of professional services firms. It introduces the *Client Management Model*™, an assessment process created by the author, to enable firms to determine their level of Client orientation and relationship development. It is evident from the author's recent *Client Care Survey* that for Client management to be successful, it is necessary to ensure that a number of key elements, supported by effective behaviours and processes, are in place. It is also generally accepted that characteristically professional services firms rank behind their consumer and service sector counterparts when it comes to marketing, sales (business development), service and employee engagement. Also, although professional services firms have audit processes, tax procedures and legal frameworks, many do not apply this structured approach to marketing their firm and managing their Clients. It would seem logical to have in place processes for marketing, business development and Client service.

Clients expect to be looked after by their suppliers; professional services firms aim to become their Clients' trusted advisers. This book shows how putting the Client rather than services first can yield improved results in terms of stronger Client relationships. It stresses the importance of having highly engaged employees and applying best marketing and business development practices in a highly competitive and dynamic marketplace. Attention to these factors provides opportunities for any professional services firm to develop and grow in new, profitable directions. Readers are encouraged to complete a Client Management Review as they finish each chapter and later, through a diagnostic tool, to create their own *Client Management Profile*™. In collaboration with the author, this data can also used to update the *Client Management Index*™ to enable benchmarking against other firms.

The words 'Client' and 'Customer' are deliberately capitalised throughout to emphasise their rightful place in the hearts and minds of everyone in a firm. In this book, when the firm is mentioned, it relates to those people who are Client-facing, whether fee earning or otherwise.

Acknowledgements

My first interaction with Clients in a business context was not particularly spectacular. As a design engineer, it was my task to prepare drawings of furnaces for Clients in the automotive and related industries. These furnaces used nickel and chrome heating elements and a supply shortage of these metals meant that my company had to forecast its requirements for the year ahead. Having spent two months preparing this information, I discovered by chance, to my amazement, that the company had used it to purchase the materials and then sell them while in mid-ocean at a massive profit – letting down at least 40 Clients. Deliveries were going to be late by many months. This episode signalled my search for an alternative working environment and, from then on, my Clients or Customers would come first, whether internally in engineering projects at Procter & Gamble or industrial Customers of 3M and those Clients of my subsequent employers.

The idea of creating a book about Client management came to me just after my retirement from Grant Thornton. Making a difference in this area has always been important to me. My passion for Clients needed an outlet! This book is the result of many conversations with work colleagues, key practitioners in professional services firms, past colleagues in my consultancy career and meetings with many Clients and prospects over the years. With the kind help of the Managing Partners' Forum, a *Client Care Survey* was created. The responses and subsequent interviews helped me to frame the chapters and to develop the *Client Management Model*™, the *Client Management Profile*™ and the *Client Management Index*™. Many thanks to you all.

My thanks also go to the many top executives and business leaders whose collective wisdom, designs and ideas feature throughout this book. In particular, I am grateful for the support of the following people who kindly shared with me their views on Client management: Alessandra Almeida Jones, Linklaters LLP; Scott Barnes, Grant Thornton UK LLP; Sue Best, ICAEW; Vikki Bingham, GVA; Anne Blackie, Grant Thornton UK LLP; Fran Bosan, Omobono Limited, Marketing Services; Mark Burns, Clarion Solicitors; Dave Chadda, Bid Specialist; Richard Chaplin, Managing Partners' Forum; Douglas Commaille, DCLW Consulting; Darren Cox, Grant Thornton International, Richard Crook,

Savills; Anthony Culley; Dana Denis-Smith, Obelisk Legal Support; Dr Charles Doyle, JLL; Nicola Duke, Mills & Reeve; Allan Evans, BDO; Rob Fear; Louise Field, Bird & Bird; Philip Gardner, Knight Frank; James Harkness, Harkness Kennett; Mark Jeffries, Mills & Reeve; Rolland Keane, Penningtons Manches; Ben Kent, Meridian West; David Kerr, Bird & Bird; Sir Nigel Knowles, DLA Piper; Christian Marroni, Freshfields Bruckhaus Deringer; Claire Mason, Man Bites Dog; Diane Nagy, DTZ; Bradley Neill, Grant Thornton International; Ashley Nicholls, The Recruitment Site; Mandy Reynolds, Stephens Scown; Jean Stephens, RSM International; Clive Stevens – Reeves & Co; Caroline Sumnall, Covington & Burling; and Keith Wells, Redstone Consultants.

Finally I would like to thank everyone at Gower Publishing who helped to produce this book.

The Challenge

The Challenges Faced by Today's Professional Services Firms in Managing Clients[1]

'Clients are hard to win and hard to keep. So much about looking after that precious relationship is obvious but frequently not done because we are too busy delivering the basic service. Those who do the obvious will win!' – Mark Burns, Clarion Solicitors.

'I think Client service is one of the few differentiators for professional services. We measure annually the business that we attract through referrals and word of mouth recommendations.' – James Harkness, Harkness Kennett, Management Consultants.

'Completing this survey has made me realise that it is an area that we must develop in a more structured manner. We believe that we look after our Clients extremely well, as evidenced by our retention levels, but we have no mechanism to measure the validity of this view.' – Anon. accountants.

'It's a given that we know the law and can apply it – service has to be the differentiator. However, it's easy to say we have great Client service, the art is how to communicate and demonstrate this.' – Mandy Reynolds, Marketing Director, Stephens Scown, law firm.

'The rewards that come from great Client service seem to me to be the biggest kept secret in the Western world. Get Client service right and you can't help being a successful firm.' – Clive Stevens, Reeves & Co., law firm.

'We have Rule number One: Clients First.' – Anon. law firm.

---

1 Comments from the *Client Care Survey* conducted by the author in the summer of 2013. Permission to reproduce these was granted when completing the survey.

'Client care is a relatively new term for most law firms in Canada – many have yet to grasp the value of Client feedback as a first step. It would be most impactful if Clients were more vocal as to why dialogue matters to them. I fear that best practices might be introduced at some firms to appear competitive rather than as a sincere expression of caring.' – Anon. law firm.

'Exceptional Client service requires a supporting culture and an unswerving commitment from the board and the Clients. Make your offer to Clients who value service. Develop your sales and marketing strategy accordingly. Don't burn time and money on a non-receptive target.' – Allan Evans, BDO, accountants.

'Great Client care is like a good marriage, you need to keep the level of interest and intrigue up, be thinking about them when you are not around, pleasantly surprise them little and often. If you do not do these things do not be annoyed if your Clients start to flirt with other firms. React positively and you may avert a divorce!' – Anon. accountants.

'We are currently working on a Key Account Management programme with an external consultant. This is being piloted with a number of offices with the expectation it will be rolled out firm wide at a later date.' – Anon. accountants.

'If I had a mantra to sum up what I think good Client care looks like, it's "Be bothered". If you are, the likelihood is you and your Clients will do well.' – Fran Bosan, Omobono Limited, marketing services.

Introduction

It is only in recent years that professional services firms (accountants, lawyers, property consultants and so on) have been developing their commercial approaches to attract, develop and retain their Clients. Characteristically, they tend to lag behind their consumer goods and service industry counterparts in this area. Their Clients are more sophisticated with a different purchasing mentality and fee earners who may provide excellent advice are not always attuned to the role played by, and the strategic importance and benefits of, effective Client management. In fact, this can be a powerful differentiator and can have a positive impact on a firm's profitability.

What this Book is About

Effective Client Management in Professional Services explains how to develop successful Client relationships. Most firms would agree that a key measure of a successful Client relationship is the level of trust that has developed. The book takes the reader on a pragmatic journey and follows the *Client Management Model*™, based on the author's 30 years of experience in professional services marketing and Client management. The book starts by explaining the benefits of having a Client orientation as distinct from a practice or fee-earning mindset. In every subsequent chapter the Client is the focus and the 12 elements of the *Client Management Model*™ unfold. Working through the book offers an opportunity to progressively audit a firm's Client management processes, behaviours and activities. Improvement plans can then be put in place.

The book explains how to create a Client-centric culture. It examines how Clients buy professional services,how firms can identify the potential target organisations that match their competencies and how to attract the right portfolio of Clients.

Through many examples the book shows how to establish which Clients are likely to be the most lucrative and provide the desired financial returns. It also includes a particular emphasis on brand, differentiation and positioning the firm, Client satisfaction and the importance of metrics. The reader then continues their journey through the Client relationship cycle and process used by many successful professional services firms. Once firms are engaged, it explains how to ensure appropriate care and to build the relationship with Clients so that the firm can develop and grow its income in an environment of high Client trust. It explains how Clients become loyal and can contribute to service development, and how to calculate their economic referral value to the firm. It also shows how it is possible to measure the impacts of excellence in Client service through the use of the *Net Promoter Score*. Business development and bid management processes and tools are explained. Given the increasing level of consolidation in the professional services sector, it considers the impact of mergers and the causes and remedies of Client defection. Developing a culture of innovation is also discussed.

Anecdotes, case studies, exercises, scenarios and tools assist in providing insights into Clients, their buying motivations and how they can become loyal, not just satisfied. Results of a recent *Client Care Survey* also feature, being complemented by interviews and quotes from senior partners, managers and specialists in a variety of professional services firms. There are many scenarios that may resonate with readers. The *Client Management Model*™ enables firms to benchmark their Client management approach against that of their peers. Readers can also determine their own *Client Management Profile*™ using a template provided and the *Client Management Index*™ for their firm. Managing Clients effectively implies paying attention to a wide range of factors beyond the fee earning itself – it requires more effort from everyone in the firm, but in return can yield lucrative outcomes.

Who Should Find this Book Useful

This book is primarily for anyone in, or wishing to join, a professional services firm interested in making a difference by improving the care, management and development of its Clients. It may also be of value to users of professional services firms who may wish to compare the Client management practices of their suppliers.

Jack Berkovi

Chapter Summary

Chapters 1–12 relate to the *Client Management Model*™.

Chapter 1   Orientation

Developing a Culture of Client Orientation explains: the impact on Clients of a firm's structure; Client service models; the importance and benefits to all parties of having a Client-facing firm rather than a practice or service orientation; the characteristics of a Client-facing culture; the Client/management needs dilemma; Client expectations; setting objectives and Key Performance Indicators that reflect Client orientation; the importance of employee engagement; making a difference; recognising excellence; the evolution of strategic marketing and its impact on Clients; Client representation at board level; and the importance of knowing the firm's top Clients.

Chapter 2   Buyers

How Clients Buy Professional Services explains: the Client's buying process; how to profile the buyer; buyer motivations and influencing roles; analysing the decision-making unit and its power and influence; organisation mapping; the importance to Clients of hiring top talent; the value of referrals; and how international Clients buy.

Chapter 3   Portfolio

Managing the Client Portfolio explains: the importance and value to the firm of reviewing the Client base; analysing sources of fees before deploying limited resources to manage all Clients; selecting and managing Clients according to their strategic and potential lifetime value to the firm; strategic Client management – how to grow business with existing Clients through greater analysis of their business drivers and requirements and greater understanding of their structure; the importance of sharing Client data across the firm;

the benefits of comparing the firm's development plans for different Clients; managing your Client portfolio; and the challenges of organising for, and managing, international Clients.

Chapter 4   Satisfaction

Client Satisfaction and Loyalty explains: the importance of monitoring and measuring Client satisfaction to gain insights; the questions that need answering; how to organise focus and reward in the firm around Client satisfaction; identifying gaps in performance; satisfaction parallels with the hierarchy of needs; causes and remedies of service failure; how to establish a Client Satisfaction Programme; the use of Client panels to keep in touch with your markets; the value of the *Net Promoter Score* in tracking Client loyalty; estimating the economic value of the most loyal Clients and rewarding excellence in Client satisfaction.

Chapter 5   Care

The Role of Client Care discusses: the behavioural aspects of Client care; what a firm needs to do to ensure that its Clients feel highly valued and are at the core of its culture; how to establish a Client Care Programme; 'Touch Points' and 'Moments of Truth'; understanding and acting out the Client experience; and the relevance to Clients of an active Client care policy and charter.

Chapter 6   Brand

Brand, Differentiation and Positioning and their Impact on Clients discusses: describing the firm; brand creation and development; the importance of the firm's brand, the promise; examples of successful brands; branding; what's in a name; how firms differentiate their offerings; how to develop a value proposition; and the importance of positioning a firm.

Chapter 7   Reputation

Gaining Reputation with Clients explains: sources of reputation; media relations and its impact on Clients; thought leadership and its impact on Clients;

thought followership; the importance of media training; issue-based campaigns; sponsorship; networks and group membership.

Chapter 8   Relationships

Client Relationship Development explains: the aim of relationship management; the importance of regular communication; Client panels; the Client relationship development process; types of Client relationship; relationship evaluation process; relationship tracking; Client segmentation; Client data analytics; Clients that defect; Client relationship management and systems; launching a CRM programme.

Chapter 9   Development

Establishing an Effective Client Business Development Programme explains: the importance of business development culture; prospecting, targeting, meetings and listening; how to structure the business development (BD) operation; how to establish effective, strategic Client relationships with your firm; metrics – sales pipeline measurement; strategic Client planning and management; aspects of BD planning; and the importance of leveraging alumni relationships.

Chapter 10   Attraction

Attracting New Clients explains: how to grow your Client base strategically and profitably; using testimonials to attract Clients; the importance of having a website that is more than just a shop window for your firm; providing Client-researched content that is easy to find, dynamic and retains interest; tracking, and acting on, Client interaction; the power of referrals to attract new Clients; attracting Clients through effective campaigns – how to manage the stakeholders and activities to ensure success; and attracting Client interest through events – how carefully targeted events can enhance the firm's reputation in a sector, location or service by focusing on Client interest.

Chapter 11   Proposals

Developing Winning Client Proposals and Bids explains: the elements of winning proposals and bids; the bid management process; how to ensure that proposals and bids are appropriately structured; bid evaluation process; Features, Advantages, Benefits and Evidence; managing the bid team.

Chapter 12   Innovation

Innovations that Impact Clients explains: the importance of innovation by professional services firms; innovations that characterise the most enlightened of today's professional services firms; the importance of having a project management capability in professional services firms; innovative mergers; current practices in corporate responsibility and partner development; and innovative service development.

Chapter 13   The Impact on Clients of Mergers among Firms

This chapter sets out the challenges, opportunities and pitfalls of mergers and acquisitions between firms and their impacts on Clients.

Chapter 14   The Way Ahead for Clients of Professional Services Firms

Based partly on discussions with leaders of professional services firms, this chapter reviews what Clients can expect of enlightened firms; consolidation of the sector, market development, competition regulation and technological advances; the impact of globalisation; the growth of digitised content marketing; and the impact on Clients of a well-managed firm.

Chapter 15   The *Client Management Profile*™

This chapter brings together the 12 elements of the *Client Management Model*™ and enables the reader to create a profile which reflects his or her firm's position. It also explains the *Client Management Index*™ that is used for benchmarking purposes.

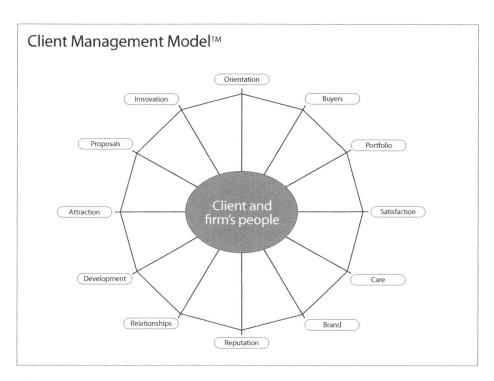

Figure I1.1   The *Client Management Model™*

The *Client Management Model™*

Each of the first 12 chapters of this book describes an element of the *Client Management Model™*, an assessment process, starting with Orientation and ending with Innovation. Note that Clients and the firm's people are at the core.

Client Management Model™

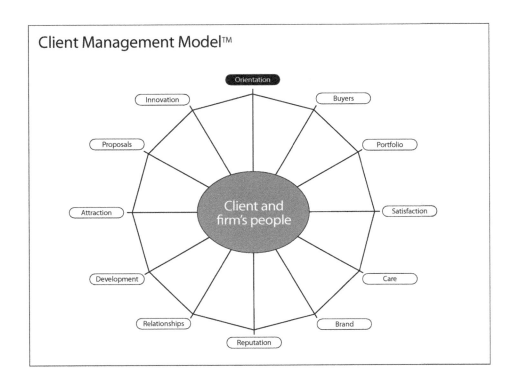

Chapter 1

Orientation:
Developing a Culture of
Client Orientation

Synopsis

Orientation, the first element of the *Client Management Model*™, explains:

- the impact on Clients of a firm's structure; Client service models;

- the importance and benefits to all parties of having a Client-facing firm rather than a practice or service orientation;

- the characteristics of a Client-facing culture; the Client/ management needs dilemma;

- Client expectations;

- setting objectives and Key Performance Indicators (KPIs) that reflect Client orientation;

- the importance of employee engagement; making a difference; recognising excellence;

- the evolution of strategic marketing and its impact on Clients;

- Client representation at the board level;

- the importance of knowing the firm's top Clients.

THOUGHT STARTERS
- How should your firm be structured?
- What are the options?
- What defines your culture?
- What is your level of employee engagement?
- Is Client-centricity part of your DNA?
- What are your Clients' expectations?

Impact on Clients of a Firm's Structure

Professional services firms have many choices in the way that their organisations are structured. However, unlike public companies, the majority of professional services firms are privately owned, often by the partners of the firm. This factor alone often creates the desire for a practice-led structure. This can often cause Clients using multiple practices in a firm having to fit in with the organisation's structure. So it is worth investing time to review the firm's current strategic position and consider the various options open to its owners and the impact of each option on Clients.

Most firms are organised along service lines, so, for example, an accounting firm will usually have separate practice groups covering audit, advisory work and tax, and within these sub-groups specialised areas such as forensic accounting, pension consulting, internal audit; a law firm may have practice groups covering corporate litigation, the environment, intellectual property and public policy. Property firms are often organised into commercial and residential. These service lines are often supported by dedicated or centralised marketing and business development teams. Such support is covered in the next, and subsequent, chapters.

So do we ever consider the impact of a firm's structure on Clients? The tendency when practice-led professional services firms meet Clients is that the practice group partner or specialist leads with facts about the firm and how their particular competences can help to solve problems. Clearly opportunities for work in other areas of the firm can be missed when a Client is only dealing with one person or team with a specific service line responsibility. Although this approach is quite commonplace, it carries with it the risk that the person or team may eventually have a dominant role within the firm with respect to the Client relationship and this can inhibit growth.

Many firms try to overcome this practice-led behaviour by having a Client management policy that assigns a second partner from a different discipline to oversee the development of the relationship. This benefits the Client, giving them access to a second external perspective on their business. It also protects the firm and Client in the case of a partner leaving, so there is still some continuity until a change is made. More importantly, it also can provide the firm with opportunities for additional assignments. Having a dual-partner responsibility can thus increase the revenue stream. By taking this more holistic approach, a broader discussion is also more likely to occur when a Client meets with two or more partners with different remits. This benefits the Client in showing that the firm's people are really interested in helping them to solve a wider variety of problems. Of course it is sensible for the lead partner to allow sufficient time for the Client to develop a trusted relationship with the firm, through delivery of excellent service, before trying to introduce too many other specialists. Another process which benefits the Client and the firm is the development of Client Service Plans that incorporate all practice areas that might be relevant to the Client. Further commentary on Client relationship development is covered in Chapter 8.

Some firms create regional practice teams providing a range of services that focus on Clients within geographical boundaries. However, this approach can sometimes lead to contact confusion and internal ownership issues with Clients having multiple sites across these artificially created regional limits. So would a firm organised with Clients in mind be possible? A sharing mentality and behaviour is a necessary pre-requisite to optimising a firm's performance. Ultimately, given that most professional service firms seek trusted adviser status with their Clients, it may be worth reviewing the level of Client orientation that really exists in a firm.

ORGANISING AROUND SECTORS

Many firms have recently created multi-practice teams that align with Client sectors, using a 'matrix' structure (see Table 1.1) – so, for example, a manufacturing team would deal with Clients from that industry, irrespective of location and services required. Practice or service line heads are still in place, but are encouraged to form cross-functional teams when facing Clients. This centralised approach tends to prevent confusion in the Client's organisation.

Table 1.1   Matrix of Sector Teams and Practice Groups

Sector team	Practice Group A	Practice Group B	Practice Group C	Practice Group D
Aerospace	X		X	
Food		X	X	X
Leisure			X	X
Mining		X	X	
Technology	X	X	X	

In Table 1.1 it can be seen that the Aerospace sector team has members from Practice Groups A and C, food Clients would be handled a sector team involving three practice groups and so on. Clients benefit by having access to industry specialists who work in various practice groups. Another example from the matrix is that Practice Group C, which could be focused on, say, employment law, straddles all the sectors. Over time it might be possible to cross-sell more services to other sectors. Table 1.1 can also be used to show the current situation and can be updated over time. Both practice groups and sectors can operate globally as appropriate to a firm's country presence, which adds a third dimension to the same matrix. This type of organisation is common in many of the mid- to large-sized firms and requires regular and timely communication within the groups that interact in the structure.

KEY CHALLENGES

It is evident from recent Client care research that looking at business through the lens of the Client, rather than that of the firm, is still the key challenge facing many professional service organisations. Structuring a firm around its Clients and markets is considered best practice, but doesn't really appear to happen in many firms because of other priorities. As we move through this book, it becomes clear that the challenge is dealing with the notion that Clients are buying solutions, not services, and that engaged employees deliver the best performance for Clients.

Another key challenge for international firms, or firms with international Clients, is the ability to provide a seamless and consistent service wherever the Client wishes to do business, especially across country jurisdictions and cultures. The management of international Clients and firms is covered in later chapters.

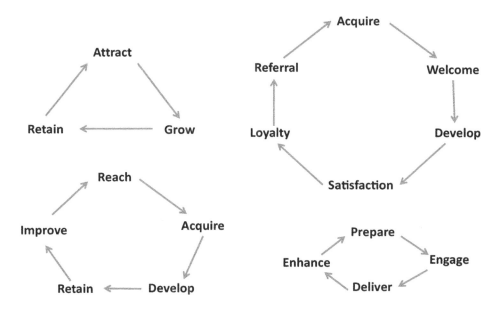

Figure 1.1   **Examples of Client Service Cycles**

Examples of Client Service Models

Client-facing firms recognise that Clients follow a cyclical model over their procurement lifetime. Many firms have developed their own Client service models often in a cyclical format, as shown in Figure 1.1. These outline the cycle of gaining interest, through evaluation, purchase, usage, repurchase and loyalty. Client-facing firms manage Clients through such cycles and know at which stage they are with each Client.

An Orchestrated Performance

Many of us enjoy well-performed music. When a large orchestra – or even a quartet – plays beautifully, there is a feeling of satisfaction in the players and their audience. We can think of the analogy of a professional services firm being the orchestra and the Clients its audience. If your firm, as the orchestra, delivers with everyone integrated, playing their harmonious parts, the result for the Client – your audience – will resonate accordingly. Your managing partner or CEO becomes the conductor of the various sections of the orchestra. Now of course not all Clients will meet the managing partner or CEO, but the principles of stewardship drill down to all practices within the firm. Consider the situations where the musicians are not playing in harmony and its potential impact on the audience. Think about situations when some parts of the orchestra have to share the stage with newcomers and integrate their performance. Clearly continuous practise is necessary for teams of experts to behave in a co-ordinated way. This approach requires dedication to the understanding of Client requirements. They tend to prefer an orchestrated, joined-up, harmonious approach rather than dealing with often unconnected soloists.

Characteristics of a Culture of Client Orientation

There are many factors which underpin a Client-oriented culture. In this section we will look briefly at its key elements of: sector focus, Client-facing processes, Client satisfaction, Client relationship management and Client-related performance objectives and highly engaged employees. Each of these will be expanded upon here and in later chapters. These elements form the basis of Client orientation.

SECTOR FOCUS

Experience has shown that the more oriented a firm is towards its Clients, the more successful it is likely to become compared with firms that focus primarily on their services. When purchasing decisions are about to be made, it is usually evidence of a firm's sector or market knowledge in depth that tips the balance in the Client's mind when all other aspects, such as reputation, technical skill and cost, are perceived as being similar. The trend within the larger and medium-sized professional services firms is to create multi-disciplinary sector or market-focused teams that can operate globally, regionally or nationally – as relevant to the Clients' requirements and size of firm. In today's competitive arena for professional services, having a Client-centric commercial strategy is most likely to bring better results than strategies that are further removed from Clients.

CLIENT-FACING PROCESSES

For a truly Client orientation, it is essential to have processes that work for the Client rather than for the firm. Employees need to understand that Clients are always seeking value propositions from their suppliers. So, rather than working in often isolated departments, it is important for fee earners and support staff to meet regularly to discuss potential opportunities with Clients and interact, ideally in cross-functional teams, to constantly add value to the Client experience. Internal communications such as intranets can help bring together otherwise separate parts of a firm. This Client-centred approach can provide regular updates on progress towards the firm's goals. Employees must also understand how the firm differentiates itself from its competitors. Many firms have deliberately organised their office space to facilitate cross-practice contact and to encourage the sharing of information across their artificial boundaries.

CLIENT SATISFACTION

Client satisfaction is the extent to which the firm meets or exceeds Client expectations. Client satisfaction information provides essential feedback to employees, however it is gained. Active listening to Clients is a skill that is not fully developed in many firms, with latent needs often going unfulfilled. Structured surveys can help people to understand how the firm is doing, and regular, less formal, contact with Clients can also pick up additional messages about the firm's performance and opportunities for further work. Engaged employees want to know how their firm is performing in the eyes of its Clients. The quality and effectiveness of Client service that they deliver is often what sets firms apart. Many firms regularly benchmark their performance with Clients against their competitors and peers to establish their market position. Enlightened firms measure Client satisfaction through formalised surveys and quickly take remedial action when needed. It is also important to have in place a Client recovery strategy and process for situations where satisfaction is below expectations. Client satisfaction is covered in more detail in Chapter 4.

CLIENT RELATIONSHIP MANAGEMENT

A further element in Client orientation is to create a Client Relationship Management (CRM) process that requires everyone to play their part in keeping the information on each Client and the status of the firm's relationship up to date. Having a CRM philosophy stresses the importance of sharing information about Clients and this helps to break down the artificial barriers that sometimes exist within and between a firm's departments and practices. The best CRM programmes are supported by systems and technology to enable rapid data searches and relationship status report outputs. With the rise in use of social media channels, many organisations have started to develop a social CRM strategy to enhance Client relationship development. This recent phenomenon is discussed further in Chapter 14.

CLIENT-RELATED OBJECTIVES

A key element in achieving Client orientation is to align employees' competencies, behaviours, development, appraisals and reward processes directly to the attainment of Client-facing objectives. KPIs that reflect Client orientation are critical to ensuring that employees know where they stand and what is expected of them. Until employees are developed, appraised and rewarded for their performance with Clients, the firm cannot expect to close the loop on Client orientation. Internal recognition of Client service excellence provides an ideal approach to developing a Client orientation.

The Client/Partner/Manager Needs Dilemma

There is often a dilemma facing professional services firms when it comes to meeting the needs of Clients and Partners/Senior Managers. This has a marked impact on culture.

Clients clearly expect firms to:

- understand their business and sector;

- provide partner/senior management level contacts;

- deliver a certain level and quality of service;

- deliver better value than competitors.

Partners/Senior Managers expect:

- to understand their Client's business and sector;

- to service many Clients;

- their Clients to think that they understand their business and sector;

- an increasing, profitable fee income from their Client portfolio;

- engaged employees that deliver excellent service and care.

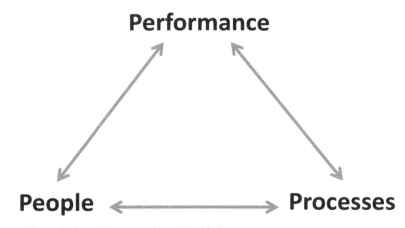

Figure 1.2   Client Expectations Model

Client Expectations

So what are Clients' expectations from a professional services firm? They may not articulate these openly, but they probably expect Client-centricity to be part of the firm's DNA. Clearly Clients want results from their suppliers in everything that is done for them. Many Clients insist on having regular partner contact when other levels of management could probably provide the solution. This is particularly relevant when firms appoint Client relationship and business development managers. We can consider Client expectations under three subset factors of performance, people and processes, as shown in Figure 1.2 and Table 1.2. These factors are drawn from interviews and discussions with Clients over many years.

Table 1.2   Client Expectations

Performance Factors	People Factors	Process Factors
Innovative solutions	People that go the extra distance	They are focused on Clients rather than on internal administration and bureaucracy
Pragmatic solutions	Highly engaged employees	Data analysis procedures
Meeting the agreed budget	Accessible partners/managers when needed	Data security
Meeting the agreed timescale	Easy to get on with	Presentation of information
Meeting service quality expectations	They understand our business issues	Reviews of future commercial opportunities

Table 1.2   Client Expectations (*concluded*)

Performance Factors	People Factors	Process Factors
Providing competitive advantages	Reliable – they keep their promises	Project management skills
Providing evidence of similar assignments	They recognise how we do business	Business reviews at appropriate intervals
Offering attractive value added services	Understanding of cultural differences	Speed of recommendations
Being effective at short notice	Are available when needed	Clear communication channels
Reliability	Can make and take decisions	Mechanism for resolving queries and problems
Giving pragmatic advice	Are trustworthy	Rapid response to adverse feedback on satisfaction
Changing their delivery team to improve results	Are confident	Responsiveness to change
Willingness to negotiate on fees	Are competent in their skill sets	Data on performance achievements versus other suppliers
Speed of implementation of solutions	Regularly challenge our decisions	Easy to understand, no unexplained jargon
Having a high level of responsiveness	Well-supported by their team	A well-managed firm
Consistency and seamlessness across jurisdictions	Are well-known in their sector	Qualitative performance measures

The Firm's Culture: Do Partners, Profits or Clients Come First?

Many professional services firms have a culture that, often by default, focuses on the reputation and technical prowess of individual partners or senior managers. These firms rely on Client relationship partners to provide feedback to their colleagues on how the firm is performing. However, this feedback is likely to be biased towards that particular partner's strengths or practice area. This rather narrow channel of communication, if typical within the firm, can also lead to the occurrence of service line 'silos' that operate almost independently of each other. Even in today's competitive environment, many partners admit that they are reluctant to share 'their' Clients with other parts of the firm, especially at the early stages of a relationship. They feel that they 'own' the relationship. In many instances this seemingly selfish, ring-fencing, behaviour can result in sub-optimal fee income and narrowly defined relationships. One comment often heard internally is that a firm's equity or owning partners think about 'me' rather than 'we'.

The more enlightened firms try to move from this rather narrow-based culture to a Client-facing mindset by encouraging more sharing of Client information and contact possibilities between partners from different service lines. This is facilitated by regular cross-functional discussions. As mentioned earlier, this broadens the potential fee income stream through a more holistic team approach and is more likely to foster an increase in revenue over the longer term. It also helps to build stronger Client relationships and raises the barriers to entry by competitors. A culture of sharing of Client information is essential within a firm for optimum business growth. Many professional services firms, realising this situation, now aim to create a 'one firm', joined-up approach when dealing with their Clients. When a firm's Client database is reviewed, it is not surprising to find that any one Client might have multiple contacts over time within the firm. Unless this contact with Clients is co-ordinated and sensitively managed, each partner may be pushing their own agenda, sometimes causing confusion for the Client. A good test of whether your systems are joined up (or not) is to ask how much income comes from a multi-serviced Client and see if you can access the answer with the touch of a button!

Many firms would admit that a key cultural factor is profitability. 'We must have a profit per employee, or profit per partner, mentality' is often said. Of course profitability has its place in overall performance objectives, but those firms that put Client focus further down the agenda may eventually find that they lose their direction in terms of market performance.

So, given all of these factors, it is worth considering what is meant by culture in a professional services firm. Many firms find this a little difficult to define or articulate to outsiders. A firm's culture embraces the attitudes, values and behaviours that follow in everything that the firm does. If your firm is trying to change its culture to a Client-facing one, what steps have you taken to assess the current situation? You can rate your firm on its Client-centricity by asking all employees questions to determine the extent to which the Client dominates people's thinking and actions. If the scores are low to medium in favour, there are clearly some issues to be resolved if the culture is to become truly Client-centric. As we will read later, the type of culture relates directly to the level of employee engagement. You can also ask your Clients to define your firm's culture and compare the results with the firm's thinking.

FROM PRODUCT TO CLIENT FOCUS

A large construction company had eight divisions, each handling different aspects of the design, build, maintain and operational functions. As the company grew, the heads of their divisions became increasingly more competitive and their behaviour became highly political. Divisional profitability became a critical key performance indicator in managements' objectives. When group performance started to deteriorate, the board was advised by one of its non-executive directors to create a new role of commercial director with the aim of removing potential barriers to progress.

A commercial director was appointed and after a short period of induction decided to conduct an audit of the Client base and the processes in place to manage Clients. This started by convening internal meetings with top management to determine how they ran their businesses; they discussed which Clients were considered 'key', the most important in terms of income and potential. It soon became evident to the new incumbent that the company's top Clients were hardly mentioned on board agendas. Clients were not represented at board level. The commercial director decided to conduct some external research, involving meetings with their top revenue Clients to discuss all aspects of dealing with their supplier. At first, this listening project caused internal ripples among top management. There seemed to be a reluctance to allow a new face to meet 'our' Clients.

However, the response from Clients was extremely positive and supportive. A number of key points arose from discussions with over 50 people in these 10 companies. The work carried out by the various divisions was generally of an extremely high standard. However, there were some unresolved service issues. One thing that stood out was the fact that the company's divisions did not appear to communicate with each other about their Clients and in particular those that they had in common. On a number of occasions Clients discovered that they were having separate meetings with people from different divisions in the same week. Those Clients dealing with more than one division were receiving separate invoices from each. It was clear that the company culture was focused within divisional boundaries, inward looking and highly competitive between divisions. One or two Clients remarked that the company was not 'joined up'.

The commercial director reported on the outcomes of the research and recommended that the company should organise itself around its Clients, retaining the divisional competences, but showing one face to its Clients. This would require different attitudes and behaviours towards Clients, both inside and outside the company. Clients were grouped in order of income stream. Each strategically important Client would have a relationship manager responsible for monitoring the company's performance with Clients. Workshops were held to discuss Clients and became a regular occurrence, involving all fee earners and support staff. People from those divisions serving the same Client would be required to meet regularly to communicate, discuss and air issues and work together to solve problems. Clients supplied by multiple divisions would now receive one invoice from the company in the appropriate detail.

After six months, a pilot Client Satisfaction Programme was launched with the top income companies that were originally interviewed by the commercial director and the results were reported to the group board. Apart from the many service issues that needed resolving, the feedback was used to support the reorganisation of the company around industry sectors, each with a leader responsible for a portfolio of top Clients. After another year, group profitability was stabilised and began to grow; many Clients commented that the company's operations seemed much more integrated.

Employee Engagement and its Impact on Clients

It is well-known that engaged employees are a major factor in the performance of a professional services firm. People are considered engaged when they feel motivated to use their talent, creativity, inspiration and resources for the benefit of the firm. Yet many firms discover through the informal grapevine and the more formal appraisal process that all may not be well between the partners who own the firm and its employees. In such situations many employees cite the lack of direction within a firm; others are concerned about the way that they are treated. Given the importance of having engaged employees, you may wish to conduct an anonymous survey of all your people to determine how they feel about their firm and how they feel and act regarding Clients. This process is often called an employee engagement survey. People are asked anonymously what they believe are the firm's values, especially if it is evident that these are not currently clear or understood. Having conducted such a survey, it is critical to demonstrate that employees' views have been listened to and acted upon.

Typical questions in such surveys include the following:

- What are the values expressed by partners, managers and others?

- How Client-oriented are these values?

- How well are these values expressed and communicated?

- How aligned are the values of partners, managers and support staff?

- What are the biggest gaps between these?

- How well are the objectives and direction of the firm explained to you?

- How well does management support you when you want to help a Client?

- How did you make a difference to your Clients' experience of the firm?

Employee engagement surveys are becoming more commonplace as professional services firms try to establish the appropriate attitudes and feelings of those who deliver and support services to Clients. Many firms seek to secure awards for their level of employee engagement to attract new recruits. It is well-accepted that a firm that treats its employees well is likely to treat its Clients likewise. One firm recently surveyed used the phrase 'Happy Employees means Happy Clients'. Once the gaps between actual and desired engagement attributes are known, improvements can be made in areas such as flexible working, work-life balance and building the appropriate level of trust between employees and top management. The issue of transparency is also becoming more important as professional services firms grow. Improvements in all these areas can then be monitored over time. A good measure of progress is often shown by a reduction in employee churn.

Apart from such internal research, many firms enjoy the status of being among the 'Best Companies' to work for. This can be a powerful differentiator with Clients. There is an annual ranking of 100 Best Companies, created by workplace engagement specialists *Best Companies Ltd* and published in the UK's *Sunday Times* newspaper, which has become an important characteristic. Around 1,000 medium- to large-sized companies are surveyed, resulting in responses from 250,000 employees. The ranking achieved is the result of employee feedback and is now considered a critical benchmark by employers and employees in today's battle to attract the best talent. The Best Companies Accreditation uses the 'Michelin star-style' rating system and is awarded to companies that demonstrate high levels of employee engagement. Professional services firms occupied just six places in 2012 and five places in 2013, all being law firms. The rankings and accreditation clearly recognise firms that place a high priority on working culture and values, factors that are also important to Clients. Another related listing, the *Sunday Times* '25 Best Big Companies', featured three of the largest accounting firms but no law firms in 2013.

Question areas in these published surveys cover the following categories:

- How employees feel about the head of the company and its senior managers.

- How employees feel towards their line manager and day-to-day managers.

- How staff feel about their immediate colleagues.

- How employees feel about the stress, pressure and the balance between work and home duties.

- To what extent employees feel stretched and challenged in their job.

- Feelings about the company people work for as opposed to the people they work with.

- How happy employees are with their pay and benefits.

- How much companies are thought by employees to put back into society generally and the local community.

Benefits to companies appearing in these rankings include the following:

- Enjoying high-profile attention given to the accreditation in the media.

- Publicity from these lists has been proved to help attract talented people.

- Enhanced reputation in the eyes of its Clients.

- Publicity helps to retain the best employees.

Annual trends enable companies to benchmark themselves against their peers.

If it is felt that the firm needs to review and perhaps transform its culture into a Client-facing one, it is important to have leadership from the top, engaging the board and senior management team, rather than to delegate the task to a particular individual or department. Commitment from the top is critical in developing and embedding a Client-facing culture. Then for greatest impact on Clients, everyone must play their part if the culture is to be truly Client-facing. Clearly a 'Best Company' accreditation logo can be used as a differentiator for professional services firms, especially in bid submissions, and can be very effective as a magnet to attract new talent. Employee engagement surveys are best carried out annually.

AN ENGAGED TEAM

Ideas consultancy Man Bites Dog has won PR Week's 'Best Place to Work' award for the last five years and MD Claire Mason believes that her people are critical to Man Bites Dog's success. 'A professional services firm is a people business – if you don't look after your people how can you expect them to look after their Clients? People are the brand experience, look after them and they will take a pride in going the extra mile for your Clients. Ours is an entrepreneurial business where everyone is valued and has their say in how the company is run and our ambitions for the future. This two-way desire to succeed is what drives our remarkably engaged workforce and enables our pedigree pack to deliver outstanding work for our Clients.'

Making a Difference to Clients

Enlightened professional services firms make a point of highlighting and rewarding outcomes of superior Client service, featuring the little things that make a difference. In many firms, stories are rife about how people went the extra distance to exceed Client expectations. These stories are published internally and occasionally externally; they are often used when inducting new employees. A Client orientation culture surely needs to be a top business priority, with supporting objectives and qualitative targets that reflect a Client orientation. These are more likely to result in the appropriate behaviours than targets which do not directly impact on Clients.

Recognising Service Excellence

Many firms link employee reward and recognition to Client loyalty, as shown by the metric of *Net Promoter Score*. This increasingly important commercial indicator of Client satisfaction is discussed in Chapter 4. Over time this measure helps to align employee performance towards Client-focused activities. If people can empathise with what Clients experience, they will have a better understanding of what is expected of them when dealing with Clients. To assist this some firms have discussion groups to map and experience the Client 'journey'; these are often extended to include Client panels that are very often willing to give their feedback if they believe that they will receive better service. There are a number of external awards recognising excellence in Client service; attaining these can be a useful source of differentiation, especially if the firm has won the same award over consecutive years.

The Importance of Regular Contact with Clients

Due to the project nature of most Client engagements in professional services firms, there are often many slack periods when the firm is not carrying out an assignment or dealing with a matter with a particular Client; for example, a patent lawyer who acts for a company may only be required at the onset of each new product development in the Client or for renewals. An accounting firm's audit Client will encounter the team when the work is carried out, with a lull in between financial periods unless queries arise. Leaving Clients 'unattended' in slack periods may create dissonance in how they feel about the firm. However, Client-centric firms are always finding ways to keep in contact with their Clients through all available communication channels, regardless of whether there is a current assignment.

The importance of this regular contact with Clients ensures that the firm is aware of developments and issues arising in the Client's organisation and sector. It provides opportunities for dialogue aside from the workstream and can provide an array of new contacts and highlight situations that may lead to other lucrative work engagements. More importantly, regular communication contributes to Client relationship development.

The Increasingly Mobile Client

The multiple channels and technologies available today, including the more recent and pervasive social media, enable the rapid transfer of information and often complex data while people are on the move; this rapid increase in mobility has transformed the communications landscape, and many professional services firms have invested significantly in mobile technology using social media to keep in touch with Clients and prospects. In fact, many Clients now have more technological power in their hands than many of their suppliers!

NEW CEO SIMPLIFIES THE ORGANISATION TO IMPROVE CLIENT FOCUS

The First 100 Days

Scott Barnes was elected CEO of business advisers Grant Thornton UK LLP in 2008. He presided over a firm structured to serve large corporate entities, small and medium-sized businesses (SMEs) and public sector bodies. In 2007 the firm had merged with Robson Rhodes. Within his first 100 days, he set an ambitious target of doubling profit per partner by 2012 and simplifying the complicated organisation structure. His vision was that the firm would be the leading player in its chosen markets. He made his toughest decisions to restructure the firm within his first six months of tenure. He felt that this was essential to take the firm forward.

Measurement

'A balanced scorecard[1] approach and process was introduced, with four blocks of priorities. These covered Clients, finance, markets and people, with just a few key targets set in each area. An example in 'Clients' is to increase the level of measured Client satisfaction in the highest scoring zone from 60 to 75 per cent. An example in 'finance' is to double the profit per partner within five years. An example of "markets" will be to increase share of public sector revenue by 20 per cent in five years. An example of "people" is that all employees will have a formal, agreed personal development plan within three months.'

Scott believed that having a few objectives in each area was easy for everyone to take on board. 'The targets applied to every part of the firm. People who were not immediately Client facing were set objectives to support those who were. It was necessary to improve internal communications so that everyone knew

---

1 The Balanced Scorecard, attributed to Drs Kaplan and Norton, is an approach to communicating actionable strategies. It includes a mix of hard (quantitative) and soft (qualitative) factors.

how the firm was performing in the four scorecard areas. Regular meetings are still held to review progress in all priority areas. This improvement saw a higher level of employee engagement than ever before. All available channels are used, blogs, intranet, office visits by board members. A set of values was established and a "CLEARR" acronym was launched – standing for collaboration, leadership, excellence, agility, respect and responsibility. These values are constantly used in recognising the firm's talent with awards for outstanding Client service and so on.'

Growth Aspirations

The UK firm has achieved continuous growth since 2008 and now, to keep up the momentum and partner/employee motivation, has an ambition of being a £500m revenue organisation by 2015. The firm has increasingly centralised around Client service, and has won numerous awards in a variety of fields from auditor of the year, through best tax team to employee engagement. A series of road shows to discuss opportunities were held around the country involving half of the partners.

Challenges

Scott believes that the biggest challenge for his firm is to create more resilience in its business model aiming for £500m with a large proportion of recurring or predictable income, rather than have too many spikes of activity. 'As we exit the recession we are aware that there will be a war on talent and recruiting the best will be challenging.'

In 2013 Grant Thornton UK was voted 'Global Firm of the Year' by finance directors and CFOs in the British Accountancy Awards. In 2014 Grant Thornton International was voted Best Managed International Firm in the MPF Awards for Management Excellence.

Setting KPIs to Improve the Firm's Results

Most professional services firms have service line revenue budgets that form the foundation of management objectives and reward. The use of the *Balanced Scorecard* has already been mentioned in the above interview. An example is shown in Table 1.3. It is important in a Client-facing firm to have measures that are challenging, but achievable. Quantitative Client satisfaction scores can be analysed across a firm's offices, regions, sectors and service lines. Such measures can also be drilled down to an individual level to enable comparison between partners and other service providers. These measures provide the drivers for improving the firm's standing and reputation with Clients and prospects. Targets can therefore be set and compared across the firm to encourage improvement. This approach also allows for a gap analysis to be carried out periodically, uncovering any anomalies. The use of moving annual totals is also valuable in assessing a firm's ongoing performance. This technique enables year-on-year comparisons of any factor that is measured and clearly shows trends that can be acted upon as necessary to maintain the desired service levels.

In more recent years many firms are reviewing more closely their return on the investment made in marketing and business development. As an example, it is important to be able to measure the outcome of events as this is one of the most popular activities used by professional services firms to attract prospects and Clients. The growing use of technology means that return on investment in web-based advertising and social channels is more measurable than traditional media.

Table 1.3   Example of a *Balanced Scorecard* for a Financial Year

Clients	*Increase* Net Promoter Score *from 50% to 60%. Increase multi-service Clients by 10%.*	**Markets**	*Increase penetration of technology sector by 5%. Increase unprompted brand awareness by 5%.*
	Increase new Client revenue by 10%. Increase proposal success rate by 5%.		*Establish aerospace sector team. Create 10 new Client-approved case studies.*
Finance	*Cut invoice days outstanding from 120 to 90. Increase profit per partner by 5%.*	**People**	*All employees to complete appraisals by June. Complete firm-wide engagement survey.*
	Reduce external agency fees by 10%. Create automated credit control system.		*Attain higher ranking in 'Best Company' ratings. Reduce employee churn by 5%.*

Event Planning KPIs

Many professional services firms use events to interact with Clients and prospects, which are often thought to be the most effective way of keeping in touch with the market. Yet experience shows that a high proportion of events are not supported by robust objectives and performance measures. Let us suppose that we have planned a seminar on a topic of relevance to

Chief Finance Officers (CFOs). We plan the event, target the audience, book the venue, prepare the invitation and send it out. On the day 60 people arrive and the event 'goes well'. For many firms this level of success is sufficient as the audience clearly enjoyed the event. Next month we have another seminar and so on. But do we ask ourselves enough results-oriented questions about the planning and monitoring of outcomes of these events?

Here are some examples:

- What is our overall objective of the event?

- Is it just to impart information to CFOs?

- Is it to convert prospects into Clients?

- What is the target set for attendance?

- What mix of prospects and Clients do we desire?

- Who will follow up attendees?

- What conversion rate do we expect in the longer term?

- Do we really need an event to achieve our objective?

- Who will report on the outcome of events? At what frequency?

Examples of answers to the above are as follows:

- We aim to secure at least £100,000 of new business from each seminar within a year of the event.

- We will research topics to ensure relevance to our target audiences.

- We will always invite an equal mix of prospects and Clients, aiming for at least 50 attendees.

- We will assign people to meet and greet specific prospects and Clients related to their field of expertise.

- We will monitor follow-up meetings to check the rate of conversion from general interest to a proposal for an assignment and the rate of conversion from proposal to fee income. We aim to exceed our current conversion rate of five per cent.

- We aim for a 10 per cent uptake from invitations.

- Compared with other activities, events are yielding the best level of sales leads.

- A report on an event detailing the measures is expected by the person responsible after two weeks.

- Ongoing follow up is to be reported on a monthly basis.

The Evolution of Strategic Marketing and its Impact on Clients

Most professional services firms have clear, consistent processes for carrying out their services. They require these to meet Client expectations and maintain their high standards of service delivery. However, when it comes to marketing and business development, many appear to be lacking in processes. Marketing is often thought of by many partners and managers as a separate department that produces collateral; the business development function is still relatively new in many firms. Those firms that understand, and have clearly defined responsibilities and processes for, these commercial functions usually have a greater awareness of their Clients' requirements; this helps to promote Client-centricity.

Compared to consumer and service sectors, strategic marketing is relatively new to professional services. In the early days of consumer marketing, marketers used to talk about the '4Ps' of marketing strategy used to guide marketing planning (these being product, price, place and promotion), known as the traditional *marketing mix*, as shown in Figure 1.3.

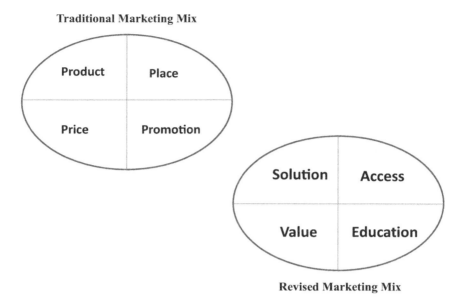

Figure 1.3   Traditional Marketing Mix: Revised Marketing Mix for Professional Services

However, in professional services, as shown in Figure 1.3, the 'product' is clearly replaced by the service or, better, the 'solution' provided, the 'place' relates to its accessibility, the 'price' relates to value and the 'promotion' is usually about education. So the 4Ps are replaced by the 'SAVE' acronym:[1] Product = *Solution*; Place =*Access*; Price = *Value*, and Promotion = *Education*. Bringing a marketing discipline to professional services is a relatively recent development. When effectively deployed, it provides Clients with clear messages about the firm's brand, positioning, differentiation and value proposition. These will be discussed further in Chapter 6.

Client Representation at Board Level

Many professional services firms have designated responsibility for Client care to the head of marketing or business development, but often do not have anyone at board level that represents the voice of the Client. In a Client-centric firm everyone understands the impact of effective, proactive Client

---

1   This acronym was first coined by Motorola Inc. in its drive to market solutions rather than products. It is certainly applicable to the marketing of professional services.

service. It is clear from the recent *Client Care Survey* that Client satisfaction and service are placed lower down the business agenda than perhaps they should be. Often it is only when a valued Client is lost through service failure, with the consequent loss of revenue, that a firm decides to take action to improve Client satisfaction. Recent research[2] has shown that the financial health of a professional services firm is directly related to the high quality and delivery of Client service and the strength of the Client–Adviser relationship. Clearly those Clients that are extremely satisfied and loyal will continue to use the firm and thus provide a predictable income stream. This is enhanced when loyal Clients become advocates and recommend the firm to others. Yet how many boards have someone to represent the voice of, and champion, the Client?

Knowing the Firm's Top Clients

An excellent indicator of the level of Client-centricity in a firm is its ability to answer simple questions about top Clients.Can you and your colleagues:

- Name your firms top 10 highest fee-earning Clients?

- Name the firm's top 5 Clients by sector?

- Name the firm's top 10 international Clients?

- Name the firm's top 10 Clients by practice area?

- Name the 10 Clients yielding the highest operating margins for the firm?

Clearly you would expect the Head of the Tax practice in an accounting firm to know the top 10 tax Clients, the Head of Patents in a law firm to know theirs and so on, but once you move out of their speciality area, answers are usually more uncertain. Yet many of these Clients are often referred to as the firm's 'Crown Jewels'. Enlightened, Client-facing firms can access this information at the touch of a button!

---

2   Effective Client–Adviser Relationships 2012 report – *Financial Times*, Managing Partners' Forum and Meridian West.

Knowing the Firm's Most Loyal Clients

Another indicator of a Client-facing firm is when the majority of employees know which Clients are the biggest advocates of the firm through their willingness to talk about and refer to the firm with colleagues and friends.

Publish Your Client Successes

It is considered good practice to continually raise awareness of the firm's star Clients, interesting stories, recent big wins and so on. Many firms are even happy to publicise their successes with the Client's agreement through press releases and articles to the media, demonstrating more evidence of Client-centricity.

TEN REQUIREMENTS FOR A CLIENT-ORIENTED FIRM[1]

If you believe that your firm is still some way from being fully Client oriented, you might find these useful in changing the current position to one of higher Client focus.

- Cultivate a close contact with the Client.
- Strive to be in a position of trust in relation to the Client's needs, expectations and wishes.
- Check the satisfaction of your Client with your services on a regular basis.
- Concentrate on all areas of performance in which you can add value for the Client.
- Consider your Client in your decision making, in theme groups, meetings, planning and even in internal business considerations.
- Require from all Client-facing employees that they meet their Clients at least annually.
- Adapt to and, if necessary, structure your firm's processes around the needs and perceptions of your Clients.
- Structure your organisation according to the market.
- Develop a Client Recovery Strategy and use it when Clients are dissatisfied.
- You should only hire and encourage Client-friendly employees.

[1] Adapted from Haines & McCoy, *Sustaining High Performance. The Strategic Transformation of a Customer-Focused Learning Organization*, 1995.

Client Orientation is Essential

Orientation has shown that many of today's professional services firms have an opportunity to reap the benefits of having more focus on Clients; however, some are still paying lip service to the approach, as evidenced by the recent *Client Care Survey*. They put other things first. There is enough evidence out there in the market to validate the benefits of Client orientation. The challenge is there to align strategy and Clients, but this requires sensitive planning and strong leadership. Those firms with the highest Client satisfaction ratings are more likely to be the most successful, achieving profitable Client relationships in a highly competitive arena. The signal will come from Clients who recognise and say that 'Client-orientation is part of that firm's DNA'.

Developing a Culture of Client Orientation

CLIENT MANAGEMENT REVIEW QUESTIONS

1.   How Client-centric would you rate your firm?

2.   How easily can you access total income, split by practice area, from a Client?

3.   How easily can you access the names of the firm's top 10 Clients (by income/sector/revenue/growth potential)?

4.   How engaged are your employees?

5.   How well do you know your Clients' expectations?

6.   How Client-friendly are your processes that interact with Clients?

7.   How much is Client-centricity part of your firm's DNA?

8.   How much does Client service feature in the firms' values?

9.   How Client-related are your objectives?

10. How much do your KPIs relate to performance with Clients?

11. How often are Client matters discussed at board level?

12. How often do you meet with your Clients?

These questions also form the basis of the *Orientation* section of the *Client Management Profile*™, which can be found in Chapter 15.

Client Management Model™

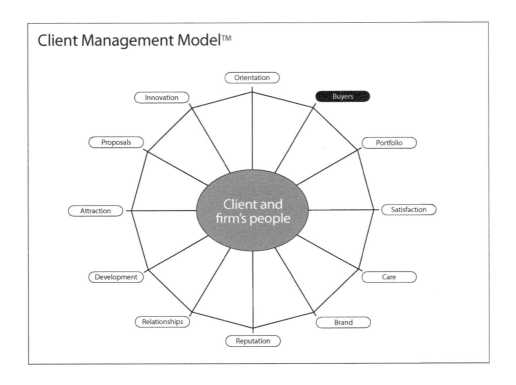

Chapter 2

Buyers:
How Clients Buy
Professional Services

Synopsis

Buyers, the second element of the *Client Management Model*™, explains:

- the Client's buying process;

- how to profile the buyer;

- buyer motivations and influencing roles;

- analysing the decision-making unit and its power and influence;

- organisation mapping;

- the importance to Clients of hiring top talent;

- the value of referrals;

- how international Clients buy.

THOUGHT STARTERS OF A BUYER OF PROFESSIONAL SERVICES
- Can we work with these people?
- Are they competent to do the work?
- Can they deliver on time and on budget?
- Are they reliable?
- What is their track record in our sector?

Initial Thoughts

The purchase of professional services can often be quite complex for both parties involved. Although Clients are essentially 'buying' people, reputation and experience, the decision to buy relies to a great extent on the eventual development of trust between supplier and provider. At the early stages of considering purchase, the person with buying authority must carefully evaluate the people who aim to deliver the service, the reputation and quality of that service and likely value for money. At this introductory stage, there is usually no commercial relationship between buyer and supplier. Procurement of professional services usually involves a number of people at different levels and with differing interests and agendas – these multiple decision makers can reside in a complex web, so it is important to have a process to understand and map these.

Compare this relatively complex purchasing situation with buying a product which you can try out, examine and even try before you buy. Due to the nature of advice given by professional services firms, it is not always possible to know the overall scope and cost of a matter or a project, so the development of trust between Client and supplier is critical. Of course, this takes considerable time and only develops once an engagement occurs, the true test of how the two organisations will work together.

How Clients Think and Feel

Many people often take for granted that all buyers are similar and will negotiate their suppliers down to a price regardless of the type of service required. While many consumer or service industry companies have identifiable buying teams, the 'buyers' of professional services can be found in many parts of the organisation depending on where the need arises.

Buyers of professional services generally go through a logical thinking and procurement process, given the relatively complex nature of the purchase. The following exercise, based on surveys and business development feedback, was used in workshops, particularly with partners of accountancy and law firms who were interested in understanding more about buyer thinking and behaviour.

HOW CLIENTS THINK AND FEEL

Your Account Manager and a prospective Client have had a really good meeting. During the meeting, the Client noted eight points.

Put the following eight statements[1] in the order in which you think they occurred in the mind of the prospect. For example, if you think that statement F is the first, place a 1 next to that statement and so on.

Table 2.1   How Clients Think and Feel

Ref	Statement	Your Order
A	That idea will help to develop our business.	
B	I am not certain whether they can be consistent.	
C	They are concerned about our company's performance. Normally suppliers are only interested in getting more business from us.	
D	Let's hope their support team understands the details.	
E	I need to have a revised timetable.	
F	I hope that they can explain how this will work.	
G	On balance, I think that we will give them a chance.	
H	It's interesting that they asked those questions, it happens to be a critical issue for us.	

For the most likely order, see Appendix 1.

---

1   Adapted from the original, attributed to my colleague Anthony Culley in Marketing Improvements Group.

CREATING A BUYING SCENARIO

A property surveyor wanted to increase the current 20 per cent rate of conversion from leads to firm instructions, so it was decided to hire a consultant to create some land agent-seller scenarios. The consultant spoke with a number of partners across their agency network and came up with six different types of seller, representing the main source of enquiries received by the surveyor's agents. Six different agent-seller interview scenarios were created and each would feature a partner who had to take turns as an agent in one scenario and a seller in another. Partners were given time to prepare for both sessions. Each interview was filmed and non-participants could watch the meeting from an adjacent room.

What became clear early on in the first interview was that the agent was not really listening to the seller but was keen to explain how good his firm was in selling land. In other scenarios the sellers gave out a number of interest signals that were clearly missed by the agents. It was also evident that agents were not giving sellers enough reasons to use their firm.

Each scenario was reviewed by the participants and their colleagues, so that opportunities and pitfalls could be highlighted. After six of these sessions the partners agreed that they should listen much more closely to establish the requirements of the seller and present clear benefits of being instructed.

The process was rolled out countrywide to other partners and then senior managers, and resulted in the conversion rate rising to over 30 per cent within six months.

A bonus from the exercise came when a number of Clients gave feedback about how engaged they felt during their meetings.

Getting to Know the Buyers and their Organisation

Initial meetings between supplier firms and buying influences will often proceed just like any social interaction. However in these times of rapid data transfer and social media, a buyer's first point of contact with your firm may well be through the internet. This contact is known as a Moment of Truth and, like every interaction of this type, represents an opportunity to connect with your firm and build a stronger Client relationship. Managing Moments of Truth is discussed further in Chapter 5. In a business meeting context it is useful for the supplier to take notes, with the buyer's prior permission, so that these can be reviewed with other colleagues at a later internal meeting.

The initial contact between the firm and a prospective Client that may have arisen from an enquiry or referral often involves one person in each organisation. For example, in a publicly listed company, your firm's tax partner meets the finance director or your corporate lawyer meets their general counsel. As discussions progress over time, a mutual rapport develops. The partner has a clearer understanding of the structure of the organisation and some idea of who might influence procurement of the firm's services. Equally the prospect has some idea about the firm's capabilities and credentials. A number of tools are used by many professional services firms to better understand how prospects organise their purchasing; these include buyer profiling, decision-maker analysis and mapping, each of which is explained later in this chapter.

In a first meeting, both parties are trying to get to know and understand each other. If the Client's requirement is considerable in scope, the 'buyer' is probably meeting with many other suppliers. It is sometimes possible in the first meeting for the supplier to determine what drives the buyer's organisation, how they make their purchasing decisions and who is involved. With regard to the former, the procurement process may be highly structured, as in the public sector, while for the latter, there can often be several levels of influence that need pursuing.

By listening closely to what Clients say and asking the appropriate probing questions, the supplier may uncover issues faced by the buyer's organisation and what motivates the buyer. Following a few meetings with the buyer, it should be possible to uncover these motivational factors and in turn know how best to deal with them. It is also important to understand where the buyer sits in his/her organisation in terms of hierarchy, seniority and buying influence. For example, your contact may specify what is required of their suppliers, but may not be the final arbiter. The head of finance may be the budget holder and may also use the service. Your buying contact may know you from a previous assignment in another company and may have brought you in to continue the trusted relationship. Such contacts are very important to nurture, as such loyalty and trust are usually only developed through personal experience, work quality and time.

The aim for the supplier is to gain the trust of the buyer and be selected to take on an initial assignment. Given the right outcomes, the supplier aims to become one of *preferred* status. These situations can also lead to the establishment of structured *framework agreements*, which reduce the time taken to start new work. Such agreements are particularly appropriate to the public sector, but are also common in larger corporate entities.

When a firm is confronted with a buyer, it is dealing with many factors including:

- Budget holders.

- Cultural issues.

- Influencers.

- Jurisdictional issues.

- Motivations.

- Personal agendas.

- Power.

- Procurement process.

- Relationships.

- Service users.

- Technical aspects.

Understanding what motivates a buyer often takes a number of meetings before these become evident. It's important to be aware of the level of seniority and power held by the buyer in their organisation – how much influence do they have over the CEO? What is the strength of their internal relationships?

We can look at these factors in stages. Even with background information about the organisation, it is not always easy in the first meeting for you to determine the buying influences of your contact. If you know the person from a previous company, you may have a better idea of their seniority and influence over the buying decision, but you cannot assume that the buying processes will be the same as it was with the previous structure.

If you have had a few meetings with the prospective Client, you may have started to form a view on what motivates them. By asking the right incisive questions, you can learn about the various people in the company and you will discover more about the likely end users of your services, who holds the budget and so on. Some companies have a policy that screens out suppliers at an early stage if they fail to meet certain defined criteria.

When a purchase of advisory services is part of a complex project, like a merger or acquisition, many people will usually have sway over the final decision to select a supplier. As such, it pays to meet as many people at the appropriate levels in the organisation so that you can have a greater chance of success in being selected to meet their requirements.

It is useful if you can have several meetings with a prospective Client in order to understand and note their interests, concerns, achievements, affiliations, preferences and their level of purchasing influence. You can then draw a mental picture of their key motivators. Various profiling tools are available to help understand these buyer motivations. One of these tools considers four factors: achievement, influence, affiliation and security. The following section gives examples of these factors. These are often described as 'signposts' to the different types of buyer behaviour that might be encountered by anyone aiming to do business. It can be useful to profile buyers using a structured approach. Table 2.2 summarises the four buyer motivations.

Table 2.2   Buyer Motivations Summary

Achievement	Influence	Affiliation	Security
Likes challenges	Enjoys debates	Non-assertive, warm	Self-image
Systematic	Takes the lead	Avoids coldness	Likes to be seen as effective
Business-like	High visibility	Informal	Concerned about change
Proud	Opinionated	Happiness of people	Sets easy targets
Takes risks	Status-conscious	Seeks company of others	Supports others
Planner	Volunteers to lead	Avoids conflict	Presents to people on side
Performance reviews	Presents own ideas	Conversationalist	Plays safe with decisions
Targets	Seeks recognition	Relationships important	Financial soundness
Works alone	Represents a group	Likes group working	Lacks self-confidence
Learning	Dominant	Sympathetic	Dislikes criticism

Source: Marketing Improvements Group.

Buyer Motivations in More Detail

ACHIEVEMENT FACTORS

- Likes to set realistic challenges and get things done.

- Is systematic in his/her approach to tasks.

- Is business-like and likes dealings to be to the point.

- Takes great pride in a completed task.

- Is good at taking risks.

- Actively plans his/her own development and progression.

- Looks forward to performance reviews.

- Likes to set measurable targets.

- Does not work well under close supervision.

- Enjoys new learning situations.

INFLUENCE FACTORS

- Enjoys a good debate and likes competing with people.

- Likes to take the lead in situations.

- Likes to have a high profile at work.

- Quickly forms an opinion and persuades others of its correctness.

- Is concerned about the status he/she has.

- Will volunteer for leading positions.

- Takes every opportunity to present ideas to management himself/herself.

- Enjoys recognition publicly for what he/she has done successfully.

- Likes to act as a representative or spokesperson for a group.

- Tends to dominate conversations with his/her own views.

AFFILIATION FACTORS

- Tends to be non-assertive and warm.

- Is visibly disturbed by indifference and avoids cool or cold people.

- Will begin conversations with a non-business-related discussion.

- Is actively concerned about the happiness of others at work.

- Actively seeks the company of other people.

- Avoids conflict with others if possible.

- Works hard to keep the conversation going and dislikes silence.

- Works hard to create warm personal relationships.

- Prefers to work in group situations.

- Shows sympathy to those who are less fortunate.

SECURITY FACTORS

- Is concerned about how others regard him/her.

- Is concerned that others see him/her as effective at work.

- Is cautious about changes which will affect him/her.

- Tends to set targets which can be comfortably met.

- Tends to react to others opinions rather than initiate them himself/herself.

- Waits until he/she knows people well before introducing his/her ideas.

- Tends to play safe when making decisions.

- Is concerned about the organisation's financial soundness.

- Lacks self-confidence.

- Reacts badly to criticism.

A guide to dealing with these motivations is shown in Table 2.3 below.

For an exercise on buyer profiling that has been used to profile many suppliers, see Appendix 2.

Table 2.3   A Guide to Dealing with Different Buyer Motivations

Achievement	Affiliation	Influence	Security
Praise in writing	Make sure social chat comes before business	Let the Client change your proposal if necessary	Sell the benefits of change
Comment on his/her certificates and trophies	Don't refuse the offer of tea or coffee	Emphasise how your proposal will affect status	Keep things in black and white – avoid grey areas
Emphasise things that will beat his/her competitors	Share an interest in his/her family/social life	Ask for his/her suggestions	Make your proposal easy to buy – nothing too risky
Keep things clear – don't be vague	Have regular informal meetings	Let him/her lead the discussions	Regular communication to inform/reassure
Show interest in personal career goals	Assist in selling proposal to his/her boss	Recognise his/her valuable contributions	Encourage, praise and thank regularly
Build measurable goals into the proposal	Don't be critical of others in front of him/her	Let the Client steal your ideas	Offer testimonials or referrals

Source: Marketing Improvements Group.

TRACKING BUYER MOTIVATIONS

Imagine that you are meeting a director in a large corporate entity who is interested in buying your firm's services. Your proposed approach would involve many changes for successful implementation. During the meeting the director appears resistant to introducing new processes and is concerned about how he will be seen in his company as champion of change.

You discover that the director is keen for his company to lead the market and is seeking advantages over his peers. When you have established his key issues, you suggest a process which he seems to find appealing. He agrees in principle and wants to make a few changes to the proposal layout. In fact he says that he will put a few of your points to his CEO this afternoon.

He is also concerned whether your ideas have worked elsewhere and needs reassurance. Finally he suggests that you meet over dinner in a few weeks' time to review how the proposal has been received by his colleagues.

This example contains a mixture of buyer motivations. Using the guide enables the selection of appropriate actions. See highlighted areas in Table 2.4.

Table 2.4   Using the Buyer Motivations Guide

Achievement	Affiliation	Influence	Security
Praise in writing	Make sure social chat comes before business	Let the Client change your proposal if necessary	Sell the benefits of change
Comment on his/ her certificates and trophies	Don't refuse the offer of tea or coffee	Emphasise how your proposal will affect status	Keep things in black and white – avoid grey areas
Emphasise things that will beat their competitors	Share an interest in his/ her family/social life	Ask for his/her suggestions	Make your proposal easy to buy – nothing too risky
Keep things clear –don't be vague	Have regular informal meetings	Let him/her lead the discussions	Regular communication to inform/reassure
Show interest in personal career goals	Assist in selling proposal to his/her boss	Recognise his/ her valuable contributions	Encourage, praise and thank regularly
Build measurable goals into the proposal	Don't be critical of others in front of him/her	Let the Client steal your ideas	Offer testimonials or referrals

Decision Maker Analysis

Depending on the complexity of an issue, the decision to use a professional services firm may rest with several people in the prospective Client; there could be many 'buyers'. Although the ultimate user of the service may be a key buying influence, they may not be the budget holder. Generally there are multiple decision makers and hierarchical layers, so before proposing any solutions to the first contact made, it is clearly important to understand the Client's organisation and how it operates. It may be important to meet others, if possible, to scope the requirement in more detail and to uncover any possible hidden agendas.

In complex selling situations, the acronym *DMU* is often used when discussing multiple decision makers in Clients. DMU stands for Decision Making Unit and is a term used to describe the group of those people who make, or influence, purchasing decisions. It is important when planning meetings with Clients to assess the stances of the likely parties that will decide on future purchases. It is also important to consider who in the Client organisation might veto a solution, perhaps on technical, financial or even cultural grounds. The DMU is often located in different sites in a Client's organisation.

Analysing and Mapping the Client DMU

There are a number of ways of classifying 'buyers' in multiple decision-maker situations. Suppose you are meeting a prospective Client and you encounter someone who is clearly a technical specifier; while they may spell out exactly what is required technically, they may not be the budget holder. Equally, you may have had a meeting with a department manager who is very keen on your proposed solution because it will make life easier for his team, but this manager tells you that they can only put forward your ideas and may not have much influence over the purchasing decision. It is possible that the buyer knows you well and recommends your firm to colleagues.

For more complex buying situations, it is important to identify those people with purchasing power and influence so that you can position your ideas accordingly. There are a number of tools and methods for classifying buyers used by practitioners in consultative selling which have developed over many years. The 'BACPOD' influencer's tool, attributed to my colleague

	Influencer Role	Characteristics	Focus	Asks	Function
B	BLOCKER	Concentrates on the downside versus the up sides	Political Personal Negative	'Will it suit me personally?'	Devil's advocate
A	ANALYSER	Judges measurable aspects of proposals Recommends Can't say yes Can say no – veto power	Product/service solution effectiveness	'Does it meet our requirements?'	Screens out formally or approves
C	COACH	Found in buyer, seller or outside Both provides and interprets data about the situation	Your success with your proposition	'How can we pull this off?'	Acts as a guide to achieve success Gives access to the opportunity
P	POLICY MAKER	Position of authority Heavily Influences yes or no Veto power	Strategy Long term relationship Trustworthiness	'Does it fit with our business strategy?'	Assesses your proposition versus their strategy
O	OPERATOR	Use/supervise use of your product/service Will live with your proposal Direct link with your success	The job to be done at work	'How will it work for me?'	Makes judgements about impact of your solution on operating performance
D	DEAL MAKER	Direct access to funds Releases funds Discretionary use of funds Veto power Can say yes	Bottom line impact on organisation Price/performance	'Will you give me better terms?'	To get the best possible deal from you

Figure 2.1   Summary of BACPOD Buying Influencers

Source: Rob Fear, Marketing Improvements Group.

Rob Fear in *Marketing Improvements Group,* has proven effective with many years of use. This helps to analyse those people who make or influence the purchasing decision and is particularly applicable in highly strategic projects. Essentially the people in the buying structure are assigned 'roles' or 'hats' to distinguish their behaviour and responsibilities.

Many people with buying influence in the Client may wear more than one of these 'hats', so it is useful to prepare a matrix of people and the relevant 'BACPOD' factors. Being able to classify buying preferences and behaviours is often the key to winning a bid, yet many firms still rely on gut feelings rather than such analysis. The elements of the 'BACPOD' tool are explained in Figure 2.1 and an example of its use is shown in Table 2.5. In summary the acronym stands for: Blocker, Analyser, Coach, Policy maker, Operator and Deal maker.

Table 2.5   Using the BACPOD Tool

Position Role	CEO	Financial Director	IT Director	HR Director	Marketing Director	Technical Director
Blocker						X
Analyser		X	X			
Coach				X		
Policy maker	X					
Operator					X	
Deal maker		X				

It is also useful to build up a relationship picture of contacts and their decision making power and influence – see 'Client Mapping' later on in this chapter.

The following case is an example of a missed opportunity where DMU analysis may have helped to avoid a poor outcome. This is based on a situation that occurred some years ago.

SELLING TO THE RIGHT PEOPLE

A large European banking group was interested in a cash management system allowing improved contact between bank tellers and Customers. It would enable removal of the glass security screen that was an obstacle to good face-to-face contact. It would replace the existing manual cash counting process and the computer system would automatically link to the cash withdrawal.

Local bank trials were well received and the IT department confirmed that it could organise the system changes required. Head office agreed in principle to a pilot of the changes.

The supplier then received notification that the project had failed to secure the required budget. The supplier decided to contact head office to determine why the proposal has been rejected. They were rather surprised at the decision since they had positive feedback from bank managers and their staff, the local IT departments and the finance head.

The supplier discovered that the bank's corporate marketing and facilities management people had not been involved in discussing the proposal. The proposed changes would mean that each bank would have to undergo a considerable and costly facelift. It would also require a communications programme to be created and implemented to raise awareness and benefits of the changes among the bank's Customers. Marketing and facilities teams were already in the process of upgrading the 'banking experience' and had already commissioned new designs prior to the new ideas being proposed.

If the proposed approach had included the head of corporate marketing and facilities at an early stage, it may have succeeded.

If a firm is about to suggest a solution to a Client's problem, it is important to ensure that the right people are involved in the Client's organisation. It clearly pays to map out, and meet where possible, the likely decision makers and influencers, especially within a complex organisation structure. Client mapping is a useful technique to inform decisions on who to target in an organisation.

Client Mapping

Given the often complex structures in Client organisations, much of the contact information about its people is usually held on a firm's databases; however, any specific data about the interrelationships and hierarchies is generally held by the relationship partner/manager. Reaching the right people who make or influence decisions is often difficult, so some form of organisation chart is usually needed.

Client Mapping is a technique that is often used when trying to understand a prospect or Client organisation structure. It helps to unearth the multiple layers that may exist and helps to avoid the pitfalls of not knowing the influences and levels in the Client organisation. The approach and process of Client mapping is quite straightforward. Usually the Client contacts are shown in one shape and those in the firm in a different shape. The seniority within the hierarchy on both sides is shown by numbers. The strengths of influence and relationships, where known, are shown by arrows. These maps are relatively easy to produce once some information is known about the Client's organisation. Once drawn, the gaps become clear. An example map, attributed to my colleagues in *Marketing Improvements Group*, is shown in Figure 2.2.

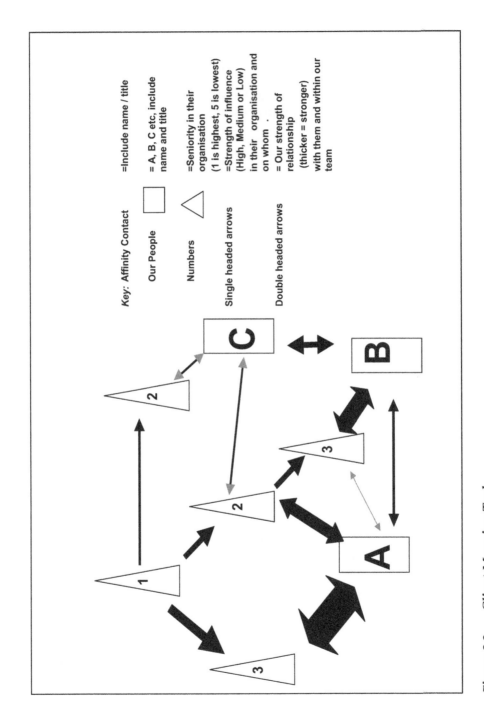

Figure 2.2   Client Mapping Tool

HOW TO DRAW A CLIENT MAP

- Involve everyone that has knowledge of, and relationships with, the Client's organisation.
- Explain to them the idea and benefits of Client maps.
- Ask everyone with knowledge of the Client to write down their understanding of their structure.
- It is then useful to start by drawing symbols on a flip chart to represent the Client's organisation and hierarchy. This is shown by triangles in Figure 2.2. Names and job titles are added; seniority is then added using numbers relating to level of management. For international Clients, country locations should be added.
- The next step involves placing other symbols, say rectangles, to represent the people in your firm who know the Client. Again, if international Clients are being mapped, member firm contacts can be added by country.
- The next step requires some knowledge of the influence between the Client's people. This is shown by single headed arrows showing the direction and strength of influence.
- The final step is to use double headed arrows to indicate the strength of relationship between and within the two organisations. The thicker arrows indicate the stronger relationships.

Once the map is drawn, it becomes clearer to the firm where action is required to improve the strength of relationships, understand the hierarchy and plan to fill any gaps. Different colours for Clients and the firm can be used if this makes it easier to understand the symbols.

*From Figure 2.2 it can be seen that Client person **1** has a strong influence over two of his colleagues, and a slightly less influence over a third. Our person **A** has a strong relationship with Client person at seniority level **3**, but our relationships with higher levels in the Client are weaker. Our team member **B** has a stronger relationship with team member **C** than with **A**. There appears to be **no relationship** at the highest level.*

Getting to Know Your Peers in the Client's Organisation

Given the relatively complex nature of the purchasing of professional services, it is considered best practice in larger engagements to arrange for suppliers to meet their peers over time to better understand the culture and organisation structure of their Client. Although the matter, project or assignment is often carried out between specialist advisers and a particular department or division, it is useful for top executives in the firm and the

Client to meet each other for the more strategic, broader discussions. Even informal events are effective in this context. Given today's advances in technology, it would also seem logical for the IT heads to meet at some point. As an example, this interaction could facilitate the linkages of systems to share data and reduce paperwork between organisations. Some firms arrange meetings of their human resources heads to compare ways of attracting and retaining the best talent. This form of contacting and relationship building takes time, but the investment pays off not only in terms of opportunities for other projects but also raises the barrier to competitor entry. The recent *Client Care Survey* revealed that this form of peer interaction is often limited to the people involved in the workstream.

Talent Management and Development

Clients are essentially 'buying' talented people and their associated ideas and skills when they select a firm. When they meet members of the firm, they expect evidence of how it goes about recruiting, developing and retaining the best talent. Professional services firms can provide some of the best career opportunities for talented people of all disciplines due to the diversity of Clients served and often their global reach. Because of growth and churn, the larger professional services firms can be recruiting hundreds of new graduates each year. In many of these firms a new employee is encouraged to map out their desired career path and, given the right performance, can achieve their personal aspirations. Employees usually have a broad choice of available training and development programmes; some firms create their own academies or universities for this purpose. Others have deliberately created 'fast-track' career paths for their highest performers and succession plans to bring on the best potential partners. Some firms will even sponsor academic qualifications as part of the employee 'package' if it enhances their reputation and retains people.

Corporate buyers expect their organisation to be dealing with suppliers that have talented people who understand their business so that they can keep abreast of commercial developments in their markets. Public sector buyers expect their suppliers to have an understanding of their sector and its different procurement methods; the larger contracts often require considerable preparation and non-billable investment at the pitching stage. Not-for-profit organisations are usually more restricted in terms of expenditure and may have quite a rigorous procurement process.

The difference between a firm's employees that just do the job and those that go beyond a Client's expectations is a key differentiator in today's competitive arena. Those people who go the extra distance stand out in the Client's eyes and will make Client retention easier when competitive situations arise.

It is an industry requirement that specialists in professional services firms must regularly update their technical skills to ensure Continuous Professional Development (CPD) and retain the required operating standards. This is expected by Clients when they seek professional advice. However, although they heed the CPD protocols, many partners and senior managers in professional services firms would admit to having little training or development exposure in Client care, questioning skills and business development skills. Yet it is behaviours in these areas that enable specialists to build strong relationships and stand above their counterparts when technical ability is considered equal by Clients selecting a firm to instruct.

Having a high level of employee engagement, as discussed earlier, is a pre-requisite for firms to retain their best talent, as there is still considerable movement of people between professional services firms. The skills of marketing and business development are generally transferable between different sectors, so a new incumbent can make their mark relatively quickly in a new environment. Other firms sometimes think 'outside the box' and recruit people from the service or consumer sectors to provide fresh thinking.

Recruiting the Best Talent

Recruiting the best talent is one of the main challenges for today's professional services firms. They use various methods to attract new talent. Some have their own resources to advertise new opportunities, whether for recent graduates or experienced people. The firm's website is often used for this purpose. These firms also provide substantial bonuses to employees if they find suitable external candidates for vacant roles. Many firms take space in university open days and recruitment fairs to meet potential graduates.

The use of external agencies or recruitment specialists is also widespread in professional services. These suppliers have built large databases of potential candidates and such outsourcing can often provide a swift response to a Client's requirements, especially if an employee has left the firm at short notice.

Social media sites are becoming more important when seeking new talent, especially LinkedIn, which regularly features job opportunities in a wide variety of sectors. Many new positions are not advertised widely to retain confidentiality in the market, as these may give competitors insights into a firm's strategy; specialist recruiters may be used in this situation.

Those firms with international reach also have the opportunity to provide temporary secondments between network members. This usually provides tremendous experiential benefits to people looking for international career development, and some roles eventually become permanent.

CHALLENGES FACED IN HIRING THE RIGHT TALENT
Resourcing in Tough Times

Ashley Nicholls, founder of The Recruitment Site Limited, believes firmly that: 'Talent management is recognised as being one of the most challenging and important functions of global businesses today. Faced by budget constraints and frequent revisions to strategies and team structures, the need to recruit effectively and swiftly has never been greater. Some professional services firms have responded by in-sourcing their resourcing teams, moving away from the traditional models of agency recruitment, in an attempt to save money. However, this can be a false economy and a potential risk as firms attempt to source the best talent themselves, replacing the knowledge, experience, networks and connections of recruitment agencies with less experienced in-house teams. Furthermore, the availability and mobility of workers only adds to the pressures faced by Resourcing Managers as access to thousands of potential employees via social media sites, like LinkedIn, or directly via advertisements on their websites, creates a multitude of potential applicants that need sifting through to identify the genuine talent.'

Resourcing Out of Recession

'Forward-thinking corporates ensure that they are ahead of the game when resourcing out of a recession. Having spotted a turn in the market, these proactive firms begin to implement their resourcing plans to support their longer-term strategic aims, ahead of the competition. By being first to market, they will have the pick of the excellent talent at a fair investment and won't get drawn into the recruitment churn when the momentum in recruiting really picks up. Firms who wait until full economic recovery miss the great candidates. Then they may well find themselves in a situation where the power and control has shifted from the corporate to the candidates, who will be attending multiple interviews, receiving multiple offers and can force salaries up with those employers keen enough to secure the best talent. It is key at this time to ensure existing staff are motivated, well rewarded and their contributions recognised to avoid them succumbing to the inevitable headhunting calls that they will receive enticing them with the promise of pay rises, better working conditions and job satisfaction.'

Great Talent Moves Around

'Professional services firms face tremendous competition to secure the crème de la crème of talent to compete in an overcrowded market place. Experienced professionals will often move from one firm to another, spreading and sharing the knowledge, skills, learning and development across the firms, diluting the ability to differentiate as best practice is recreated and distributed across the industry. Hiring talent from outside the industry can bring in fresh perspectives and ideas and break this cycle of rotating talent.'

The Importance of Referrals

Buyers of professional services often receive referrals from third parties; these can be from similar organisations known to the buyer or through a third party such as a bank. So it is important for professional services firms to have good relationships with potential referral groups. These can also include the firm's alumni.

How International Clients Buy Professional Services

Many internationally based Clients have sophisticated procurement policies and need suppliers that are able to match their global presence. For example, a global corporation based in New York may have satellite offices and operations in most major cities around the world. The corporation has decided to minimise the number of suppliers used globally and has therefore sought firms that can deliver a consistency of service wherever they do business. Suppliers will be expected to understand cross-border transactions, governance, cultural and jurisdictional differences, and logistics.

It is not unusual for international Clients to establish *preferred supplier agreements* that span the countries or jurisdictions where they have a presence. The decision-making unit in such Clients is clearly complex and consequently it may take many months, or even years, to become a preferred supplier. Firms that can match the geographical footprint of their Clients' operations are in a strong position to provide a seamless service. However, any firm operating internationally must have in place policies, procedures and systems that can interact with the Client to ensure quality and consistency of service delivery everywhere. Managing international firms and their Client relationships provides additional challenges, requiring attention to detail and sensitivity regarding country differences and cultures. This set of capabilities is discussed in the next chapter along with organising to manage international Clients.

Knowledge of Buying Processes and Structures is Vital to Win New Business

Buyers has shown that as Clients become more demanding it is vital that the firm understands more than just the Client's requirements – they need to know how the Client selects suppliers, how they choose between them, what motivates them and who has power and influence over the buying decision. Talented people attract buyers, so it is important for firms to nurture this relatively scarce resource and expose them to prospective Clients. Enlightened firms have become smarter in their understanding of how Clients buy and DMU analysis; this makes the winning of new business easier. Organising to serve international Clients is becoming more important as buying decisions are affected by global forces.

How Clients Buy Professional Services

CLIENT MANAGEMENT REVIEW QUESTIONS

To what extent:

1.   Does your firm explore and record each Client's buying process?

2.   Do you explore and record each Client's buying motivations?

3.   Is DMU analysis used to determine buying influences?

4.   Do you classify buyers with the BACPOD (or similar) tool?

5.   Do you map contacts in the Client's organisation alongside yours?

6.   Do you know how much business comes from referrals?

7.   Does your appraisal process rate performance with Clients?

8. Do you discuss Clients' buying habits and trends?

9. Does your firm develop its employees' competences related to Clients?

10. Does your firm regularly benchmark itself against its competitors?

These questions also form the basis of the *Buyers* section of the *Client Management Profile*™, which can be found in Chapter 15.

Client Management Model™

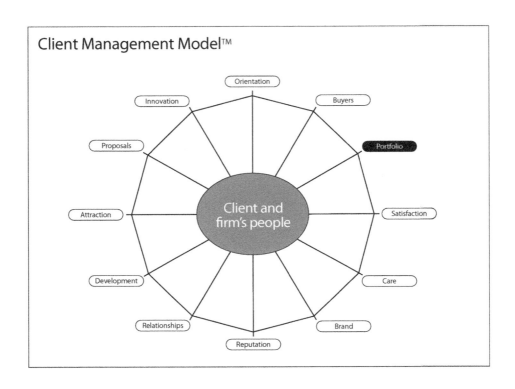

Chapter 3

Portfolio:
Managing the Client Portfolio

Synopsis

Portfolio, the third element of the *Client Management Model*™, highlights:

- the importance and value to the firm of reviewing the Client base;

- analysing sources of fees before deploying limited resources to manage all Clients;

- selecting and managing Clients according to their strategic and potential lifetime value to the firm;

- strategic Client management – how to grow business with existing Clients through greater analysis of their business drivers and requirements, and greater understanding of their structure;

- the importance of sharing of Client data across the firm;

- benefits of comparing the firm's development plans for different Clients;

- managing your Client portfolio;

- the challenges of organising for, and managing, international Clients.

THOUGHT STARTERS
- What typifies the Clients you serve?
- Are you serving the right Clients?
- What is a strategic Client?
- What is the role of a strategic Client manager?
- How well do you manage international Clients?
- What metrics should you use?

The Evolving Commercial Model

As professional services firms grow in size, skills and handle different types of Client, strategic decisions are usually necessary about the direction, structure and scope of its operations. Some firms decide to specialise in one specific area, for example, a law firm may focus on mergers and acquisitions or patents, while an accounting firm may have a strong advisory practice. Others grow their skills base across disciplines to offer a broader range to Clients or decide to expand geographically regardless of the services offered.

It is only relatively recently, compared with their consumer and services counterparts, that professional services firms have taken on a more commercial approach to running their organisations and communicating their offerings. This is partly due to the increased level of competition as the market for professional services has matured. While gross profit per partner is an important measure of a firm's performance, many firms have not yet considered the introduction of marketing and sales functions to bring more focus to growing the business profitably and seeking new markets. Client service is considered important by most firms, yet the recent *Client Care Survey* research reveals that few real measures of Client satisfaction are actually in place.

The commercial function of marketing is often misunderstood by many professional services firms. At a recent networking event, one firm's managing partner admitted that initially marketing was 'a group of fairly expensive people producing pretty brochures'. Selling is often considered taboo in such organisations. Some fee earners clearly believe that Clients will select their firm just because of its reputation. It is also relatively recently that brands and branding have started to emerge and develop within the increasingly more competitive professional services arena to differentiate between firms.

When marketing is truly effective, it brings a professional, strategic, approach of determining Client requirements and then satisfying them profitably through competitively differentiated solutions. Professional marketing people are usually excellent communicators and are trained to understand this and the importance of securing profitable sources and streams of income. They possess the skills to analyse fee income by Client type, service, region, office and sector. This analysis often reveals the strengths and weaknesses of a firm's current operations and provides insights into its possible marketing strategy. Professional marketers also know the power of effective communications directed at the right audiences through the appropriate channels. When marketing is operating effectively, it pervades the firm so that everyone feels Client-oriented. True marketers are not usually satisfied until Clients are part of the firm's DNA, as revealed by employee engagement surveys and, most importantly, from Client feedback.

In professional services firms, the sales function is usually referred to as business development (BD) or Client service (CS). The marketing team devises strategies and targets specific Clients to 'open doors' for the BD team, usually through the generation of enquiries. The BD/CS team then follows up leads and introduces Clients to the firm, and to the relevant partners, with the aim of closing on an instruction. The commercial function usually has a team responsible for creating responses to high-value bids. When marketing is really effective, it makes the subsequent BD process easier.

The most effective commercial model has marketing, BD and bid teams working in harmony – a powerful force available and appropriately resourced to pursue and capture new Clients and to grow existing ones. As firms become more sophisticated, their approach to marketing and BD is likely to create more specific roles. The aim is to develop a portfolio of loyal Clients who consider the firm as its trusted business adviser.

The Evolution of Marketing in Professional Services Firms

In professional services firms the marketing function often evolves by the appointment of marketing managers with responsibility for a particular practice group or service line, for example, audit, tax or advisory in accountants, commercial litigation and intellectual property in law firms and commercial office development in chartered surveyors. Their role is to create credible, differentiated value propositions for their service lines with appropriate communications, through defined channels, to target audiences. This is discussed further in Chapter 6. Marketing's task is to open up opportunities for the firm. Their equivalents in consumer markets would be brand, product or category managers. As the function grows, marketing people are often assigned to regions or industry groups, such as corporate entities, not-for-profit organisations, aerospace, technology and so on.

It becomes evident that a matrix type of organisation can evolve in professional services firms, where the practice marketing team works with the sector marketing team to develop a 'package' of service line offerings to Clients in a defined sector. This form of market segmentation enables firms to understand Clients in more depth, which often differentiates firms from others in the overall market for their services. Applied marketing can transform an organisation within a relatively short time. The following case study shows how this process was adopted in a manufacturing environment.

FROM PRODUCT FOCUS TO CUSTOMER FOCUS

A leading aluminium manufacturer was reviewing its performance as its board realised that their different operations had large variances in volume and profitability. The business aimed to maximise output and profitability from each of its manufacturing sites. Each site had its own portfolio of Customers, ranging from construction companies purchasing aluminium sheet and extruded rods, to aerospace companies buying thin film and sheets, and cooking foil sold to supermarkets.

An external consultant was appointed to investigate the situation, provide new insights and recommend a way forward. Given the sensitivity of the situation, the consultant decided to conduct separate interviews with manufacturing plant managers and a selection of Customers. Levels of satisfaction were generally quite high, but many larger Customers felt that there was a lack of understanding of how the aluminium products were used in the various markets. Some Customers mentioned that they would often meet several different salespeople in a month, each selling the different types of output. The consultant reviewed the internal organisation of the manufacturer and realised that it had a very product-focused mentality. Department managers were responsible for maximising output at the lowest cost. Apart from a few isolated projects, there was very little attention given to research and development. Although there was a sales office at each factory site, there was very little communication between them, even though they had some common Customers. Each site had sales representatives whose role was to sell the output of their factory. Again, apart from an annual event, the sales people did not interact with each other.

After several months, the consultant made a number of recommendations to the board. The overall thrust of this interim report was to change the way that the company faced its markets. A three-year programme was proposed during which the company would create a matrix organisation which related to both manufacturing sites and Customers.

In the first year, each site would be assigned a product manager, whose role was to develop new uses for the variety of aluminium manufactured there. Product managers were appointed covering the different forms of aluminium; thin film, rod, rolls and sheets. In year two, market managers were appointed with responsibility for the key markets using the products. These were defined as aerospace, construction, DIY, home and windows. The market managers visited Customers and distributors in their sector to gain an understanding of their requirements.

Towards the end of year two, the market managers worked with product managers to create offerings to their Customer groups which often required output from several factories. In year three, a manufacturing office was established to forecast demand from each site based on market manager projections. The sales force was reorganised around markets, and was retrained to understand the outputs of all manufacturing sites. Towards the end of the programme, the sales team was organised to manage key Customers in specific sectors. Eventually new products and applications were being developed by product managers working with these key Customers. Within five years of the start of the programme, overall profitability had increased, stock levels were stabilised and the company expanded its production based upon demand-led market forecasts. The consultant was retained to continue development.

Sector Focus

Clients usually expect to deal with people who can demonstrate a real understanding of their business and in-depth knowledge of their sector, so it is not surprising that some firms have assigned partners with the responsibility for overseeing all Clients in a particular sector alongside their service line specialism. As an example, in a law firm, a commercial litigation partner may have an in-depth knowledge of the media sector and so would be called upon to develop media Clients. As other matters arise, so the media sector leader would introduce the appropriate colleagues. In an accounting firm, a tax partner may also lead their property sector. As the relationship with the Client develops, the partner discovers other, unsatisfied requirements. With the Client's agreement, the sector partner introduces other partners from different disciplines to meet the Client. Experience shows that Clients are often well disposed towards sector leaders rather than service line heads, as knowledge of a Client's industry is often an unspoken expectation and yet is a key purchasing determinant.

A SECTOR-FOCUSED DEVELOPMENT STRATEGY

Mills & Reeve LLP (M&R) is a top 50 UK law firm providing corporate and other legal services from offices in Birmingham, Cambridge, Leeds, London, Manchester and Norwich. Its fee income was £77m in 2013. Mark Jeffries is responsible for the strategic direction of the firm with considerable experience in leading and managing its growth.

'Since the mid-1980s M&R has merged with or acquired a number of smaller firms. This started with Francis & Co., Cambridge, followed in 1998 by the acquisition of The Lewington Partnership' says Jeffries. 'As critical mass was sought in the north of England, the firm merged with George Davies in Manchester in 2013. It is hoped to replicate this model in Leeds.'

'When M&R seeks firms to expand its national presence it carefully selects firms with the requisite skills in national sectors. Over the years M&R has achieved success in education and particularly higher education, being one of the four top firms; in health it occupies a similar market position. Other chosen sectors are private wealth and insurance. M&R is reviewing other emerging sectors such as food & beverages, technology and sport (a strength of George Davies). When entering a sector M&R puts together a team to deliver "heavy lifting" services comprising corporate finance and real estate lawyers, and then brings in the appropriate specialists to complement the offering.'

'Another important selection criterion for M&R is cultural fit; the firm has developed a distinctive approach to its people which Clients recognise in its style of service delivery. This approach has enabled M&R to be listed in the *Sunday Times* 100 Best Companies over each of the last 10 years; making it the only law firm to have done so. Its 2015 vision and values are important to M&R as articulated in two documents on their website. These values are openness and integrity, working together, respect for each other and strong Client relationships.'

'M&R has an international capability through its membership of SCG Legal (previously State Capital Group, reflecting its US origins). It has many contacts throughout this global network of law firms and is represented at SCG's major conferences. Close relationships have grown with firms in France, Germany and the Netherlands which have a good sector fit with M&R. They work together on Client service and technical training projects as well as business development initiatives to provide a coherent pan-European service offering to Clients. While cultural fit is important in its UK expansion, with international work, consistency of quality in delivery is the most critical element in choosing a country partner.'

Mills & Reeve has clear strategic goals to achieve by 2015 and is prepared to face the challenges it faces through differentiating its approach in a highly competitive arena.

Classifying Clients

It is worth reviewing the various metrics and analytical methods used by professional services firms to classify their Clients in order to gain a deeper understanding of where the firm's business is now and where it could go in the future. There are many classification options. These can inform a more strategic direction to be given to the firm's Client fee earning teams and supporting staff. This analysis helps to decide the focus and deployment of limited resources.

METRICS

When assembling a Client portfolio, it is important to have in place the appropriate KPIs. Professional services firms use a wide variety of these measures to monitor their ongoing performance. They include:

- share of Client spend – the proportion gained by the firm;

- gross margin – by Client, sector, office, etc.;

- services provided – the extent of cross-selling;

- referral value – the value attributable to reported referrals;

- overall market share in a particular sector;

- income growth by sector.

The Client portfolio can then be evaluated and flexed according to the financial needs of the firm.

CLIENT ANALYSIS

Ways of classifying Clients for focus

We will look at three classification methods here:

- Fee income level.

- Strategic.

- Opportunistic.

Fee income level

This is the most common method of classification. Many firms stratify their Clients by fee revenue, putting them into categories such as' Crown Jewels', Gold, Silver and Bronze; major, premier or key Clients, and so on. Others look at Client profitability at the gross margin level, and devise appropriate development strategies. Such approaches appear quite logical, however it is best not to distinguish between the level of care attributable to different sizes of Client – after all, in due time, a Bronze Client could become a Gold one! Of course, the resourcing of higher income level Clients is likely to be greater than lower income ones but should pay off in the longer term. Hence some firms decide on a 'premium' level of service for their top 50 Clients. The downside of this approach is that the smaller Clients may feel neglected.

Some firms use the concept of Client Lifetime Value (CLV) to assess the potential fee income level of a Client and the likelihood of a relationship continuing. This also allows better planning on investment in Client relationships and is considered a good basis for decisions about the content of a Client portfolio.

To calculate the gross CLV take the average annual fee earned from all Clients and multiply this by the expected duration (lifetime) of the Client relationship in years. To calculate the net CLV estimate the average annual cost of serving a Client and deduct this from the gross figure.

EXAMPLE CALCULATION OF CLIENT LIFETIME VALUE.

Let us suppose that your firm has 200 Clients generating an annual fee income of £10m. On examining your data you discover that the average Client engagement is 5 years and the servicing cost per Client is around 20 per cent of fees per year.

Average fee = £10,000,000 / 200   = £50,000

Gross Lifetime Value = £50,000 x 5   = £250,000

Servicing cost = £50,000 x 20% x 5   = £50,000

Net Lifetime Value per Client = £250,000 - £50,000 = £200,000

Some firms also factor in an annual Client churn rate, based on Client retention. This reduces the CLV.

Strategic

Another approach to distinguishing which Clients to service is to consider their 'fit' with the firm's strategy. Some firms choose to group their Clients by size. For example, if the firm aims to service large corporate entities, such Clients as blue-chip companies would be considered strategic. International Clients could also be considered as strategic.

If the firm has decided to focus on specific industrial sectors or geographical area, those Clients would be considered strategic. Having a strategic approach to markets enables the firm's marketing and BD teams to direct their activities and energies towards defined, targeted, potentially lucrative Clients. Some firms call these 'core' Clients and will do almost anything to retain them, aiming to achieve a minimum level of profitability. Strategic Clients are those that a firm will do almost anything for in order to retain their business.

Opportunistic

Occasionally, some Clients just contact the firm for advice 'out of the blue' and decide to engage them. These Clients can be quite lucrative and may provide single assignments or ongoing fee-earning possibilities. Many firms consider these Clients as opportunistic and will try to fit them into one of the other selection categories at some point in time, given that there is a strategic fit.

Of course, it is worth the time taken to investigate the source of the lead, as it could be through a referral.

Key Client Selection and Management

Once it has been decided how Clients might be classified, it is important to establish a process for their ongoing selection and management. From analysis of our Client base, we can decide how best to manage our Client portfolio as outlined earlier. It is clear that a firm cannot give the same time and resources to every Client, so some form of selection and prioritisation is necessary to provide focus on those Clients that are likely to be the most lucrative to the firm over the longer term. Many firms devise criteria to select which Clients require this focus. They then assign priorities and use a weighting to 'score' Clients.

These selection criteria include the following.

STRATEGIC

- Strategic alignment.

- Overall importance to the firm.

- Sector focus.

- Growth prospects and potential.

- Stage in the Client lifecycle.

- Client loyalty and advocacy levels.

- International.

- Cultural fit.

INCOME

- Revenue objectives overall.

- Current and projected revenues.

- Cross-selling potential.

- Frequency of fee generation.

- Fee penetration.

- Share of Client spend.

- Lifetime value.

- Level of repeat business.

- High referral value.

MARKET POSITION

- Size in terms of turnover.

- Regional importance to the firm.

- Prestigious, e.g. well-known.

- Market leader.

- Corporate responsibility profile.

- International reputation.

Prioritising Clients

Table 3.1 shows how to use the strategy factors to compare different Clients. To make this effective, it is important to bring together a small team for each Client that can assign scores against each factor based on their Client knowledge. This would typically include the Client Relationship Manager, BD and any Practice Team member. This exercise can then be extended to include the other classification factors.

Table 3.1   Evaluating the Strategic Fit of Two Clients

Strategic Selection Factors	Weight	Client A Score	Client A Total (W x S)	Client B Score	Client B Total (W x S)
Strategic alignment	8	8	64	7	56
Overall importance to the firm	7	5	35	8	56
Sector focus	6	9	54	3	18
Growth prospects and potential	5	6	30	6	30
Stage in the Client lifecycle	4	8	32	6	24
Client loyalty and advocacy	3	5	15	5	15
International	2	9	18	6	12
Cultural fit	1	7	7	7	7
Totals			255		218

So, in this example, Client A has the better strategic fit. When repeated for all Clients being considered, resources can then be allocated accordingly. It may also be decided to service certain Clients in different ways depending on their fit with the firm's strategy and their potential.

ESTABLISHING AN EFFECTIVE MARKETING OPERATION IN PROFESSIONAL SERVICES

A national professional services firm with around 100 partners was structured along 10 service lines, each with a practice head reporting to the managing partner. A marketing department had been set up primarily to produce sales collateral and run events. As income had remained stagnant for a period of several years, the board decided to call in a consultant to advise how the firm could grow. The consultant discovered that each service line was run autonomously, with little collaboration or communication between them about Client management or development. There was also very little analysis of sources of business. Events were held regularly and activities were created, but without much attention to follow up and return on investment. Partners held on to their Clients and were clearly reluctant to share knowledge and relationships.

Determining the Top Value Clients

Following discussions with the management team, the consultant organised a number of workshops involving a mix of service line heads and managers. Preparatory work involved some basic analysis of income. During the workshop sessions, each service line head was asked to name their top ten Clients by income. These were listed on flip charts and displayed around the walls of the room. It became evident that many Clients appeared on several lists.

What was more revealing was that some of the participants admitted that they were unaware of these 'shared' Clients! The delegates were then asked to classify Clients by sector. This gave another view of the business and highlighted relative sector strength. Another exercise mapped the contacts at each Client; this again surprised the audience. It became clear to the group that there was little co-ordination of Client contacting.

Managing Common Clients across Service Lines

Over the ensuing weeks the consultant called together groups of service line heads to discuss how they could manage the 'common' Clients that had been identified. Around 70 Clients were selected for further review. It was agreed that each Client would have a partner assigned who would be responsible for managing the overall relationship between the Client and the firm. This change would be communicated to, and discussed with, the Client. Each 'relationship partner' would be required to develop a service plan for Clients in his portfolio, based on input from each practice head, even if there was no income currently in that service line. This service plan would eventually form part of the ongoing strategic dialogue with the Client.

Introducing Professional Marketing

The consultant then suggested that each service line should have marketing support at manager level, led by a senior marketing manager who would report to the board. This investment was agreed and four professional marketing managers were appointed to cover the 10 practice areas. The marketing team created positioning and differentiation statements for each service line and produced strategies and plans aimed at specific target audiences.

This structure remained in place for around two years, during which time the firm's revenue had clearly grown through the cross-selling opportunities that were identified by the marketing team working with relationship partners and service line heads. The inertia that was associated with the earlier ways of working had disappeared.

Sector Focus

Following further analysis of the firm's business by sector, it became evident to the senior marketing manager that there were certain sectors that were growing; these were food, retail, technology and transport. The board agreed to the recruitment of a sector marketing manager whose role was to create campaigns relevant to each growth sector. Over time this role was extended to include other emerging sectors and the larger value sectors were assigned a sector marketing manager. Sectors were then targeted for business development.

Client Satisfaction

A Client satisfaction programme was established, starting with the firm's top 70 Clients. This revealed further business development opportunities which were followed up. The service line marketing managers were given new roles to oversee strategic marketing channels and to create a positioning and package of service lines for each channel.

In the five years since the intervention of the consultant, the firm's income grew on average by 8 per cent, year-on-year.

Organising to Serve International Clients

Many professional services firms operating out of London often manage their international business from there, sometimes through associates. London is seen by many firms as a global business centre and a hub for their operations. As business has become increasingly global for many Clients, especially those in the media and technology sectors, a local presence is more desirable to these Clients. A firm present in many countries is more likely to take on Clients whose operations also match that presence. If it is possible to broaden the firm's reputation by keeping a single brand and name, this is more acceptable to international Clients.

When law firm Bird & Bird decided to expand abroad, it sought the best entrepreneurial lawyers with local knowledge who could set up and run an office in their country. This has the advantage of management control and consistency of branding, keeping the Bird & Bird name intact. Many professional services firms are set up as networks, many are independent organisations under an international umbrella with common frameworks; others are structured globally. Another route to serving international Clients is through joining industry networks. An example of this approach, mentioned earlier by law firm Mills & Reeve, is the US-based SCG Legal, a global network of law firms.

Industrial corporations, such as those in the automobile sector, were among the first to recognise their purchasing power as global markets opened up. Purchasing decisions in global manufacturing are often made at HQ and then instructions to suppliers are cascaded down through the country operations. Supplier rationalisation and supply chain management have revolutionised these corporations and their purchasing has become more cost-effective over time.

Similarly, in internationally spread professional services firms, there is an expectation from Clients of a seamless, consistent service everywhere. As stated earlier, the challenge is to provide the same Client experience in all locations. This has to be the goal of an effective global firm. Cultural differences aside, this situation provides professional services firms wishing to have a global footprint with the biggest challenges.

CONSISTENCY WITHIN A GLOBAL NETWORK

Most professional services firms are international these days; Allan Evans serves on BDO's global board to ensure consistency in processes, structures and disciplines across the network. 'The same experience must occur wherever BDO does business. This is critical for mid-sized firms. For example, the *Net Promoter Score* system is becoming mandatory for all member firms.'

The Challenges of Managing International Clients

Many Clients of professional services firms have operations in many countries, so if a firm is represented locally, there is an opportunity to serve them. Clearly the management of international Clients has its challenges, especially as most professional services firms operate in global networks of independently owned organisations. Many questions arise when shaping international policy and Client management, for example:

- How well is your firm organised to deal with multi-country (and therefore multi-jurisdictional) Clients?

- How consistent is your branding and marketing communications across the network?

- Does your network provide a seamless, consistent service in all locations?

- Will Clients have sufficient access to key partners in all locations?

- How do you manage Clients in countries where your firm is not represented?

- Can your processes and systems cope with international communications and transactions?

- How will you manage Client expectations across geographic boundaries?

- How will you decide which Clients to manage globally?

- Who will take responsibility for managing global Client relationships?

- What pricing policy and structure is needed for a seamless operation?

- How should you communicate on cross-border enquiries?

- How should you respond to bid opportunities from international Clients?

- Which country will take the lead with a multi-country Client?

- How will Client satisfaction be monitored and reported?

- How frequently should your Client service teams meet or be in video conference?

- How well are your Client satisfaction programmes aligned in all countries?

- How will your business development initiatives be co-ordinated?

- What projects of interest to international Clients can you manage involving your network?

Many operational issues arise, such as:

- language capability;

- transfer pricing;

- IT systems compatibility;

- work planning processes;

- risk management and containment;

- recruitment;

- legal and compliance variations;

- governmental rules;

- data protection and security;

- changes in country representation of the firm;

- cultural differences;

- project management.

Most professional services firms operating in global networks have established a central international headquarters staffed with people who oversee, and assist with, the development of the network by:

- Setting the strategic direction of the global organisation;

- Helping member firms to achieve the strategy;

- Providing guidance on legal and risk management compliance;

- Encouraging collaboration and sharing of resources between member firms;

- encouraging regular communications with, and between, member firms;

- ensuring that minimum standards are met across a wide variety of metrics, such as branding, marketing communications, BD and Client satisfaction;

- vetting and selecting new members for the network;

- administering new members and integrating them into the network;

- terminating membership where necessary;

- locating potential member firms where a country or service line is under-represented;

- managing international projects of benefit to member firms, for example, market research;

- managing the financial aspects of the HQ;

- co-ordinating cross-jurisdictional bids;

- facilitating contacts throughout the network.

HOW LAW FIRM BIRD & BIRD INTERNATIONALISED ITS BUSINESS

Just over 20 years ago, recognising the rapidly evolving needs of its core Client base, law firm Bird & Bird made a strategic decision to deliberately grow by global expansion. In 1998 Managing Partner David Kerr proposed his vision for the firm at the partners' retreat – the time had come to internationalise the firm through a single partnership, replicating the successful London model. At the time Bird & Bird's international presence only existed in Brussels and Hong Kong. Meanwhile, the firm's target Clients, particularly those in the technology sector – a rapidly growing market for Bird & Bird – were looking for a range of internationally available services. Although the firm was experiencing steady growth at the time, Kerr warned that there was a strong possibility of losing business to global competitors who were already building their international networks – the firm could even cease to exist in five years if they didn't act quickly.

Kerr explains that he had identified two routes to the internationalisation of the firm. The first, quite popular in the market and relatively easy to accomplish, was to have a loose international network where the firm did not share profits. The second, more innovative, option was to create a single partnership sharing a common financial interest. This latter model was agreed by the vast majority of partners and started to take shape by the millennium.

Rather than following the typical acquisition model, the agreed vision was to identify high-profile individuals in large non-sector-specific firms in the countries where Client demand was driving expansion and persuade them to join the firm. These people would be well-known in their field and local market and possess the entrepreneurial spirit to build and grow a business under the Bird & Bird brand in their country. In fact, many of these people had already worked with Bird & Bird. Kerr was frank with his partner colleagues when he said that one of the measures of the success of this strategy would be when the majority of the firm's partners were based outside the UK.

A small corporate development team headed by the firm's finance director was established to manage the firm's expansion, with a new CFO to manage the existing operations.

In 2000, Bird & Bird looked to France as their first new venture, already working with Clients such as BT. Their Brussels office had identified a strong potential candidate in a French firm who was eventually persuaded to set up a Paris office. Following the success of this venture, subsequent expansion was rapid, with offices opening in Sweden (2000), the Netherlands (2001) and Germany (2002). These were followed by an office being established in Italy (2003) as a result of a recommendation from Bird & Bird's thriving German practice. By 2004 Bird & Bird had over 100 partners and it opened an office in Beijing. Offices were opened in Spain in 2005, in central and Eastern Europe and Finland in 2008, in Singapore in 2009, in Abu Dhabi in 2011, in Denmark in 2012 and in Dubai in 2013. Today the firm also has partnership agreements with firms in Australia, Malaysia, Portugal, Switzerland and Tunisia.

During this period of rapid expansion the corporate development team and partners were encouraged by the realisation that the Bird & Bird brand was quickly developing a strong reputation around the world, and by the willingness of its long-standing London Clients to extend their business to the international Bird & Bird offices. David Kerr anticipates that the firm will continue to expand.

Innovation with Clients

Another factor in the success of the firm's international reach strategy has been the determination to prioritise the Client service experience in every Bird & Bird location. One example of differentiation has been the creation of bespoke Client portals online with secure access for Client personnel and third parties to provide co-ordinated global legal services, visible matter management, transparent billing and easy access to documentation and know-how. This dynamic process is managed by a team of Client Relationship Executives. Whilst highly regarded by Clients, this offering also has the benefit of raising barriers to competitive entry.

The Way Ahead

In terms of their expansion, Asia and South America are cited as the next markets for development. With many of its Clients selling their technology globally, Bird & Bird is aiming to be the leading technology law firm outside the US, as well as developing in those markets where technology plays an increasing role such as energy, aviation, media and life sciences.

The Role of the International HQ

In professional service networks the international HQ is primarily administrative. While it does need to encourage strong communication links across the network, it does not usually have a fee-earning responsibility; this is left to member firms. In return for its services, member firms pay the HQ a joining fee and an annual fee to finance the international office. The location of an international office in a particular country may depend on the relative local fee income; as such, many firms establish an international headquarters in the country with the highest income level. This location can also be rotated over time among the larger firms in the network so that an international perspective is really encouraged and not dominated by one country. Most of the larger global firms convene annual international conferences. Each year a different country acts as host and usually presents highlights from its operations, followed by examples from other members. Member firms enjoy the opportunity to meet their peers and compare programmes, cultures and results. Such annual events become important when encouraging participation in new initiatives, such as establishing the *Net Promoter Score* in each member firm. Most globally minded firms operate weekly news intranets and monthly conference calls in time zone groups so that everyone can keep up with developments, such as new Clients acquisitions, members, changes in policy, awards won and other matters of interest.

HOW RSM MANAGES ITS GLOBAL NETWORK

Jean Stephens has been CEO of RSM International (RSM) since 2006, a network of audit, tax and advisory firms in over 100 countries, with 700 offices and over 32,000 people. RSM ranks 7th in global fee income and positions itself as having 'global reach with local perspective'.

Selection of Member Firms

When admitting new member firms, Jean and her team have strict selection criteria. In the first stage they conduct desk research to select firms that match their target market; some firms also contact RSM with a view to joining the network. If an exploratory meeting is held, RSM looks at the potential member's vision and strategic direction; where the firm is going, how they are building their business. RSM is also interested in how the potential member would use the network and work with other members.

The second stage involves reviewing the firm's quality infrastructure, and how leadership – the 'tone from the top' – is established. Essentially RSM looks for well-managed firms to join their network. The existing Client base is reviewed along with the firm's ambitions and its match with the existing network in terms of sectors, international reach and size. Although fees and referred work are often discussed, the synergy between firms and the network is considered more important. In prospecting meetings, RSM looks for firms that have the right fit and with which it can build strong, long-term collaborative relationships.

A third stage involves technical due diligence; procedures and processes are reviewed and compared with both internationally accepted norms and RSM standards. Any gaps are reviewed and may make or break the potential firm's chances of joining.

Consistency

RSM has many policies to ensure that consistency is maintained throughout the network of member firms. RSM emphasises high quality of Client service in all its communications. A monthly managing partner bulletin is distributed to all member firms along with an internal news bulletin for RSM staff. A global leader for quality and risk was appointed recently to underpin the RSM commitment and focus on quality and service as 'second to none'. RSM also has a global audit methodology along with standards for tax and risk assurance. It aims for consistent policies and application; it is also moving to a paperless methodology.

RSM runs the RSM Academy, now in its 8th year – a leadership and specialist training programme for managers and junior partners to increase their international Client skills and capabilities. It has also created global engagement leaders for management of multi-country Clients.

An annual inspection programme is in place for robust monitoring of member firms' plans, training and accountability. Member firms are expected to report on time and have the opportunity to critique each other on specific Client engagements. RSM holds annual conferences in all regions, as well as a three-day annual global conference. Aside from this, the regional operating groups, Centres of Excellence and other technical committees further encourage partners and internationally active staff to meet regularly to share best practices, develop an understanding of other cultures and build cross-border teams.

Impact of Mergers, Acquisitions and Departures from the Network

If a member firm decides to join or leave the network the situation is handled very sensitively by RSM management especially with regard to its impact on Clients. RSM aims to minimise this impact by agreeing an appropriate transition programme with affected firms. For the Clients there is always priority on continuity of service and changes in advisory teams in such periods of change and uncertainty.

Managing International Clients

RSM's international business development project – 'Connected for Growth' – provides member firms with the skills and tools needed to engage in cross-border business development strategies. As part of this initiative RSM has developed pricing and scoping tools to enhance value to Clients and project management tools to aid Client satisfaction. Connected for Growth also includes a skills development programme providing high value training to create Global Engagement Leaders.

The Use of Data Analytics to Segment Clients

Many firms hold a massive amount of transactional and other information about their Clients. By using sophisticated software programmes and analysing this information, suppliers are able to predict with some accuracy the future behaviour of Clients. The use of Customer data had its beginnings in the consumer sector and has now moved to the services sector. An example is retailers that use mined transaction data to send money-off coupons to their Customers for goods related to the previous purchase. Another is in hotels that send out special offers to loyal Customers.

It will be interesting to see what developments occur in professional services, where Client data is just as prevalent, although existing in lower volumes. It is likely that the more informed firms will use data analytics to better target prospective Clients by drilling down into the detail available. This topic is discussed further in Chapter 14.

MANAGING GLOBAL KEY ACCOUNTS

Darren Cox was appointed Global Key Account Manager at Grant Thornton International following over 20 years' prior experience of Key Account Management (KAM) in the legal and financial services sectors. His role is to formalise the global KAM Programme within the Grant Thornton global network.

'For KAM to be successful, a strategic approach is essential. Many senior partners have had various levels of exposure to KAM in the past, and there can be resistance to any attempts to make improvements or changes. KAM requires application of a focused business strategy that concentrates on those Clients that are of the highest corporate value in terms of income, profitability and growth. A Global Key Account Manager is the firm's champion of the Client and reflects the Client requirements and concerns back to the firm.'

The requirements of a KAM Programme are considerable for an effective outcome:

- A board level/management team KAM programme sponsor.
- Alignment with the firm's strategic plan, signed off at board level.
- Having the appropriate behaviours in place to manage the Client relationship, often through coaching and mentoring.
- Selection of the right Clients.
- Determining the appropriate value proposition for each Client (see also Chapter 6 for more information).
- Conducting needs assessments so that action plans are realistic in addressing the opportunities that present themselves.
- Clearly defined team member responsibilities and KPIs.
- Ensuring there is a mechanism in place to reward the non-billable time invested.
- Having the budgetary flexibility to support KAM, effective management will see investment of upwards of 30–40 per cent of a high earning partner's time.
- Measurement and reporting, ideally by a third party, against agreed annual objectives.
- The ability to measure and monitor the profitability of business with the Client.
- A full time resource spending at least one day per week on each Client.
- An appropriate supporting structure to underpin the Client relationship and monitor satisfaction.
- Sensitivity to cultural differences within the network regarding ways of working, sharing of information with other members and the level of candour.
- Sensitivity towards the differing requirements and preferences of international Clients.

- A feedback process involving the Client, overall relationship review at least annually to review joint progress and agree actions where appropriate along with major matter reviews as appropriate.
- Celebration of success: don't discount the importance of internal communication.
- Accepting that we learn from our successes and also failures, while there will be hard earned wins not all plans turn out as expected; the aim is for continuous KAM improvement.

One of the key challenges with KAM is that there may be only a few contact points in the network that have the appropriate depth of relationship with the international Client. It is how you utilise these contacts to help build cross-service line revenues.

To implement a KAM Programme requires a number of ongoing activities. For example, facilitated workshops can be held with two Client teams at a time, which can challenge each other's plans and bring different cultural insights across jurisdictions. These sessions are followed by regular reviews through video- and tele-conferencing.'

'In my experience KAM works better in some cultures than others; KAM is usually driven from the West, and some member firms in some countries within regions such as Asia & Pacific may find KAM a struggle at first. For this reason a KAM programme needs to consider this and ensure that key stakeholders are engaged early into the process. The use of fit-for-purpose templates and guidelines supported with an organisation structure are useful prerequisites for an effective KAM Programme.

Regular contact between Client team members is also essential to maintain the necessary momentum and meet the Client's requirements. A dedicated internal portal is available to enable sharing of documentation across the firm. Monthly calls are made in the Western hemisphere and the Eastern hemisphere. A balanced scorecard is used by managing partners to ensure that partners deliver their KAM KPIs and that these are acknowledged during the partners' appraisal.

In a global KAM Programme one of the key elements is the selection of Clients. This requires engagement of key stakeholders from across the firms in identified growth markets across the network. The process takes considerable time and effort and the assessment is scored using a number of strict criteria, including:

- Fit with the firm's global industry groupings.
- Whether a formal master service agreement or preferred supplier agreement is in place.
- Revenues in excess of $1m per year for the past three years with growth potential.
- Multiple service line opportunities identified.

- Geographic fit with the firm's capabilities.
- Established relationships with senior head office buyers/influencers within the Client.
- Availability of the lead partner for non-billable time.
- Local business development resource available to assist with the delivery of parts of the global plan relevant to their jurisdiction.

"KAM Client team member collaboration and focused Client engagement will result in increased workflows and deeper relationships with senior buyers and influencers. The ultimate aim is to achieve/maintain trusted advisor status. This effort helps to ensure on-going revenue growth and Client loyalty. This result in turn has the added internal benefit of supporting the expansion of the KAM programme".'

Portfolio Management is a Strategic Priority

Portfolio has shown how professional services firms can manage their Clients in many different ways. Strategic classification is a useful way of informing best use of resources. Those firms that have addressed the variety of Clients served and taken decisions to manage them strategically are more likely to be successful than firms who are prepared to handle any Client that comes along. The role of strategic Client Manager is becoming critical when managing both large and international Clients. Managing global Clients is also discussed in Chapter 14.

Managing the Client Portfolio

CLIENT MANAGEMENT REVIEW QUESTIONS

To what extent:

1.   Has your firm classified its Client portfolio into strategic groups?

2.   Do you review your method of classifying Clients?

3.   Do you review your KPIs to see how these are managed over the Client mix?

4.   Do you know the penetration level of the firm's top 10 Clients?

5.   Do you know and report internally your gross margins per sector?

6.   Do you know and report your income growth per sector and service line?

7.   Do you use data analytics to improve your knowledge about Client preferences?

8.   Do you create service and development plans for top Clients?

9.   Do you allocate Client Service Partners to your key Clients?

10.   Do key Clients have an allocated marketing budget?

These questions also form the basis of the *Portfolio* section of the *Client Management Profile*™, which can be found in Chapter 15.

———

Two further pointers:

- If you have international Clients, can you name the top 10?

- Review your processes for managing international Clients.

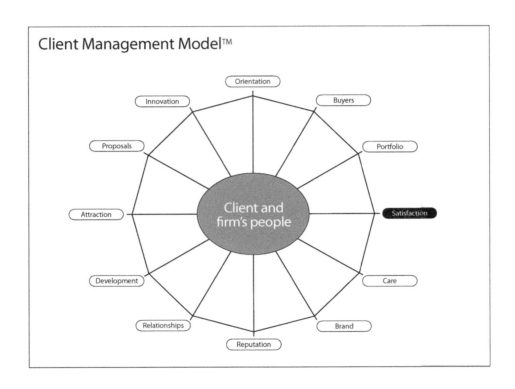

Client Management Model™

Chapter 4
Satisfaction:
Client Satisfaction and Loyalty

Synopsis

Satisfaction, the fourth element of the *Client Management Model*™, explains:

- the importance of monitoring and measuring Client satisfaction to gain insights;

- identifying gaps in performance targets and metrics;

- how to organise focus and reward in the firm around Client satisfaction;

- satisfaction parallels with the hierarchy of needs;

- the causes and remedies of service failure;

- dealing with the loss of a major Client;

- how to establish a Client Satisfaction Programme;

- the use of Client panels to keep in touch with your markets;

- the value of the *Net Promoter Score* in tracking Client loyalty;

- how to estimate the economic value of the most loyal Clients;

- rewarding excellence in Client satisfaction.

THOUGHT STARTERS
- What is Client satisfaction?
- How do you measure Client satisfaction?
- What evidence do you have on Client loyalty?
- What is the value of your referral business?
- Why is the *Net Promoter Score*[1] such an important metric?

---

1   The *Net Promoter Score* is attributed to Fred Reichheld and was introduced in his *Harvard Business Review* article 'One Number You Need to Grow' in 2003.

Client Satisfaction Yields Insights

Client satisfaction is the extent to which a firm's services meet or exceed Client expectations. It is well-known that a small increase in Client satisfaction can yield considerable additional net profit, so it pays to constantly strive for increased Client satisfaction and loyalty through continuous monitoring and improvement of the Client experience. It is vital to check regularly how satisfied Clients are with your services. The more Client-oriented firms are more likely to be doing this as a matter of everyday business. This is usually effected through various types of survey, often conducted by a third party or someone in the firm unconnected to the Client in order to remove any bias.

Monitoring Client satisfaction can often uncover new opportunities for your firm; the swift handling of any concerns revealed during a satisfaction survey can also recover a Client from the possibility of defection. It is well-known that satisfied Clients tell many others, but unsatisfied ones tell between seven and 10 people.

Those firms conducting Client satisfaction surveys use a variety of methodologies. Some manage and implement the process internally; others use a mix of internal and external approaches. Clients are grouped by the type of survey they will receive, by agreement with the relationship partners involved. The most common and cost-effective method is post-transaction, being by telephone, using a well-briefed third party. Face-to-face interviews with the most strategically important Clients are usually carried out by board-level and senior management who are not directly involved with the Client assignment or matter being reviewed. Some firms outsource this research activity for complete independence. This level of investment is an initial hurdle for some firms to overcome, but current practice suggests that it is increasing.

Other surveys are also carried out independent of any current transaction. These reveal how the firm is treating its Clients during periods of lower work activity. Where possible, interviews are recorded with permission. Listening to these can reveal issues and concerns that may not surface elsewhere; such activity can also be a great source for case studies and referrals. Verbatim comments are very powerful to those hearing them in this new context. The recent *Client Care Survey* of professional services firms has shown that not all firms consider the importance or benefits of Client satisfaction and showed that the voice of the Client is rarely represented in the boardroom.

Table 4.1   Client Satisfaction Benchmarking Methods

Conduct surveys of peer firms	12.50%
Review syndicated research	33.20%
No comparisons made	60.90%

Source: Client Care Survey 2013.

There are many benchmarking surveys available that enable firms to have a clearer picture of their relative performance in Client satisfaction. Yet the *Client Care Survey* shows that less than half of professional services firms surveyed carry out any form of competitor comparisons of Client satisfaction. Table 4.1 shows that only one in eight firms survey their peers and only one third review syndicated research.

So, what is the nature of Client satisfaction and what does it really involve? The mantra of Client satisfaction is a very simple one: 'Do the right things, right first time.' Yet few firms, if any, ever fully succeed in this aim. We all have experiences of different levels and qualities of Client/Customer service. When we receive bad service, we usually tell our friends and family; nowadays we can even vent our annoyance on the supplier's website! Of one thing we can be fairly certain: your Clients will tell their colleagues if your service is poor. Of course, we also talk about excellent service.

To address the issue of understanding the needs of your Clients, it is best to conduct detailed market research. Ideally, it should also provide clear insights into how and why Clients are judging the firm's current performance with that of their competitors in the way they service Clients. The more quantitative the answers obtained, the more useful is the data. This greatly assists in the subsequent process of determining and monitoring internal actions.

The Service Matrix – Capability vs Delivery

Market research can identify which are the most important service dimensions from the Clients' perspective. This helps to focus the time and resources involved where the greatest impact can be obtained. Market research should also seek to clarify the firm's comparative performance.

Identifying Performance 'Gaps'

The process of identifying performance gaps on service-related issues is best effected by interviewing or surveying Clients. They are first asked to rate the firm's *performance* on the service dimensions out of a maximum 10 points. They are then asked to rate one or two competitors on the same performance factors. Then they are asked to similarly rate the *importance* of each factor, regardless of supplier. This enables a matrix to be created showing how the firm and competitors performed against the same factors. Using this matrix approach, such as the one illustrated in Figure 4.1, the results can be plotted and can reveal for some firms that 'service enhancement' can be self-funding. If a large number of dimensions fall in the 'over-delivery' box, project task teams can generally find ways of saving costs without a significant adverse effect on Client service performance. These savings can fund improvement in other areas. For example, the logistics sector does not provide Clients who simply want a package delivered with superior vehicles; they use the asset saving to fund superior IT systems for those that want tracking information. Many professional services firms spend considerable sums in creating and mailing newsletters, but have not established Client reaction or preferences.

The Performance 'Gap'

For each service element, the research should ideally identify:

- the standard of performance that is acceptable and what is regarded as 'added value';

- where the firm does not meet the standard;

- which other firms and competitors are meeting or exceeding the two levels of standard.

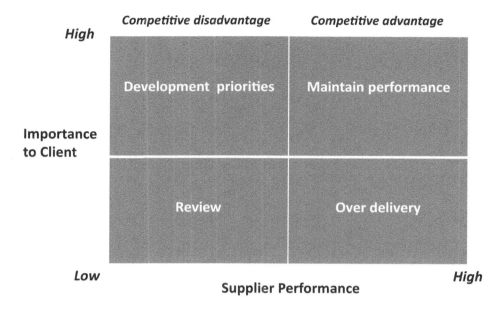

Figure 4.1   Service Matrix

There are many ways to obtain this type of information. The best research approach is based on detailed face-to-face interviews with a variety of people within the Client's Decision Making Unit (DMU). This gives greater insight into the 'prism of activity' that ultimately creates Client satisfaction and loyalty.

Law firm Mills & Reeve (M&R)[1] is careful to establish how Clients want their work to be managed and delivered. Some Clients have given feedback that they are receiving a '5 star' service, but only have the budget for a '3 star' service. In such cases, M&R redesigns and re-engineers its offering accordingly to maintain margins.

Aspects of Service

As an example, here is a list of basic aspects of service used to rate insurance companies:

- Claims payment – efficiency and integrity.

---

1   See feature later in this chapter.

- Developing our book – enterprise and active support.

- Insurance cover – fitness for Client needs.

- New business – efficiency in providing quotations.

- Policy documentation –usability and timeliness.

- Renewals process – efficiency and fairness.

- Underwriters – professional capabilities.

Using Maslow's[2] Hierarchy of Needs to Explain Client Satisfaction

For every industry, it is clear that a 'hierarchy of needs' exists, the key to development of enhanced Client satisfaction can be likened to satisfying 'basic' levels of need fully before addressing the upper levels. This hierarchy was first conceived by Abraham Maslow Although created some time ago, the model is still considered by experts as appropriate in all markets.

The five stages in Maslow's original* model are as follows:

1. Biological and physiological needs – the basic life needs – the lowest needs to be satisfied before moving to the next point below.

2. Safety needs – security, protection.

3. Belonging and love needs – affection, family, relationships, work group.

4. Esteem needs – achievement, responsibility, status, reputation.

5. Self-actualisation needs – personal growth and fulfilment.

Examples in different sectors are shown in Table 4.2. In parallel with the original needs model, Customers and Clients only move up the hierarchy when the current level of satisfaction is met.

---

2   Adapted from the *Journal of Psychology*/Abraham Maslow's *Theory of Motivation and Personality*, first published in 1954.

Table 4.2   Hierarchies of Needs

Satisfaction level	Original*	Consumer	Industrial	Professional Services	Satisfaction level
Highest	Self-actualisation	Partnership	Joint ventures	Client advocates and referrals	Enchanted
	Esteem	Category champion	Tailored products	Repeat business	Delighted
Average	Belonging and Love	Value	Augmented products	Value added	Satisfied
	Safety	Quality products	Value added	Specialist services	Indifferent
Lowest	Biological and Physiological	Distribution	Core	Core practice areas	Alienated

Many firms, in an effort to be seen as 'leading edge', spend too much time and wasted resources focusing on the upper echelons of these hierarchies before attending to the lowest levels. Meanwhile, their Clients are judging them critically on some of the simple issues – accuracy of order fulfilment, response (speed) to basic enquiries, sector understanding, quality relationships and so on.

The Root Causes of Failure in Client Service

From experience, three simple answers are apparent: lack of common goals, poor or unclear communication internally and between the firm and Client, and the level of effort a Client has to make to ensure that their needs are met. We will take each of these in turn below.

LACK OF COMMON GOALS

Often no clearly defined goals have been set detailing what are the Client service objectives. There can be a wealth of different internal responses to the concept, but unclear objectives such as 'We must respond quickly to Client enquiries' are not sufficiently defined. What is meant by a response? What does 'quickly' mean? Many firms use 'SMART' objectives to greatly clarify the position: **S**pecific, **M**easurable, **A**chievable, **R**ealistic and **T**ime-bound. Have we defined the required standards? Who will do what, how, when and why? For example, 'The Client service function will contact by telephone the person making the enquiry within three hours to provide the answer requested or to seek further information' is much better than having no policy for this situation.

Far too frequently, no clear service goals are set and communication is poor. This leaves the door open for different interpretations within different parts of the firm. It also leads to Client confusion.

POOR, OR UNCLEAR, COMMUNICATION

It is the role of management to set the corporate goals for Client service standards. With robust research, these can and should be based on matching Client expectations where this can be done profitably. Exceeding expectations can only be justified where perceived added value can be demonstrated and a commercial return obtained. If these goals are not clearly communicated and regularly reinforced, changes of personnel or new internal processes and informal networks can all too quickly create mixed messages, leading to an erosion of the original sense of direction and its replacement by a variety of divergent ideas.

LEVEL OF CLIENT EFFORT

If your firm is easy for Clients to deal with on any matter, then the level of Client effort required is much lower than if the Client has to expend considerable energy and time to work with the firm or sort out an issue. Whilst it is not easy to quantify the value of how easy it is to do business, many firms have not taken this factor into account when monitoring Client satisfaction. Almost all the details so far should have provided an illustration of what needs to be done to set the right objectives.

Dealing with the Loss of a Major Client

If a major Client decides to terminate a relationship it is important to discover the reasons for their decision, if it has not already been obvious from Client satisfaction reviews. Here are the most common reasons:

- Poor service quality and delivery.

- Fees becoming uncompetitive.

- Too many changes of relationship manager.

- Mergers and acquisitions leading to relationship changes.

- Lack of contact at the appropriate level.

- Lack of value added services.

- Regulation requiring supplier rotation.

- Lack of regular contact.

The loss of a major Client can clearly affect a firm's market reputation. Effective media relations and internal communications within the firm may limit the damage, but such a loss may signal the need for an improved risk assessment to be carried out for major Clients. Retention strategies can then be devised and implemented for those Clients at most risk of defection.

Targets and Metrics for Client Satisfaction

Client satisfaction surveys typically ask about the non-financial aspects of doing business:

- the firm's overall performance in meeting a Client's requirements;

- the quality, performance and behaviour of the firm's service delivery team;

- whether the Client would continue to use the firm and its other services;

- whether the Client would recommend the firm to others (the Net Promoter question);

- how easy it is to deal with the firm.

The recent Client care research shows that many firms monitor survey results by:

- overall performance;

- service delivery team;

- recommendation;

- sector;

- sales office.

Further examples of targets are shown from the *Client Care Survey* in Table 4.3 below. It is interesting to note that nearly 40 per cent of respondents had no formal targets and only 25 per cent used an advocacy metric such as the *Net Promoter Score*.

Table 4.3   Targets Set by Professional Services Firms for Client Satisfaction

Overall satisfaction	56.3%
Service delivery metrics (i.e. responsiveness)	44.3%
External advocacy by Clients for the firm (*Net Promoter Score*, etc.)	24.7%
Office (i.e. London)	12.6%
Line of service (i.e. audit, litigation)	27.6%
Client industry group (i.e. banking)	14.9%
No formal targets set	38.5%
Unsure	3.4%
Other areas	2.3%

Source: Client Care Survey 2013.

Developing Client Trust

Most managing partners in professional services firms will say that they want to be their Clients' trusted advisers. Very few surveys can reveal the level of trust that exists between the Client and the supplying firm. However, it is considered that repeat purchasing behaviour and a recommendation related to a high *Net Promoter Score* (discussed later) are clear indicators of the level of Client trust. Some form of scoring is best used to enable qualitative comparisons.

By listening to your Clients, you will discover many points that you can leverage to improve your relationship, fee income and, ultimately, the level of trust. How well do your teams score in commerciality, personal chemistry, understanding your Client's business and issues?

Client Care Survey Results

In this recent research, only just over a third of key Clients received annual satisfaction reports, as shown in Table 4.4 below. Given their 'key' status, this seems a very low proportion. It is also remarkable that only 15 per cent receive post-transaction reviews. These figures would therefore seem to indicate that the definition of key Clients may vary considerably from firm to firm.

Table 4.4   Who Receives Client Satisfaction Reports?

	Monthly	Quarterly	Six-monthly	Annually	Ad hoc	No reports	Unsure
Board	12.5%	12.5%	7.1%	15.8%	23.4%	22.3%	6.5%
MP/CEO	17.4%	10.3%	9.8%	13.0%	26.6%	17.9%	4.9%
Management team	16.8%	14.7%	6.5%	12.0%	24.5%	21.2%	4.3%
Practice group leaders	15.8%	11.4%	7.1%	8.7%	32.6%	20.1%	4.3%

Source: Client Care Survey 2013.

Table 4.4 shows who receives Client satisfaction reports and at what level of frequency. What is of interest here is that less than 20 per cent of respondents at board and management level receive monthly reports, yet less than 10 per cent of respondents stated that offices received regular reports.

Table 4.5   Proportion of Key Clients Receiving Satisfaction Reviews

	All key Clients	A majority	Around half	A minority	No reviews	Not sure
Annual satisfaction reviews	34.5%	12.1%	11.5%	19.0%	21.3%	1.7%
Post-transaction satisfaction reviews	14.9%	14.9%	9.8%	31.6%	23.0%	5.7%
General relationship satisfaction reviews	24.1%	18.4%	9.8%	26.4%	16.7%	4.6%

Source: Client Care Survey 2013.

Table 4.5 reveals that only 35 per cent of key Clients received annual satisfaction reviews and only 24 per cent had general relationship reviews. There is considerable room for improvement here, as many of the Clients not surveyed may feel neglected.

Table 4.6   How Many Post-transaction Reviews are Acted Upon

	All Clients	A majority	Around half	A minority	None	Unsure
Reviews with a high level of satisfaction	24.6%	17.9%	7.5%	23.1%	14.2%	12.7%
Reviews with an average level of satisfaction	28.4%	18.7%	6.7%	26.9%	8.2%	11.2%
Reviews with a low level of satisfaction	54.5%	18.7%	4.5%	9.7%	3.0%	9.7%

Source: Client Care Survey 2013.

The *Client Care Survey* revealed a low level of post-transaction follow-up. Table 4.6 shows that less than 25 per cent of high-scoring reviews and only 54.5 per cent of low scoring reviews were acted upon. Yet the mere act of following up can often lead to new opportunities with the Client, even if there was a complaint to resolve. This would seem to indicate that the level of commitment given by professional services firms to Client satisfaction is in need of considerable review and that there is much room for improvement.

Table 4.7   Who Follows Up Commitments Made after Client Satisfaction Reviews?

	MP/CEO	Management team	Marketing team	Practice group leader	No formal follow-up
Reviews with a high level of satisfaction	8.2%	19.6%	14.7%	20.7%	37.0%
Reviews with an average level of satisfaction	8.2%	21.7%	17.4%	19.0%	33.7%
Reviews with a low level of satisfaction	23.9%	23.9%	10.9%	21.2%	20.1%

Source: Client Care Survey 2013.

It is also interesting to note that top managers, i.e. the CEO or Managing Partner, were only involved in following up around 24 per cent of low-scoring reviews, as shown in Table 4.7. What is also revealing is that 20 per cent of reviews with low-scoring results have no formal follow-up. These findings would suggest that the follow-up process is also in need of review.

Table 4.8   Current Level of Post-transaction Reviews

Number of Clients	None	1–25	26–50	51–100	Over 100	Unsure
Face-to-face meetings	9.0%	50.7%	14.9%	9.0%	9.0%	7.5%
Telephone surveys	33.6%	29.1%	8.2%	3.0%	14.2%	11.9%
Web-based surveys	53.7%	10.4%	9.0%	3.7%	17.2%	6.0%
Postal surveys	66.4%	4.5%	3.0%	3.0%	9.7%	13.4%

Source: Client Care Survey 2013.

Table 4.9   Desired Level of Post-transaction Reviews

Number of Clients	None	1–25	26–50	51–100	Over 100	Unsure
Face-to-face meetings	1.5%	25.4%	22.4%	20.1%	26.9%	3.7%
Telephone surveys	11.9%	18.7%	17.9%	16.4%	28.4%	6.7%
Web-based surveys	26.9%	7.5%	8.2%	7.5%	38.1%	11.9%
Postal surveys	65.7%	5.2%	3.0%	1.5%	10.4%	14.2%

Source: Client Care Survey 2013.

Tables 4.8 and 4.9 from the recent *Client Care Survey* indicate the volume and types of post-transaction reviews undertaken, and desired, by professional services firms. There is a clear signal here that firms want to increase the number of Clients receiving face-to-face and telephone post-transaction interviews.

Benchmarking Surveys for Competitor Comparison

Many firms use some form of benchmarking to determine their relative market position. These surveys can typically rate suppliers and may cover the following areas:

- *Brand* – the importance in selecting supplier and what proportion mention it without prompting.

- *Corporate responsibility* – how important is it and is this evident?

- *International reach* – cross-border working.

- *Loyalty* – would you provide a reference to another organisation?

- *Reputation* – the importance in selecting supplier; the importance of supplier achieving awards.

- *Sector experience* – how important in selection and how well was this demonstrated?

- *Social media* – whether the Client has commented on the supplier on social media.

————

Interview questions on Client satisfaction typically focus on the following areas:

- *Client experience* – how did the Client feel in dealing with the firm?

- *Commerciality* – how well was this demonstrated?

- *Communications* – how well was this demonstrated?

- *Costs and value for money* – what level was achieved?

- *Deliverables vs proposal* – how well did the supplier meet promises made at their pitch?

- *Friendliness of the team* – how well did the firm's people get on with the Client?

- *International focus* – how was this demonstrated and used?

- *Loyalty* – would you provide a reference to another organisation?

- *Market reputation* – how well-known is the firm perceived to be?

- *Partner/expert accessibility* – importance and execution.

- *Responsiveness* – speed of response to queries, changes to requirements.

- *Service delivery* – the processes used.

- *Service quality* – the way that the service was delivered; was it smoothly executed or disruptive?

- *Team members* – how did they perform together and individually?

- *Timeliness of responses and output* – how well were timings met?

Qualitative Aspects of Client Satisfaction Interviews

In addition to the scored questions, face-to-face interviews in particular are a very useful source of verbatim comments about the firm. These can be reported back to the appropriate people for action as needed. Such qualitative comments can be used, with the Client's permission, in case studies and articles. Comments will vary considerably between Clients being reviewed.

POSITIVE COMMENTS

Here are some examples of positive comments taken from the author's research:

'The relationship partner is clearly one of the best in her field.'

'The partner takes an interest in our business and knows the sector well.'

'The partner is very bright and has tremendous insights into our operations.'

'Their international footprint matched well with our own operations and provided a seamless service.'

'They put an incredible amount of time into developing their relationships with us.'

'The team is always challenging us to review our processes for improvements.'

'Their technical knowledge is second to none.'

'We have had the same team for several years and that stability has paid off.'

'They give excellent value for money.'

'They give me the best legal option rather than lots of reports.'

'Their team built an excellent rapport with my people within a very short time from being instructed.'

NEGATIVE COMMENTS

Here are some comments suggesting that improvements are needed:

'We felt that our previous supplier was more proactive and curious about our business.'

'The firm seemed to find our international project a bit difficult to manage.'

'They need someone who oversees all the different work we require, not just a team of partners.'

'When the lead partner changed we noticed a drop in the level of contact.'

'Their technical people are ok but they don't seem to understand the realities we face.'

'They need to be more joined up in their communications.'

'They don't seem to understand where our business is heading.'

'They sometimes take ages to resolve my invoice queries.'

'Once they had merged we hardly saw anyone from the enlarged firm.'

Analysing Client Satisfaction Survey Responses

Responses to two key questions – on overall satisfaction and on recommendation – can be used to classify Clients. For example, those Clients scoring 8–10 on these questions could be called 'Loyal', those scoring 5–7 'Indifferent' and those scoring 0–4 'Unhappy'. Responses from Clients can then be grouped into the following categories:

- Those Clients that award high points for satisfaction (Loyal), i.e. at least 8 out of 10.

- Those Clients who are neutral about satisfaction (Indifferent).

- Those Clients who are clearly not satisfied (Unhappy).

Reports can then be produced indicating overall and individual performance.

Establishing a Client Satisfaction Programme

Many firms have yet to consider the need to invest in monitoring and measuring Client satisfaction. Some of these firms tend to operate on the principle that 'If all is going well and the Client pays the invoices, all must be well' and 'The Client will soon tell us if something is wrong'. That's often too late. So what are the key elements of an effective programme?

LEAD, PLAN, RESEARCH

To create a Client Satisfaction Programme requires leadership, careful thought and planning; it is also critical to have board-level support at the outset. As stated earlier, Client satisfaction has to be research-based to be successful. This research usually starts by organising a number of interviews with top-value Clients, conducted by people in your firm who are not working directly with the Client. This task is often carried out by senior marketing people, but can be effected by a third party. Many Clients accept the digital recording of such interviews on the understanding that they will only be used internally and to improve the service and relationship. Digital recording is an effective way of providing accurate transcripts that can be produced internally or outsourced to a specialist agency.

DISCUSS CLIENT FEEDBACK TO ESTABLISH SERVICE GOALS

The interviews are then distributed and discussed internally with a number of senior people, including the lead partner for that Client. This group, which is ideally cross-functional, can then determine the firm's mission in serving its Clients. What drives Client satisfaction is best discussed at top level so that any changes that may be required have their support. If your firm plans to increase its focus on its Clients through some form of Client Satisfaction Programme, internal communications will play a crucial part. Client service goals need to be established and communicated.

SECURE TOP-LEVEL SUPPORT AND REGULAR COMMUNICATIONS

As mentioned earlier, the key to a successful Client Satisfaction Programme is having top-level support and full employee engagement through regular communications. When everyone understands how they can make a difference to the Client experience, through communication around the firm of success stories and reward systems, they will create a culture that is clearly noticed by Clients. When case studies are produced featuring loyal Clients, these can be used when pitching for new work and can also be a good source of material when new employees are inducted.

ALLOW TIME FOR NEW BEHAVIOURS TO HAPPEN

The development of a Client satisfaction mentality can take several business cycles to become part of the firm's fabric and culture; however, the investment in time and resources pays off in the longer term. People often need training and development in Client-related competencies, developing new skills and habits, and especially understanding the importance of obtaining regular formal and informal Client feedback.

APPRAISE AND REWARD EXCELLENCE

Appraisals or performance reviews should also reflect the firm's Client management objectives. Employees should be recognised and rewarded for excellence in Client service. They also have to be told how Client concerns were carefully resolved so that they can learn about Client retention.

> ## CLIENT SATISFACTION OBJECTIVES AND METRICS
>
> To take a particular example, let's look at some top line objectives set by a professional services firm:
>
> - Acknowledge non-Client enquiries within a working day of receipt.
> - Respond to Client enquiries within two hours of receipt.
> - Achieve at least 75 per cent level of Client satisfaction in loyalty zone within two years of the start of the programme.
> - Ensure that the lead partner visits the Client at least twice per year.
> - Resolve invoicing queries within two hours of receipt.
> - Communicate any team changes within a working day.
>
> Whilst each of these service goals and external Key Performance Indicators (KPIs) focus on meeting a specific and stated set of Client expectations, all of them have specific internal agendas. On the other hand, very few, if any, of them can be achieved by one department working in isolation. Teamwork is vital in achieving consistently high Client ratings.

Attention to Detail

- The initial research is usually conducted with an external supplier.

- Create a cross-functional project team to define the external standards (KPIs).

- Identify with the various functions through a series of workshops where and how their activities help or hinder achieving the external KPIs.

- Define new or enhanced ways of working to ensure that the processes which internally created the right result were fully understood and could be acted on effectively.

For each KPI, the functional teams define the required inputs and outputs to achieve the Client service goals – who should do what for whom, by when and how well!

Developing KPIs

Internal KPIs are then defined by the people involved for themselves for the tasks they would be carrying out. Subsequently the cross-functional teams sort out the discontinuities that exist between the specific functionally proposed KPIs.

The process involved – putting cross-functional groups together to discuss specific requirements – is a very strong catalyst for developing a significant decrease in the 'silo mentality'. People begin to share their ideas and experience with each other as well as their frustrations. Working together to find solutions always enhances teamwork, provided that a common agenda exists.

Using the *Net Promoter Score* to Rate Client Satisfaction

A key question in Client satisfaction surveys relates to the *Net Promoter Score* (NPS). This is an important metric of the loyalty that exists between a Client and a supplier. This one critical factor encapsulates both the value of the Client and the potential referral business. It is therefore not surprising that many professional services firms are using this metric. The Net Promoter question is often phrased as follows:

> *'How likely are you to recommend our firm/product/service to your friends/business colleagues?'*

> *(Score 0 = not at all likely, 5 = neutral, 10 = extremely likely)*

To calculate the *Net Promoter Score*, take the percentage of Clients scoring 9 and 10 (the Promoters) minus the percentage scoring 0–6 (the Detractors). Scores of 7 and 8 are usually considered as 'the Passives'. For an example of how to calculate the NPS and the potential economic value of Promoters, see later on in this chapter.

GVA REPORTS ON CLIENT SATISFACTION AND NPS

In its 2013 Trading Report, leading property firm GVA reported the following survey results:

Overall satisfaction: 7% unsatisfied (score 1–6), 66% satisfied (score 7–8), 27% very satisfied (score 9–10).

Likelihood to recommend: 8% Detractors (0–6), 47% Passives (7–8), 45% Promoters (9–10).

Thus, their NPS was 45% – 8% = 37%.

Another Example of Calculating the NPS

Let us suppose that we have the scores from 20 Clients who have answered the question: 'How likely are you to recommend our firm to business colleagues or friends?' Scores out of 10 are shown in Table 4.10.

Table 4.10 *Net Promoter Scores* from 20 Clients

Client	Score	Client	Score	Client	Score	Client	Score
A	7	F	10	L	5	R	8
B	9	G	6	M	7	S	6
C	5	H	4	N	8	T	9
D	7	J	9	P	3	U	4
E	9	K	10	Q	9	V	10

CALCULATING THE NPS

To calculate the 'Promoters', we calculate the percentage of those Clients scoring 9 and 10, which is 8 out of 20, i.e. 40%.

To calculate the 'Detractors', we calculate the percentage of those Clients scoring 0–6, which is 7 out of 20, i.e. 35%.

The remainder (25%) are the 'Passives', with the potential to move up or down in loyalty.

The NPS for these results is therefore 40% – 35% = 5%.

NPS is considered an excellent indicator of Client loyalty. Research in 2009 by Richard Owen and Laura Brooks in *The Ultimate Question* showed that the higher the NPS, the higher is a firm's potential long-term revenue growth and profitability. As a firm is able to increase its NPS, and decrease the 'Detractors', so it will reduce Client churn; it will increase the likelihood of cross-selling other services to the Client and reduce the overall costs to serve. It is clearly also important to investigate those Clients with 'Detractor' ratings as they are likely to defect unless something is done to improve their score and move them to at least the 'Passive' state. Equally it is useful to look at the underlying reasons as to how the 'Passives' could become more loyal before they tend to 'detraction'.

Probing NPSs

In the above example we looked at the scores of 20 Clients across the business. Let us suppose that we want to establish which sectors are yielding the best NPSs. In Table 4.11 the same 20 Clients have now been coded into four sectors, coded a to d. It is interesting to look at each sector's NPS.

Table 4.11   *Net Promoter Scores* with Sector Codes Added to Clients for Further Analysis

Client	Score	Client	Score	Client	Score	Client	Score
Aa	7	Fb	10	Lc	5	Rd	8
Bb	9	Gc	6	Ma	7	Sc	6
Cc	5	Hc	4	Na	8	Td	9
Da	7	Jd	9	Pc	3	Uc	4
Eb	9	Kb	10	Qa	9	Vd	10

CALCULATING THE SECTOR NPS

In Table 4.11:

- For sector (a) we have a Promoter score of 20%, a Passive score of 80% and a Detractor score of 0%, so the NPS is 20%.
- For sector (b), we have a Promoter score of 100%, a Passive score of 0% and no Detractors, so the NPS is 100%.
- For sector (c) we have a Promoter score of 0%, a Passive score of 0 and a Detractor score of 100%. The NPS is -100%.
- For sector (d) we have a Promoter score of 75%, a Passive score of 25% and no Detractors. The NPS is 75%.

This analysis has enabled us to put the sectors in order of NPS; clearly sector (b) is the highest performer at 100% and sector (c) has serious problems that require immediate attention.

Another cut at the analysis can be effected by line of service, or by geographical location such as a sales office or even down to the lead partner; again this may reveal areas of high and low NPS for review. By drilling down into these subsets, it is possible to assign appropriate resources to take action.

Hewlett Packard's Senior Vice President of Customer Support & Services stated in the report *2020 – Return on Service** that the company has moved from using delight metrics to track approval ratings to the NPS as its dominant Customer satisfaction metric.

HEWLETT PACKARD RAISES THE BAR WITH
NET PROMOTER SCORE[1]

Customer service metrics are central to HP's service strategy. Richard Bailey, Senior Vice President of Customer Support & Services, says the IT group has long used delight metrics to track its approval ratings with Customers, but in 2013 it moved to using *Net Promoter Score* (NPS), which has become its dominant Customer satisfaction metric. 'Over the last few years we have enhanced the way we measure Customer satisfaction. In doing so, we are able to engage with our Customers during each aspect of their relationship with us, whether they are in-warranty or out-of-warranty' Mr Bailey says. HP chose

[1] From the report 'Service 2020 – Return on Service', published by BDO and written by the *Economist* Intelligence Unit, 2014.

NPS for two reasons, he says: 'NPS is probably the highest bar you can set in terms of the tool set. And it's more than just looking at one Customer Touch Point – it requires you to be more inclusive and makes sure you are delivering a great Customer experience throughout the organisation: from marketing to support and services.'

Characteristics of Loyal Clients

So how does a Client move from being satisfied to become loyal? As discussed earlier, we can map the 'life cycle' of a Client. This cycle begins with a Client as a 'prospect', moves into the first purchase stage to become a Client, then on to repeat purchase. At this time the Client may be sufficiently satisfied that they will provide additional assignments. Over time, as trust between the Client and the supplier develops, the Client may agree to provide the occasional reference. This is a movement towards loyalty. Perhaps the Client then agrees to a case study which is published on the supplier's website. This situation can develop whereby the Client is willing to show their loyalty publicly, for example, being prepared to talk about a case study presented at a seminar or conference. When a Client freely recommends your firm in this way, it is clearly a demonstration of their advocacy.

Other examples of advocates are Clients who agree to be filmed in an interview about their business, recommending how your services overcame some of their challenges. These case studies provide excellent material for developing employee understanding about Clients. Some firms measure the amount of Client referral business they receive and set an internal target for future referrals.

Calculating the Value of the 'Promoter' Clients

Clients that recommend a firm are clearly of high value as their unprompted, or stimulated, comments to others can lead to considerable potential increased business at little additional investment for the firm. It is possible to estimate the referral value of such Clients. Many loyal Clients are prepared to talk freely to potential Clients about their suppliers. To estimate the value attributable to these Clients, it is necessary to ask three additional questions to the 'Promoters'. Let us call our firm 'A'.

These additional survey questions are as follows:

- 'Did you select firm "A" because of a referral from a business colleague or friend?' (Yes or No)

- 'Have you referred business colleagues or friends to firm "A" during the past 12 months?' (Yes or No)

- 'How many referrals to firm "A" did you make in the past 12 months?' (Number)

It is considered best practice to ask these additional questions of Promoters after allowing a little time to elapse following the overall Client satisfaction survey.

VALUING THE PROMOTERS

To estimate the value of referrals, all you require in addition is the average expenditure per Client. Let us suppose that our research reveals that, on average, 60% of Promoters said 'yes' to the first two questions and in answering the third question made four referrals in the past year. If we already know that we acquire 10% of our Clients through referrals, we are achieving 60% × 4 × 10%, or 0.24 Clients per Promoting Client. So for every just under five referrals from 'Promoters', firm 'A' can expect to gain a new Client. If the average revenue per Client is £50,000, the potential value to our firm of a 'Promoter' is 0.24 × £50,000 = £12,000. We could perform similar calculations to investigate the potential loss from 'Detractors'. Clearly we should also examine the economic impact possible by moving Clients from 'Passive' to 'Promoter' and from 'Detractor' to 'Passive'. These moves will also have a positive impact on a firm's revenue.

Further Research with 'Promoters'

The NPS is based on the potential referral value of Clients. To determine a Client's *actual* referral behaviour requires additional research into *how* the Client makes referrals. In today's highly active social and other networks, it is worth establishing which networks are favoured by your Clients, as these are the most likely ones used for referrals. These networks can then be used as channels for marketing and business development activity. Once we have a strong relationship with a loyal Client, we should be able to extract this additional information.

CLIENT FOCUS PROGRAMMES AT MILLS & REEVE

Client care is an important feature of the development of law firm Mills & Reeve (M&R), led by Nicola Duke, Head of Client Care, who is responsible for two programmes: the first relating to outstanding Client service delivery and the second to key Client relationship management.

The Outstanding Client Service Programme relates to how the firm delivers advice. Rather than just offering options, the firm recommends an appropriate course of action; this approach again is a source of differentiation. For measurement, the *Net Promoter Score* is used firm wide in Client surveys along with the balanced scorecard for objective setting. In the early stages of this programme some partners found it difficult to distinguish their responsibilities for service delivery on particular matters from the responsibilities of the Client partner for the overall relationship. The firm's partner remuneration system encourages cross-selling to, and sharing of, Clients. Client service teams meet regularly across the UK via video conferencing and conference calls. There are opportunities to share best practice across the firm. Some sectors also have Client panels, leading to new service development; an example of this is a subscription-based procurement portal providing direct access to relevant documents.

For the Key Client Programme, external consultants were appointed to interview the firm's top 30 Clients and tasked with providing a detailed report on the strength of relationship between Client and M&R. The combination of this research and Client feedback has enabled M&R to differentiate itself in its markets. Initially there was some resistance from Client partners to setting up or laying the groundwork for interviews. Excuses were sometimes given such as 'They are just about to go out to tender so we should do the interview later' – yet this is the very moment when Client feedback would be most useful!

Key Clients are selected not only on the basis of turnover and profit but also their longer-term strategic importance in the context of the firm's sector strength and plans. The firm is conscious however that the type of relationship required by Clients varies within its different sectors; so, for example, the relationship with a corporate Client will be biased towards transactional activity whereas the relationship with a public sector Client will usually follow a competitive tender for a fixed period of between three and five years. M&R is careful to establish how Clients want their work to be managed and delivered. Some Clients have given feedback that they are receiving a '5 star' service but only have the budget for a '3 star' service. In such cases, M&R redesigns and re-engineers its offering accordingly to maintain margins.

The NPS is becoming one of the most important Client satisfaction metrics; it can be used across the firm with any department that interacts with Clients. To many firms it is the dominant measure of the Client experience.

Establishing an International Client Satisfaction Programme

Many professional services firms have established some form of Client satisfaction processes, monitoring and reporting. Those firms that are part of an international network may not have local control over how Clients are managed. This can result in considerable inconsistencies. Some firms set operational standards in an attempt to overcome these, but cultural and other local factors often inhibit or modify the outcomes. As mentioned earlier, accounting firm BDO makes the NPS a mandatory requirement of all its global members.

The same elements as mentioned earlier are required to establish a Client Satisfaction Programme with the added dimensions of globalisation. To raise the standard of Client management by introducing a global Client Satisfaction Programme requires commitment from the international board of management. A small, multi-country team is usually established to manage the programme comprised of a mix of 'well-established' to 'beginners' in Client satisfaction measurement. A typical process for globalisation of Client satisfaction would be as follows:

1.   Audit the current situation in all locations.

2.   Report back on the gaps between the best and least effective operations.

3.   For countries starting a programme, conduct local research with their Clients based on best practice.

4.   Establish a global standard for all members to follow based on the best that exists now.

5.   Discuss and test the standards with pilot group of locations ranging from best to least effective.

6.   Revise the standards where necessary.

7.   Roll out the programme region by region.

8.   Create regular communication on the programme results.

9.   Report on *Net Promoter Scores* by location.

10.   Assist local members with improvement programmes.

11.   Establish strategic Client management where appropriate.

The effectiveness of such a programme relies on the attention to detail throughout the process. For example, if a set of Client satisfaction questions has been agreed, it needs to be tested for cultural differences and understanding. Experience shows that many Eastern cultures are not as open or transparent as their Western counterparts, so there may be some reluctance from Clients to answer some of the questions. When establishing standards, such factors have to be taken into account.

Table 4.12   An Example of a Client Satisfaction Audit Summary of a Global Network

Item Region	Client feedback	Surveys effected	Face-to-face interviews	Telephone surveys	Web based surveys	Net Promoter Score	Strategic Clients
Asia & Pacific	Limited	Very few	Starting	Starting	In place	N/A	N/A
Europe	Regular	Routine	With top Clients	With most Clients	With smaller Clients	In place with variable results	In most countries
Middle East & Africa	Limited	None	Some	Starting	Starting	N/A	N/A
Far East	Regular	Routine	Majority of Clients	Very few	Some	Starting	In some countries
Americas	Regular	Routine	With top Clients	Smaller Clients	Few	In place with good results	In place

A partial audit summary is shown in Table 4.12. This shows that there are regional differences. Within each region there are also likely to be variations of implementation. One way forward could be to have a representative European team working with Middle East & Africa colleagues and another working with the remaining regions. Such a programme may take several years to establish to the required standards, especially where the process of surveying and interviewing Clients has to start from scratch.

CLIENT SATISFACTION PROGRAMME AT SAVILLS

Richard Crook, Head of Business Development & CRM, says 'Savills has always focused on Client satisfaction, using external consultants to conduct Client interviews. Recently this programme has been increased in volume and now includes members of Savills' internal research team and board members, such as the CEO, to interview key Clients. Post-transaction surveys are usually sent out with invoices as this is usually a good test of the Savills platinum service. Social media are also used to monitor trending about the firm. The residential business uses "mystery shopping" techniques to test the quality of its office locations.

Savills measures ratios like:

- repeat vs. retained vs. new business;
- how many service lines are sold per Client;
- satisfaction and favourability scores;
- *Net Promoter Scores* (these have increased over the past two years).

Given Savills' global reach it is developing these measures as management tools to maintain their leading position.'

Rewarding Excellence in Client Satisfaction

Many firms have implemented a reward policy to drive up Client satisfaction. This takes into account factors such as:

- increase in fee income over a defined period;

- increase in Client satisfaction survey score/*Net Promoter Score*;

- reduction in Client churn;

- increase in number of services purchased by the Client.

The challenge with rewarding excellence in Client satisfaction is to ensure a fair approach, given that many people collaborate in delivering Client service. Some firms provide a Client team bonus structure based on Client expectation feedback, for example if the team:

- Consistently exceed expectations, bonus = inflation + 5 per cent of salary.

- Exceeds expectations, bonus = inflation + 3 per cent of salary.

- Meets expectations, bonus = inflation indexed salary.

- Does not meet expectations = no bonus.

Client Satisfaction Breeds Loyalty

Satisfaction shows the importance of keeping in touch with Clients as work progresses, through leaner times, to seek qualitative and quantitative feedback from Clients on their experience with the firm and act on it. However, achieving a 'satisfied' rating is usually not enough to retain a Client – the tipping point occurs when the firm augments its service delivery with added-value offers and finds innovative ways of increasing Client loyalty.

Use of Client satisfaction metrics like the *Net Promoter Score* can signal potential opportunities and defection warnings for a firm. Use of Client panels and testimonials helps to retain Client loyalty over time. Those Clients that provide additional business opportunities through referrals and testimonials should be nurtured as their loyalty value can be assessed.

Establishment of a Client Satisfaction process is now considered best practice in professional services firms. It requires board-level leadership and the involvement of all Client-facing and supporting employees. A fair reward structure based on meeting or exceeding Client expectations will usually drive up satisfaction ratings and contributes to a stronger Client relationship.

———

Client Satisfaction and Loyalty

Chapter Review Questions

To what extent does your firm:

1.   Regularly benchmark its service against competitors?

2.   Identify each Client's requirements and preferences?

3.   Identify service performance gaps?

4.   Use a performance/service matrix for groups of Clients?

5.   Monitor Client effort in dealing with the firm?

6.   Set targets for Client satisfaction?

7.   Use the NPS with all Clients?

8.   Regularly review Client satisfaction surveys at board level?

9.   Regularly update its Client satisfaction targets?

10.   Know its NPS by sector?

11.   Know its NPS by service line/practice area?

12.   Know the referral value of its Promoter Clients?

These questions also form the basis of the *Satisfaction* section of your *Client Management Profile*™, which can be found in Chapter 15.

Client Management Model™

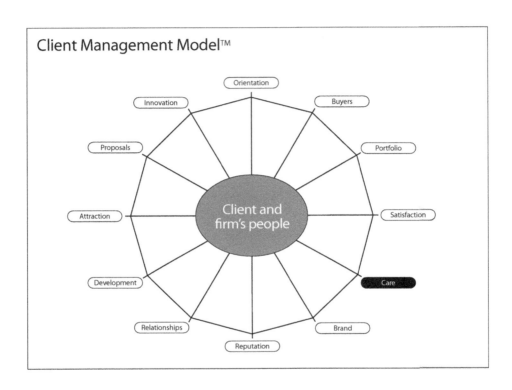

Chapter 5

Care:
The Role of Client Care

Synopsis

Care, the fifth element of the *Client Management Model*™, discusses:

- the behavioural aspects of Client care;

- what a firm needs to do to ensure that its Clients feel highly valued and are at the core of its culture;

- how to establish a Client Care Programme;

- 'Touch Points' and 'Moments of Truth';

- understanding and acting out the Client experience;

- the relevance to Clients of an active Client Care Policy and charter.

THOUGHT STARTERS
- What is meant by Client care?
- Who is responsible for Client care?
- What does the Client experience when dealing with your firm?
- What is best practice in Client care?
- What is a Touch Point?
- What is a Moment of Truth?

Client Care

Effective Client care comes naturally to many people, especially if the firm encourages Client-centricity. Any interaction with a Client or prospective Client is an opportunity to build a trusted relationship. Although looking after Clients may seem an obvious characteristic and requirement, many firms surveyed recently admit that there are many improvements to be made. For effective Client care, everyone who deals directly or indirectly with Clients needs to understand that the firm exists to serve its Clients – not the other way round! How many times do we overhear colleagues talking about their interactions with Clients: 'Oh, that was just … one of our Clients … wanting us to change our invoicing date. Some chance!' or 'That Client … is always complaining.'

Given that Client care implies looking after Clients, many firms have a Client Care Policy (see later) and document situations where Client care is needed. They communicate the appropriate action required to all employees. They also use these to train and develop the appropriate employee behaviours when interacting with Clients.

Establishing a Client Care Programme

These training situations leading to the development of an effective Client Care Policy and Programme can come from:

- general observations;

- discussions of 'Touch Points' and 'Moments of Truth' (see later in this chapter);

- Client satisfaction reports;

- Client panels;

- feedback from Client meetings;

- research surveys.

Many firms conduct regular Client care training; some have an ongoing programme to ensure that their Client Care Policy is applied consistently.

To establish and embed a Client Care Programme requires considerable planning, Client research and, ideally, commitment from the board. Everyone in the firm has a responsibility to exercise excellent Client Care, but to succeed, they must have an appreciation of what constitutes good and bad Client care.

A best practice Client Care Programme could include the following elements:

- Client Care Policy discussions.

- Workshops to discuss Touch Points, Moments of Truth and act out scenarios.

- The importance of listening.

- How to make Clients feel important – building Client rapport by asking questions.

- How to say 'Yes' more often to Clients.

- How exceeding Client expectations builds the relationship.

- How to interpret and appreciate Client feedback.

- Client satisfaction surveys.

- Client satisfaction report reviews.

- Face-to-face discussions with Clients.

Who Manages Client Care?

Responsibility for the establishment of Client Care Policy and Programmes needs to be at a senior level in the firm to ensure the highest level of commitment. Ideally a board member should bear the responsibility. As a function, responsibility for Client care often rests within, or sits alongside,the marketing and/or business development teams. Enlightened firms appoint a board member to oversee policy creation and to champion stories about Client care around the firm. The human resources team are often used to develop training programmes and workshops with marketing and BD input.

As a minimum, a firm should appoint a Client Care Manager to champion the behavioural aspects and manage Client satisfaction research. The key to a successful Client Care Programme is regular internal communication along with employee training and development.

A MANTRA FOR CLIENT CARE

'If I had a mantra to sum up what I think good Client care looks like, it's 'Be bothered'. If you are, the likelihood is you and your Clients will do well.'

Ms Fran Bosan, Omobono Limited, Marketing Services.

So what does excellence in Client care look like? Here is an example from the retail sector.

GOING THE EXTRA DISTANCE

Mr Crosby visits his local camera shop and asks for a zoom lens to fit the model he is carrying. He says that he wants to take photographs at his cousin's wedding tomorrow. The sales assistant searches the database and says that unfortunately they don't have the lens in stock at this branch, but he can have one in a few days' time. Mr Crosby orders the lens and says to the assistant that he wishes he had come to the shop earlier in the week.

Next day, early on the morning of the wedding, Mr Crosby hears his house bell ringing and, on opening the front door, sees the familiar figure of the camera shop sales assistant holding a box. 'Good morning Mr Crosby. Managed to get this lens for you from another branch – hope you enjoy the day.'

We can all remember situations like the above case where someone went the extra distance to help us. It is also well-known that unhappy Customers tell their friends and family about poor service. In these times of rapid communications, such stories can reach millions in seconds across the Internet and have the power to enhance or destroy reputations.

Client Touch Points

Client care is a behavioural process that involves taking notice of everything relating to Clients and their interaction with the firm. Attention to detail is a key requirement of effective Client care. This section explains the importance of understanding Client Touch Points, how they need to be identified and managed to ensure that any latent business opportunities are leveraged when they fleetingly occur. If we can understand what makes up the Client experience, we will make large strides in providing service excellence. Every positive interaction with Clients helps to build your brand loyalty.

A *Touch Point* is a term often used to describe any encounter where people can exchange information, provide a service or handle a transaction. There are many Touch Points when an existing Client, or non-Client, is in contact with our firm. It is how these Touch Points are identified that can differentiate between successful and unsuccessful firms and brands, and lead to the best experience for the Client. There are clearly thousands of Touch Points occurring during the lifecycle of a Client relationship. Explaining Touch Points to employees is a critical part of their understanding of Client care.

Examples of when Touch Points can occur are as follows:

- Visits by prospects or Clients to reception areas.

- Telephone calls from prospects seeking information.

- Letters or emails asking for advice.

- Response from a prospect to a direct marketing campaign.

- Meeting someone from your firm at a conference or other event.

- Feedback to your website.

- Clients attending a function and meeting your people.

- Clients reading an article and asking for more information.

- Prospect meeting someone from our firm while travelling.

- Prospect completing an online survey or section in your website.

In each of these instances we should be conscious of observing and managing the interaction; for example, here are some that the author has observed.

IDENTIFYING TOUCH POINTS: THE VISITOR SCENARIO

A person arrives at a firm's reception desk at 10.45 am and asks for a Partner by name, explaining that they have a meeting at 11 o'clock. Typically the receptionist welcomes the person, asks for their name and organisation, creates a name badge, passes it to the person and asks them to take a seat while they contact the Partner.

Think of the possible situations that could occur during the short waiting period.

The Visitor – Identifying Possible Touch Points

Many are left unmanaged, yet provide further opportunities for contact with the firm.

Here is a list of some of the possible Touch Points:

- Is the reception area kept tidy?
- Is it welcoming?
- The visitor may be a Client or a non-Client – has the receptionist established this by searching the firm's database?
- Has the visitor been offered some refreshment? Of course, this may happen at the meeting.
- Has the visitor been alerted to your publications display?
- The visitor is seen making notes while viewing a video about the firm.
- Whom should the receptionist contact to meet the visitor, a PA or the Partner?
- The person may wish to visit washroom facilities – a place where some firms discreetly display their latest advertising campaign material or articles.
- The visitor overhears conversations between other visitors about your firm.
- The visitor picks up a daily newspaper and reads an article featuring your firm.
- Before the visitor leaves, if appropriate, did you establish their feelings about their experience?
- Do you follow up after such visits to establish Client feedback?

Moments of Truth

Another term, like Touch Points, often used in discussing Client experiences is 'Moments of Truth'.[1] Whereas Touch Points describe any likely interaction between a Client and a firm, a Moment of Truth is the *actual instance of contact* that gives the Client an opportunity to form or change an impression about the firm. An example is a telephone conversation between a prospective Client and your firm or through an internet search. How that enquiry is handled will leave an impression on the prospect. Many firms track the initial Moments of Truth by adding information to their Client database – for example, Table 5.1 shows part of an activity record for a target prospective Client in the technology sector. Understanding these Moments of Truth in the Client's journey from interest to purchase is critical as each interaction, if well-managed, helps to strengthen the Client experience.

Table 5.1   Prospect Activity Record

Date	Requests	Activity	Contacts in the firm
14.12.12	Seminar information	Sent seminar details	Celia Dalton
15.02.13		Intellectual property seminar	Bill Turner
25.02.13	Technical report on IP	Sent technical report	Celia Dalton
19.04.13		Director's lunch (follow up from Feb. seminar)	Bill Turner
24.06.13	Conference details	Sent conference details	Peter Gill
22.07.13		Technology conference	Jim Ryman

Moving Activities into Progressions

This record gives some indication of the prospects' desire to learn more about the firm. Within a seven-month period, we have had many recorded touch points of interaction. Bill Turner appears to be building a relationship with the prospect. Celia Dalton, Jim Ryman and Peter Gill have also responded to various requests. At some point there will need to be a co-ordination meeting in the firm to decide how to take forward the potential business with the prospect. As an example of next steps in the above, progressing the technology event

---

1   The term 'Moments of Truth' is attributed the CEO of Scandinavian Airlines, Jan Carlzon, when he turned the loss-making business into a Customer-driven organisation during the 1980s. He cited examples of Moments of Truth in the airline and its hotels had the whole organisation trained in understanding and managing these Moments of Truth. The subsequent behavioural changes turned around the airline's fortunes.

might be an appropriate point to re-contact the prospect to seek their interest in meeting over lunch the firm's technology sector leader and possibly an IP specialist.

MEETING SOMEONE AT A CONFERENCE

Many initial contacts are made through unplanned situations arising at events such as conferences. Attendees usually have similar issues and needs, and may be seeking solutions to business problems.

A brief encounter at a conference often involves a short conversation, an exchange of business cards, a chat over coffee or lunch during a break. This 'Moment of Truth' gives a prospective Client an impression about your firm and an opportunity to follow up if the interaction was favourable.

Many conference and event organisers provide visitors with a delegate list. It can be useful to scan this for potential or target contacts and trying to meet them briefly during the proceedings.

The Client Experience

It is considered good practice to really understand the Client experience – the things that happen during the 'journey' taken by a prospective Client that ultimately becomes a regular, loyal Client and potentially an advocate of the firm. The Client experience can be described as the ongoing accumulation of the Moments of Truth, a series of ongoing impressions gained about the firm, its work, its people and its culture. A 'spectrum' view defines the Prospect-to-Client journey as moving from 'cold' to 'hot'.

At first the 'cold' prospect may have some knowledge of your firm through its reputation in the marketplace. At this stage of awareness we imagine that the prospect is satisfied with current suppliers and has no desire to change. However, we may be able to create some activity to tempt the prospect to make contact with our firm. But what is the benefit to the prospect? Will your activity help the prospect in some way? Will it create sufficient dissonance in the mind of the prospect that they will make contact? It's worth remembering that prospective Clients are often your competitors' best Clients, so others are also vying for the same Client's time and interest.

Experience shows that people are usually interested in improving their company's performance, so prospects will often participate in benchmarking and other surveys. If your firm has uncovered something significant in the prospect's sector, it could result in creating sufficient interest and curiosity in the prospect's mind that they will ask for a copy of the survey report or attend a presentation of the survey results. Another successful approach in gaining a prospect's interest is to produce articles in specific journals that they might read.

After several interactions and 'Touch Points' with your firm, albeit at a distance, the prospect may decide to meet with one of the partners for an exploratory discussion. This is a 'warm' breakthrough that needs careful attention! Many firms misread this opportunity as a 'buying signal', but at this stage it is only a declaration of further interest. It is clearly important to do some background research on the prospect before having the first meeting; after all, it is common courtesy to show some knowledge of the prospect's company and its business.

When meeting your firm, prospects have expectations about the interaction: 'What are these people like to deal with?' and 'What do they know about my business?' The key to a successful first meeting is the creation of a rapport between the prospect and the firm. If the setting is relatively informal, it is usually best to ask the prospect a few questions about what led them to make contact with your firm. What or who was it that triggered their interest? By focusing on the prospect's interests, the firm gradually understands the prospect's position and the likelihood of changing suppliers. Perhaps, after a few meetings, you can discover the satisfaction drivers and motivations of the prospect.

A PASSION FOR CLIENT CARE

Allan Evans, partner at accountants BDO, is passionate about Client care. BDO has a managed Client programme – irrespective of size and complexity all BDO Clients receive a high level of Client service; however, some Clients may require a different, tailored service related to size, work complexity and international scope. Compared to smaller Clients, these Clients may require a broader team of several partners.

Client feedback is sought annually within a structured national programme. In addition, feedback is sought on a project by project basis at several points in the year. Allan states 'In these times of the reach and immediacy of social media, you will always hear from Clients anyway.' BDO encourages a continuous dialogue with its Clients.

'If you are going to take Client care seriously, be prepared to publish your targets and results and measure down to the individual level. Share satisfaction scores with Clients. We aim to be as transparent as TripAdvisor with data which is shared on our intranet site and openly shared with our Clients and future Clients.'

'BDO benchmarks its service with other firms. Rewards are influenced by satisfaction results. Both good and bad results are shared and discussed with Clients.'

Excellence in Client Care Leads to Achieving Preferred Supplier Status

Many Clients have sophisticated procurement processes that allow a 'preferred supplier' status to be conferred on a firm. This gives the firm a competitive advantage over other suppliers. In due time, after a year or two of successful transactions and high Client care and satisfaction ratings, it may be possible to test the Client's loyalty to the firm by pitching for business held by other incumbents. If the Client becomes an advocate, opportunities may arise for the firm to seek references from its Client; some of these may be expanded into case studies that can be used as a shop window for prospects. By now it is likely that the Client has achieved 'strategic' status within the firm and is involved in the joint development of new services, Client panels and speaking about their experience with the firm at events attended by prospects. These activities are included in the firm's strategic Client plan, which is ideally shared and discussed with the Client at some point. An example of a strategic Client plan format is shown in Chapter 9.

WALKING THE CLIENT JOURNEY

In the service sector suppliers of media-enabling technology operate in a highly competitive arena. One particular supplier of broadband had entered the market and was aiming to increase its market share of households and businesses using its equipment. It grew in size over time and had articulated a mission for their brand to become 'the best in the market' and communicated this mantra to all of their staff. It wanted its staff to 'live' its brand. However, as feedback from the marketplace was mixed, and often poor, it called in external branding consultants to investigate.

Discussions with field engineers who handled repairs and replacements revealed that they were not happy in carrying out their work. In fact they felt very grumpy, because they were being given high targets which were almost impossible to achieve. For example, they had a target of 30 minutes per visit and were often held up in traffic in between calls. Clients often complained about poor service – engineers arriving late. The field engineers called them grumpy Clients. The brand promise was not being realised where it mattered – in front of the Clients, but also in the minds of the service employees.

However, it was not easy to convince management and their internal staff about these issues, as they were not in the field where these situations occurred. Their view was 'It's part of the job'. So the consultants decided to create a scenario to represent the field situation. They hired actors to 'walk the Client journey'. One actor played the part of the grumpy Client with a faulty set top box and the other a grumpy field engineer. Several situations were played out in front of employees. These included:

- Tardiness

The Client complained to the engineer that he was an hour late and didn't contact the Client to let him know. In turn the engineer said that he didn't have time to call because the traffic was so bad.

- Equipment exchange

The engineer looked at the equipment and decided to exchange the box for a new one. However, the Client complained that the previous two engineers had done this with no improvement.

The scenario showed that the field engineer was not attuned to the behaviour of the Client, even if the problem was eventually resolved.

The consultants then interviewed each actor and asked whether their behaviour had improved or worsened the situation. Each agreed that they had not really considered the impact of their behaviour on the situation. The field engineer stated that he had only been trained to repair products and admitted a lack of understanding of how to deal with 'difficult' Clients.

> The consultants recommended that field engineers be trained in understanding and dealing with different types of Client behaviour. Further scenarios based on engineer and Client feedback were created to enable the field engineers to practise with 'Clients' in a training environment. After several months the field engineers were given a longer time to handle each visit, were expected to make prior contact with Clients to advise their time of arrival and warn them of any traffic issues; the level of Client complaints had reduced considerably.

Establishing a Client Charter

This section sets out why it can be useful to have a Client Charter and includes some of the key pointers for an effective Charter. Many professional services firms have created a charter to state their mission with Clients. Some firms retain these solely for internal use; others publish their charters to the outside world, often through their websites and in reception areas.

Clients expect superior service from their suppliers. Many Clients benchmark procured services across and between supplying organisations, so, for example, they might compare the quality of service from their lawyers with that of their accountants. Some organisations create a specific charter mark that can only be displayed by member firms attaining their standards.

Examples of basic Charter statements include the following.

Contact with Clients

- We will answer the telephone within three rings.

- We will advise you in advance when key team members will be on leave and who will be their temporary replacement.

- We will acknowledge all written communications on the day of receipt.

Client Management

- We will advise Clients about our Client satisfaction process.

- We will ensure that our Clients receive an interview annually with a member of our Client Care team.

- We will agree and deliver work as promised, to the highest level of quality, on time and to budget.

- We will have regular meetings with Clients to fully understand their business.

- We will seek feedback on all aspects of service and act on any findings.

Pricing Policies

- We will agree costs at the start of an assignment and advise the likelihood of any unanticipated changes.

- We will supply a table of hourly rate charges for senior partners, partners, senior managers and managers.

Here are some examples of published charters.

COODES SOLICITORS
Service Standards

We will:

- Tell you who is dealing with your matter and who your contact is. We will keep you informed of any changes.
- Do our best to communicate with you in plain English and keep legal jargon to a minimum.
- Explain to you the legal work that is needed. We will keep you informed of your legal rights and provide you with the necessary advice to enable your matter to be completed or resolved as effectively as possible.
- Progress your matter as quickly as reasonably possible and inform you of the up to date position and the timescale for future actions on your behalf.

- Update you when appropriate as to whether the likely outcome of your matter justifies the likely costs and risks of continuing.
- Deal with your enquiries and communications as quickly as reasonably possible. We will endeavour to return telephone calls the same day, and reply to letters within two working days.

Charges and Pricing

- We offer a range of pricing options for the work that we do.
- At the start of your matter we will establish with you the pricing option that is the most suited to your individual requirements.
- We will keep you informed of the likely charges for the matter at least every six months and also if there are any unusual or anticipated costs.
- We will inform you if there are any unusual or additional charges prior to incurring these charges.

Client Care

- We will consider carefully all your comments about our service. If you feel that you are not receiving the service that you hoped for, please tell the person dealing with your matter immediately.
- We may ask you to complete a feedback form at the end of your matter which we will use to help us improve our service.
- We operate a complaints procedure which is available on request.
- We treat all Clients fairly and do not discriminate against anyone because of their age, race, sex, sexual orientation or disability.
- We will represent your interests and keep your business confidential.

THE INDEPENDENT SURVEYORS ASSOCIATION

- The Independent Surveyors Association is a National Network of like-minded professional surveyors and valuers with considerable experience and skill committed to providing a service of quality and Putting the Client First.
- By instructing a chartered surveyor entitled to display the Charter Mark of ISA, a Client can be confident that the member:
  - Is not only a member of the Royal Institution of Chartered Surveyors and as such committed to rigorous professional standards, but also has at least three year's post-qualification experience as a principal, partner or member of senior staff.
  - Operates as an independent firm and, as such, will act personally and directly for the Client, but with ability to call on the wealth of specialist disciplines and skills provided within the National Network.
  - Will engage in discussion with the Client and explain any aspect or findings in further detail.
  - Confirms terms of appointment and the fee basis on acceptance of instructions.
  - Offers total loyalty to the Client and absolute discretion.

- Responds promptly to telephone calls and correspondence.
- Is committed to act in a timely manner and to an agreed time-scale.
- Reports clearly and concisely in plain English.
- Is committed to act courteously.
- Maintains a procedure for addressing complaints according to established principles set by the ISA and the RICS.

Taking on New Clients

Most professional services firms have some form of start-up or 'on-boarding' process when they take on a new Client. Due to the nature of the work, there is usually an engagement contract stating the terms and conditions relating to the work. It is interesting to note that although firms celebrate new business internally, when it comes to the Client, the process is rather formal and can often feel somewhat cold to a Client.

However, when taking on a new Client, apart from the necessary contractual formalities, there are many opportunities for further, early engagement. For reasons of consistency, some firms centralise their Client take-on procedures. Taking on new Clients should provide a trigger for a firm to develop the relationship. For example, a 'Welcome Pack' can be given, or sent, to a new Client, explaining more about the firm, providing contacts and seeking feedback on issues of interest. Many firms set up a welcome meeting with a new Client, where they are introduced to the lead partner and where the firm's relationship management process can be outlined. Some firms have a welcome event where they invite recent new Clients to an informal gathering of partners from different practice areas. This has the benefit to Clients of exposing them to other Clients and partners, showing the scope of the firm's activities. The firm benefits by making new connections that may be useful later in the relationship.

The Client take-on process is one of the earliest opportunities to demonstrate Client care and show how the firm treats its Clients at the initial stage of the relationship. It is best practice to appoint an independent manager to oversee the relationship development and this person should be introduced to the Client at the earliest possible time. By involving someone in this role who is not directly involved with the work in hand, the firm can introduce another practice contact for the Client. This process benefits the Client by providing another sounding board that might be useful occasionally.

It is also important for the firm to seek feedback from new Clients at the early stages to see how both sides are faring as the work proceeds. This may uncover concerns from the Client that can be handled or opportunities that need follow-up.

GREAT CLIENT CARE

'Great Client care is like a good marriage; you need to keep the level of interest and intrigue up, be thinking about them when you are not around, pleasantly surprise them little and often. If you do not do these things do not be annoyed if your Clients start to flirt with other firms. React positively and you may avert a divorce!' – Anon. Accountants.

Client Care in Action Helps Client Retention

Care has explained the power and benefits of having clearly stated guidelines regarding the way that a professional services firm treats its Clients. Enlightened firms have invested considerably in providing excellent Client care. They do this by ensuring that their employees are trained to recognise and act upon opportunities to enhance the Client relationship, aside from the contracted work delivery. Some firms have created their own Client Care Policy that explains exactly what the firm's stance must be with all Clients. Its standards and messaging should align with the firm's brand promise. The Client Care Policy should ideally be published for employees and Client alike. This policy can incorporate a Client Charter. It can be featured on marketing communications, in website pages and in social media whenever the opportunity to publish it arises. The policy should be reviewed at least annually to ensure that it is refreshed. When Client care is well managed, it is part of everyone's DNA and happy Clients will tell their colleagues and business friends.

Client care can be a powerful differentiator. It involves developing the level of trust between firm and Client, the information provided and how it is communicated and the level of customisation of everything the firm does for the Client.

Client Care

CLIENT MANAGEMENT REVIEW QUESTIONS

To what extent does your firm:

1.   Have a published Client care policy?

2.   Regularly discuss Client Touch Points?

3.   Use Moments of Truth to discuss Client care behaviour?

4.   Discuss the Client journey and experience internally?

5.   Discuss the Client experience with its Clients?

6.   Have a Client Charter?

7.   Publish its Client Charter internally?

8.   Display its Client Charter on its website?

9.   Train all employees in the elements of Client care and service?

10.   Involve Clients in developing your Client care approach?

These questions also form the basis of the *Care* section of your *Client Management Profile*™, which can be found in Chapter 15.

Client Management Model™

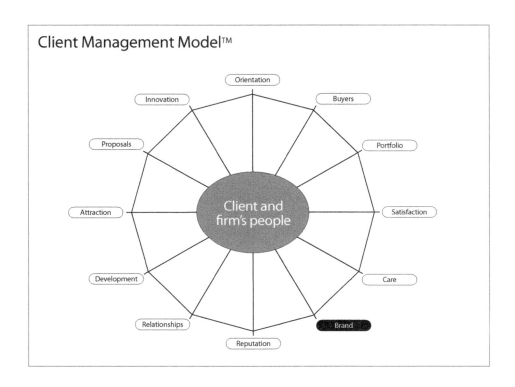

Chapter 6

Brand:
Brand, Differentiation and Positioning and their Impact on Clients

Synopsis

Brand, the sixth element of the *Client Management Model*™, explains the following points:

- describing the firm;

- brand creation and development;

- the importance of the firm's brand, the promise – examples of successful brands;

- branding;

- what's in a name?;

- how firms differentiate their offerings;

- how to develop a value proposition;

- the importance of positioning a firm.

THOUGHT STARTERS
- What are your brand values?
- What is your brand promise?
- Who manages your brand?
- Does your behaviour reflect your brand values and promise?
- How are you different from your competitors?
- How should you be positioning your firm with Clients and other groups?

Describing the Firm

One of the most recent marketing developments in professional services is the creation of brands. Many law firms still retain and use their full names, based on their unique tradition and history. As firms merge, their names often become longer to retain the identity of the merged firms. However some law firms, and many of the larger accounting and property firms, have simplified their names to become shorter and often more memorable, mnemonic, descriptions. For example, property firm Jones Lang LaSalle recently re-branded as JLL. One easy test of this issue is to call a firm with a long name and hear how its telephonists describe the firm – they often use a shortened form! What is more, Clients may do the same. Many of these names include the creation of a distinct emblem or logo. This trend is likely to continue as brand identity and ease of recognition become more important differentiators with Clients. Such branding style lends itself to today's technology and is highly visible in websites, blogs and social media channels. It also works well, and is important, in international markets.

The increasingly important roles and reach of marketing communications and information technology are having a marked impact on Clients. Now it is possible, especially with mobile technology, to reach Clients rapidly using a variety of channels and techniques. Equally Clients expect firms to respond rapidly to their questions and issues. In fact, as stated earlier, many Clients have access to a wider range of technologies than their suppliers. Just consider the power and speed of today's mobile 'smart' phones and tablet computers, literally in the hands of Clients.

Brand

Many professional services firms have invested considerable sums in researching and developing their brand. From an external perspective, your brand is what the Client or non-Client experiences, whether they are receiving information or meeting members of your firm. From an internal perspective, your people are the brand in the sense that their attitudes and behaviours to the outside world reflect the ethos and culture of your firm. Energising the brand through employees is one of the key challenges facing professional services firms.

THE BRAND PROMISE

Underlying the brand is the brand promise: what the Client can expect from your firm. This is often not explicitly stated, but is implied in all that supports the brand. It is vital that all members of your firm understand your brand, what it stands for and how they can impact on the brand's effectiveness and the firm's reputation with Clients and prospects. The challenge about 'living' the brand is that it is a daily duty of everyone in the firm, yet this is not always the practice.

It is also important to regularly research the relevance and position of your brand in your served markets, especially unprompted brand recognition, by asking the appropriate questions, for example: 'Name the first supplier that comes to mind for accounting/legal services other than your current supplier.' There are many available benchmarking surveys of professional services firms that are regularly conducted. A frequency of every two years is considered a good investment.

MESSAGING

Messaging describes the brand promise and everything related to the brand; the words and behaviours that your firm uses to express these things. Marketing communications need to be 'on message' – these should always reflect the essence of the brand. It has been said that 'the people are the brand' – if the firm's culture has the brand essence in its DNA, it will be evidenced from employee engagement and behaviour in the workplace.

LIVING THE BRAND

You would think that firms who have created a brand expect its promise to be fulfilled at all times. Yet few firms actually check how well, or badly, this expectation is being implemented by its employees. 'Living' the brand requires appropriate attitudes and behaviour that come from highly engaged, well-trained people. As Claire Mason, of *Man Bites Dog*, says; 'People are the brand experience, look after them and they will take a pride in going the extra mile for your Clients.'

Some firms refresh their brand image in an effort to position or reposition their offering to their markets. However, if employee behaviours and the firm's deliverables do not match the desired changes, the cost and time involved will be in vain. Any changes to the brand are best derived through detailed market research with Clients and prospects. Clients' perceptions of a brand come from every aspect of your firm, whether by letter, email, telephone conversations, events, face-to-face meetings, publications, social media content, visits to premises, merchandise and the work delivery team.

For most professional services firms, the brand is one of its most important assets, to be guarded and monitored vigilantly. It is therefore not surprising that many firms now assign a brand manager to this task. The role of global brand manager is one recently created by the larger firms with international reach where the firm's reputation and consistency of branding are clearly important.

THE CHALLENGES OF MANAGING A GLOBAL BRAND

Bradley Neill became International Brand Manager of Grant Thornton International Ltd in May 2013, having previously been Brand Manager for the UK firm. He is responsible for a number of key areas with respect to the Grant Thornton global brand. Bradley's biggest asset is his background and experience in corporate design; this is proving very important within the professional services industry.

Global Brand Compliance

Bradley works closely with five regional marketing managers representing member firms to ensure consistent application of the brand around the world, as the firm has strict standards which must be adhered to. In his early months Bradley discovered that a lack of local marketing resources led to brand non-compliance, so he now works with these members to align the brand's visual identity. Another area where it is easy for standards to slip occurs when a new member firm is inducted. They have to become used to using the new brand

and remove any traces of their original identity. This is especially relevant when integrating merged firms, where previous branding, cultures and processes have to change to fit the new regime. A smooth integration is desired but is often a challenge to implement.

Raising the Quality of Marketing Communications

One of Bradley's key tasks is to raise the quality of all printed or digital material across the global network. In 2015 he plans to implement regional design hubs to raise the level of marketing output and brand compliance. Rather than have one global print or design supplier, Bradley has established an accredited list of local suppliers that meet the required standards following a robust due diligence of their operations. Most of these suppliers were already in use, but the list has been tightened. The key is to appreciate local cultures and differences in order for member firms to buy into the change in processes.

Brand Strategy

The firm has already invested significantly in its brand platform, what it means to employees, Clients and local communities. There are many interpretations of the brand promise across the world; these need aligning with the core messaging already in place. The current strapline 'An instinct for growth' has met with wide acclaim by both employees and Clients. Now the firm is establishing the appropriate employee behaviours through global training and development initiatives so that they can implement the growth agenda mantra that underpins the brand in most markets.

Protecting the Brand

Bradley deals with the legal aspects of the brand to ensure its protection in various jurisdictions, working through regional management and legal teams. Regular audits of the brand are conducted to sense check what exists in member firms. In a recent survey around 65 per cent of member firms responded quickly to questions about their print and digital use of the brand. The brand is seen to stand out from those of its larger competitors and design agencies have been highly positive about its implementation. A brand refresh was recently carried out and this reignited the enthusiasm that was already in place.

Brand Creation and Development

Although there are many ways of approaching brand creation, best practice indicates that brands are created by starting research inside a firm before moving outside. Firms should be wary of brand creation processes that only look externally. The following is an example of a brand creation process that works.

11 STEPS TO CREATING YOUR BRAND[1]

1   Building Additional Value to the Business

Brands are economic assets, and are of underestimated importance in their own right to businesses today. Today, a firm's brand, as distinct from any physical assets it may possess, can be valued annually. In a world of mergers and acquisitions, the brand value is a core element of the final transaction price. The Apple brand was valued at $98,316M in 2013, with Accenture's valuation rising 8 per cent year-on-year.

2   Understanding the 'Brand Equation'

'Brand Equation' is in fact no more than what people do every day and every time they decide to buy; it explains how people engage with a brand.

3   Dissecting Stakeholders' Perspectives of the Brand

'Stakeholder' experiences and perceptions are important and used to be limited to Customers/Clients; the commonly held view was that the source of all wisdom lay solely and exclusively with them. What is now needed is a more 'holistic' perspective that could probe into the business, its model, its supply chain and, of course, down to its delivery.

4   Creating the Brand Equation

How do we create a 'Brand Equation' using a profile, and what are the dimensions that every brand must possess? The concept of the 'Brand Equation' is viewed by looking at four key elements: **Inherent Forces; Competitive Advantage; Rational** and; **Emotional**.

5   Market-Driven Brand Assessment Criteria

Part 1 – Applying the Inherent Strengths within the Brand

This addresses how to shape your brand authority and credibility into a strong set of inherent/latent dimensions that build a strong branded business, and how to set about rethinking your business definition to optimise the opportunities branding may offer.

Part 2 – Giving Your Business a Superior Value Proposition

This explores the image and performance dimensions by which your Clients/Customers will assess your brand in the market against the competition, and how you can differentiate your firm from your competitors.

---

1   A preview of a forthcoming book by Douglas Commaille, DCLW Consulting.

6   Client-Driven Brand Assessment

Part 1 – Building Emotional/Persuasive 'Capital' for Your Brand

The strength of a brand authority or credibility is never enough to anchor into the psyche of your Clients/Customers. Its imagery, personality and emotional 'hooks' need refreshing, re-vitalising and even re-expressing as the market evolves. The emotional and persuasive dimensions are important triggers in developing the overall perception of the brand and in building brand loyalty and affection.

Part 2 – Leveraging the 'Performance' Record of Your Brand

Rethinking how you see what your firm does, combined with strong competitive difference, creates a deeply rooted 'rational' and performance-based brand assessment. These are what Clients/Customers assess you by – after the product/service itself – and assure repeat purchase, and can also drive constant re-assessment of the brand's competitive advantage

7   Brand Essence or Brand DNA

The information from stages 1–6 is collated to extract the DNA of the brand. At this point, we are developing an expression of what your firm and brand 'stand for'; e.g., Think VOLVO – think 'safety'.

8   Crafting the Brand Values

This stage explores the role of brand values in defining the brand in the market, and why they are so important. Everyone has personal values and a moral code that they think has importance and significance to their day-to-day lives; this is no different from a brand perspective. Brands need strong values because they are what the world connects to and buys into: Disney, Virgin and Body Shop use Brand Values to define themselves in the market and build the loyalty that all successful brands need.

STEPS 9 TO 11: EMBEDDING THE BRAND INTO YOUR FIRM AND MARKET

9   Connecting Branding to the People

Brands only really work if the people who manage them and represent them understand what it is they stand for. This is not often something that is immediately obvious in many branded businesses, where Client/Customer perception and experience is secondary to operational issues. Sadly, some of the biggest businesses forget this: how many of us have come up against intractable inflexibility, mind numbing bureaucracy, or businesses that simply appear to 'load the dice' against the Client?

10   Brand Strategy and Implementation

Your business is your brand and your brand is your business. That is why Brand Strategy is integral to the business and cannot, and must not, be developed in isolation from it. The Brand Strategy applies all the elements previously discussed in terms of the market and commercial exploitation of the brand, not least, how the brand connects with Client aspirations and business objectives.

11   Living the Brand

It's important to understand what happens when we need to create the actual Brand Experience. This is usually the point at which many businesses give up through lack of attention to detail, disinterest and/or economy. However, this is where the **great** brands are built and grow, and where the 'also ran' brands fail. It is the test bed of Client acceptance and the final reality check in the journey.

BEST BRAND

An interesting exercise was used with partners of professional services firms wishing to raise their brand profile. In a workshop environment they were asked to name the brands in any market that most impressed them. Such brands as Apple, BMW, Coca-Cola, Disney, Google, HP, IBM, Mercedes, Nike, McDonald's and Virgin were mentioned. For each of these brands the delegates were then asked to list their attributes. For example those attributes for Apple were innovation, product quality; those for BMW and Mercedes were style and product quality, those for Disney were entertainment and Customer service, those for Virgin were great products and Customer service, and so on. It was interesting to note that no professional services firm was mentioned.

Delegates were then asked why their own brand was not listed. Many said that it was easier to have brand recognition in consumer markets and the service sector than in professional services. However, all agreed that it was important to have brand aspirations such as being the best in their chosen market segments. This was followed by a discussion on the values that could be attributed to their brand. This led to discussions on how they could energise their brand through the behaviour of their employees' understanding of the brand's values and aspirations. The outcome of the exercise was to define a research project to understand what employees, Clients and prospects thought of their brand. The gaps identified between the firm's perception of its brand and those of Clients/prospects enabled the firm to realign its strategy and close the gap over time through a series of brand-related projects.

What's in a (Brand) Name?

Many professional services firms have evolved through mergers and acquisitions. When considering the brand name for these firms, especially those trading internationally, decisions have to be made about such factors impacting Clients as:

- ease of understanding of the firm's name in global markets;

- ease of recognition;

- pronunciation of the name;

- simplicity, saving time;

- easier to use a short form name in digital environments where space is often limited.

For these and other reasons, many firms have reduced their names in some way, for example: PricewaterhouseCoopers has become pwc; Linklaters & Paines became Linklaters; Freshfields Brukhaus Deringer is generally known as Freshfields; Ernst & Young is now EY; and in March 2014 Jones Lang LaSalle was rebranded as JLL (see Chapter 14). This trend is even happening in the globalising consumer world, for example, Procter & Gamble is now simply P&G.

'BRAND' IN PROFESSIONAL SERVICES? NEW THINKING NEEDED

Only recently have professional services firms begun to hitch themselves to the 'brandwagon', and still very few show any signs of having learned from others' mistakes. In fact, many are making those same mistakes. The most fundamental of which is to confuse 'brand' with 'branding'.

A Brand is a Promise Kept

A brand is a promise kept. In the best cases, brand drives everything about an organisation: its structure, its products and services, its culture, its Client service, its communication. 'Branding' is only a part of that last aspect, and can only be done and understood once all the other elements are defined and understood.

If a brand is a promise kept, then the brand has to be built from the inside out. It has to be developed with the future in mind, and around a core of authenticity. To believe that the brand is the responsibility of the marketing department is to miss the point entirely – it is an asset that should be nurtured by all the senior leaders of a business. And to limit 'brand' to names, logos and umbrellas is to devalue that asset. It should be the one thing, above all, that builds commitment to an organisation, creates preference and allows the benefit of the doubt – across all stakeholders and measurable in sharp commercial terms.

A Defining Idea is Essential

The greatest brands stand for something, beyond the everyday demands of Client or Customer service and making money. They have a defining idea that runs through everything they do and say, and is rarely tied to a specific product or service. Their values, principles and behaviours are aligned and demonstrable in support of that ideal. The professional services sector hasn't grasped this properly, or the opportunity it presents to them. Very few firms have this kind of defining idea. They position themselves in a category of several, rather than of one: see how many law firms are 'leading', or how many talk about 'relationships' and 'partner involvement'. They use the language of precedent and safety in numbers. And they become indistinguishable one from another, except in name.

But it is possible for firms to be great brands, and there are signs of some realising this opportunity. One law firm we worked with in South Africa, for example, has embraced the idea of 'prosperity'. With the understanding of their role in developing local, national and regional economies, everyone in the firm now appreciates the contribution they can make. They now bring an optimistic and generous perspective to all of their internal relationships and integration; they know how and why they will extend into other jurisdictions; they approach their Client and business development with greater clarity and purpose; they are recruiting, training and promoting people according to their brand definitions. In short, they are keeping their promise.

The People are the Brand

This now shows the benefit of putting the brand at the heart of an organisation: it is the only way of guaranteeing consistency of behaviour and communication, of internal behaviour and external experience, ultimately of promise and delivery. There's a clue in the middle of 'professional services firm': the service is through people and the people are the brand.

Keith Wells – Director, Redstone Consultants.

Branding

The purpose of branding is to create the reputation of the brand to develop trust with existing and potential Clients through communication of the brand message to target audiences. Once a brand's values and associated employee behaviours have been developed to reflect the brand promise, branding and marketing communications can then be created to ensure that this impacts on Clients. Branding is the marketing communication element that helps to underpin the brand in its markets. The importance of branding is consistency of application within, and outside of, the firm; whether through its stationery, website, signage, business cards, advertisements and anything else that bears the brand name. This applies to both digital and printed materials.

BRAND IDENTITY

Professional services firms have researched the importance of various aspects of their brand identity, for example, using colour. Blue has been a favourite for many years with professional services firms, but some Clients consider this to reflect coldness. As a result, warmer-looking colours and fonts have been adopted by some professional services firms in the past 10 years.

Consistency of brand identity is important wherever the brand might appear, so it is important to have a preferred suppliers list for all printed materials, stationery, signage and branded promotional merchandise. For consistency of application of brand image, it is also important to provide people with templates and the appropriate user training.

BRANDING AND MESSAGING AUDITS

To ensure consistent application of the brand and associated messages, it is vital to keep track of its appearance on signage and published material. Many firms use third parties to 'mystery shop', or audit, their branding performance. This typically involves people visiting the firm's premises to see how the brand is physically displayed, whether it conforms to the firm's brand guidelines and so on. They then report back their findings supported with photos as appropriate. Where there are concerns, photographs are usually examined to enable deviations from standard to be seen. Such audits also review media advertising. Reports are then sent to brand and marketing management so that any corrective action needed can be taken. Another aspect of tracking brand performance relates to consistency of messaging in all marketing communications. Again, this can be monitored and regularly audited.

DEVELOPING THE ICAEW BRAND

Sue Best is Marketing Director for ICAEW, the Institute of Chartered Accountants for England and Wales. One of Sue's first programmes was to refresh the ICAEW brand. 'We manage relationships with both its individual members and students and with corporate members and firms. Managing its reputation is critical to its successful growth. We analysed our membership by income, sector, breadth/depth of engagement and membership and measured its brand and reputation.'

'We plan to develop long-term, sustainable relationships and focus on our key members. Top member organisations are involved in our 'Premier Relationship Programme', known internally as PRP. It is felt that the programme name is important, ensuring that it communicates the right message to our people and members externally, i.e. that building and maintaining the relationship is critical.'

'Measurements are in place to check the growth in income and relationship. PRP was piloted, focusing on a smaller number of key firms first, then rolled out to include other key organisations. PRP is covered in induction training to ensure that all new joiners to ICAEW are aware of its key strategic relationships and how they are managed. Now, senior staff and directors have responsibility for managing the relationships with our key member organisations. There are regular meetings with peer contacts in the member organisations and we aim to present a coordinated approach with a single point of contact to the Client; this requires careful management of all communications. This also reflects on the ICAEW brand – this has to be consistent.'

Sue quotes Wally Olins, co-founder of Wolff Olins advertising agency – 'Overall because branding is about creating and sustaining trust, it means delivering on promises. The best and most successful brands are completely coherent. Every aspect of what they do and what they are reinforces everything else.'

Sue feels that the personal touch is very important with members – 'It's about building the relationship and that takes time. It's often the little things that count – spending time understanding their issues, being up to date with developments in their organisation and sector or simply by sending an article or newsletter with a handwritten personal note on a compliment slip often works well in developing relationships.'

Differentiation

Differentiation should be a critical part of a firm's strategy. When communicated, it explains how a firm sets itself apart from its peers. This may be how your firm works with its Clients, how a service is delivered or what the firm is famous for with its Clients.

Many firms use straplines to reinforce and differentiate their brand in some way with the aim of gaining competitive advantage. These are usually placed alongside or underneath the brand name or logo. Straplines were first introduced in the consumer sector, gradually appearing in the service sector and now to professional firms. A famous strapline in the UK retail sector is that of John Lewis, which states 'Never knowingly undersold' and is matched with behaviour – the company will refund the difference if you could buy an item cheaper elsewhere. Some straplines are used audibly in advertising. Another example is from Avis, the car rental company, whose phrase and behavioural campaign 'We try harder' – and stories on how they did it – helped it to gain market share against rivals Hertz. Others use the personality of their founder as a unique differentiator, e.g. Richard Branson for Virgin. Table 6.1 shows examples from professional services firms.

Table 6.1   Straplines Used by Professional Services Firms

Sector	Firm	Strapline
Accountants	EY	Building a better working world
	Grant Thornton	An instinct for growth™
	PwC	Building relationships, creating value
Law	DLA Piper (USA)	Everything Matters
	Shepard Mullin (USA)	Our Mission is Your Success
Property	GVA	Creating real value in property and places

If it is possible to find something that is unique, distinct and interesting about your firm, such as an award for service excellence, it is good practice to use it as a differentiator and helps to build image and reputation. Developing a value proposition will help to differentiate the firm. However, it is important to realise that differentiators are not sustainable forever. Therefore it is incumbent on firms to optimise the commercial leverage of any differentiator that it owns.

Developing a Value Proposition

A value proposition is something highly desirable to Clients that is ideally unique to your firm or cannot easily be emulated by competitors. It may also be tailored to a specific group of Clients.

THE CHALLENGES OF DIVERSITY

Defining a value proposition for a professional services firm is not straightforward. This is due to the diversity of Clients, market sectors, services and not least the regulatory, legislative issues and limitations that professional services inevitably carry with them. Global firms have an even bigger challenge that adds the dimension of country cultural differences and practices.

AN EXAMPLE OF A VALUE PROPOSITION FROM AN ACCOUNTANCY FIRM

'We focus on business issues and provide Clients with insights around their issues and the support to solve them.' This is a very general proposition that could be used by many firms.

A Hierarchy of Value Propositions May Be Needed

Larger, particularly global firms could consider developing a 'hierarchy' of propositions. This would start by developing a broad, corporate/firm-wide statement, not unlike the example above. Value propositions may then have to be defined for market segments rather than the whole firm. This may already happen during the bid process, so it should be possible to articulate value propositions per Client group. These can be market tested and then rolled out as appropriate. For a value proposition to succeed it is best tailored to a particular Client.

STAGES IN DEVELOPING A VALUE PROPOSITION

To develop a value proposition it is necessary to understand the current strengths of the brand and the firm and whether related messaging includes a compelling, value-differentiated, rationale to buy the firm's services. This involves a number of stages:

- Reviewing the brand image, its credibility in the served markets and how the firm stands out from its competitors.
- Discussions with Clients and prospects to validate these facts. There may be some aspects of the brand that are working well and others that are not perceived as value by Clients and prospects.
- From these discussions it should then be possible to state the firm's core differentiator and its benefits to Clients.
- Validate the Clients' perceptions of value as a function of time, money and degree of risk.
- Determine the drivers of Client motivation and emotional engagement with the firm.
- Create an expression of the Value Proposition that incorporates the above factors.
- Test the proposition with Clients and non-Clients to validate it before launching.

Attributed to Douglas Commaille, DCLW Consulting.

Positioning the Firm with Clients

Positioning is the way a firm describes its vision and mission to its markets, so that the message is clear and memorable and Clients can understand where a firm stands in its markets. Effective positioning statements are ideally compelling value propositions, usually including differentiating factors, to enable Clients to make meaningful competitive comparisons. Over time, Clients mentally retain various facts about the suppliers that they encounter. Clients need reminding of what sets a firm apart from others. If you have a strong differentiator, for example, you have the fastest response time to create international Client service teams in your market, you can use this when describing and positioning your firm. With the many thousands of messages from different sources reaching your target audience, you are aiming to position your firm in the mind of your Client; thus, it is important to understand what is foremost in their thinking. As stated above, it is critical to realise that some differentiators are transient – they do not last forever. Awards are examples of transient differentiators, as they are only valid for a specific time period, usually a year. Of course, if your firm has been fortunate in winning an award for several consecutive years, this position can be leveraged as a competitive advantage when sending out proposals and bids.

If your firm publishes a mission statement (what it stands for) and its vision (where it's heading), these can be used in your commercial communications so that Clients associate your brand promise with the firm's positioning message.

HOW OBELISK LEGAL SUPPORT POSITIONS ITSELF IN THE LEGAL SERVICES MARKET

Dana Denis-Smith is CEO of award-winning Obelisk Legal Support, an organisation she founded in 2010. As a trained lawyer, Dana spotted an opportunity to provide income for legally trained mums at home by offering firms a different approach to solving resource problems by using outsourced lawyers. At first, law firms found this concept and the strange obelisk logo intriguing and at first difficult to take on board, but now Obelisk's 500-strong lawyer base is proving viable for many of the largest firms, including such firms as Goldman Sachs. Obelisk's key differentiator is its flexibility.

Positioning

Obelisk Support positions itself as an organisation that provides flexible and affordable quality legal services. They classify their ex-City lawyers as:

- 'Stand-in' (someone required for a limited period)
- 'Stand out' (someone who is noted in their field)
- 'Stand-by' (someone who is ready to step in when needed)
- 'Stand-off' (third party secondment to help the Client)

Dana says that 'Obelisk was built to answer the following Client needs – which are faced by most organisations and most departments within businesses:

- Cost – there isn't an organisation around that isn't trying to cut overheads.
- Capacity – there isn't an organisation around that doesn't have headcount challenges.
- Confirmation – there isn't an organisation around that doesn't want flexibility.
- Competence – there isn't an organisation around that isn't looking to enhance quality whilst reducing costs.'

When Obelisk had just 12 lawyers on its books, Dana started to mine the talent in this group, discovering their language skills and so on. To grow the business she organised house parties across the UK with lawyer mums who wanted to return to work. Over time she has continued this approach had the strategic vision to grow to around 500 lawyers within a few years. She has also found interesting opportunities within her own company for some of these the talented lawyers. 97 per cent of her lawyers are female.

Obelisk's brand personality evokes reliability and structure. Its values are based on the acronym HAPPIER, as below.

Vision

To build the world's leading outsourcing business centred around communities of local, home-based, highly-skilled professionals.

Values

The company uses an acronym – HAPPIER:

- **H**elpful
- **A**uthentic
- **P**ositive
- **P**rofessional
- **I**nnovative
- **E**lastic
- **R**esponsive

Client's Reason to Buy

Flexible, affordable and responsive quality legal support solutions from experienced ex-City lawyers.

The Brand Challenges Ahead

Brand explains why professional services firms are relatively new to establishing their brand and leveraging its uniqueness. The very fact that Clients often find it difficult to distinguish between firms means that firms are faced with a major challenge in finding the right brand promise that can be kept; values and employee behaviours that underpin the brand.

However, it is not safe just to choose a brand name and hope that it will solve the problem. As mentioned many times earlier, the brand is a reflection of the behaviour of employees and its development starts from the inside of a firm. The values associated with a brand have to be researched and developed by creating the appropriate dialogues between employees, partners or owners and Clients. Many firms have taken what they feel is the safe route of using their name as the brand, but this may not be sufficient unless their reputation and performance clearly stands out from the competition.

A well-researched and tested brand name is the preferred way forward – if professional services firms are able to find the defining idea that pervades the firm and sticks in the minds of its Clients, then they are more likely to create a successful brand name and messaging that can stand alongside the great brands in other markets. Ideally a brand, and related Client experience of the brand, should reflect the firm's value proposition to stand out from its competitors.

Many firms go through various stages of brand evolution, yet have not taken the necessary steps to follow through with implementation where it counts – in the marketplace. Living the brand is one of the key challenges to professional services firms.

Brand, Differentiation and Positioning

CLIENT MANAGEMENT REVIEW QUESTIONS

To what extent:

1. Do your employees understand that their work behaviour reflects your brand?

2. Is your brand promise clearly stated in all of your published communications?

3. Do you regularly survey unprompted recognition of your brand with non-Clients?

4. Is your branding consistently applied in all communications and signage?

5. Do you regularly audit whether your branding is consistently applied?

6.   Do you clearly communicate what differentiates your firm from competitors?

7.   Do you have a clearly defined and stated positioning?

8.   Is your brand promise regularly reviewed with Clients?

9.   Are your brand values clearly communicated inside your firm?

10.   Are your brand values clearly communicated to audiences outside your firm?

These questions form the basis of the *Brand* section of your *Client Management Profile*™, which can be found in Chapter 15.

Client Management Model™

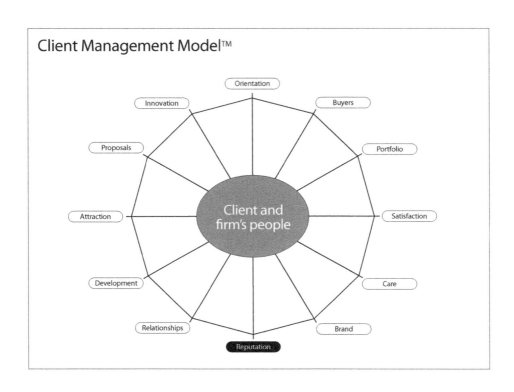

Chapter 7

Reputation:
Gaining Reputation with Clients

Synopsis

Reputation, the seventh element of the *Client Management Model*™, explains:

- sources of reputation;

- media relations and its impact on Clients;

- thought leadership and its impact on Clients;

- thought followership;

- the importance of media training;

- issue-based campaigns;

- sponsorship;

- networks and group membership.

THOUGHT STARTERS
- What affects your reputation?
- How can you use thought leadership?
- Who are your target audiences?
- What issues are of interest to your Clients?
- What can you publish?

Sources of Reputation

The reputation of a professional services firm can develop from many areas. Just as Clients 'buy' people, they are influenced by a firm's reputation. Many firms receive referrals from existing Clients because they have delivered a sufficiently high quality of service that the Client is willing to mention this to peer organisations. Whilst word of mouth is an ideal form of developing new Clients, it can be a relatively slow process and so builds up over a considerable time period.

An issue-based campaign, perhaps a piece of thought leadership, targeted at the right prospects or Clients can be very effective in rapidly building your firm's reputation and can often lead to a new revenue stream. Reputation can be gained rapidly by association with a high-profile organisation, for example, if your firm sponsors or co-sponsors a widely publicised report or a good cause.

Media Relations and its Impact on Clients

In recent years many professional services firms have established a public relations (PR) function to enable managed contact with the media and other audiences to position their firm accordingly. This function often starts at the corporate level, aiming to reach specific audiences with messages and publications that can influence the direction of the firm in its chosen markets. Others outsource the PR function to an agency. Many firms do not have an articulated PR strategy.

The larger professional services firms also have PR managers for service lines and some have sector-focused PR teams or specialist agencies. Each of these has its place in supporting the firm's strategy.

Thought Leadership and its Impact on Clients

In today's increasingly competitive arena for professional services, ideas are a major source of differentiation. Those professional services firms that stand out in their market have moved beyond providing solutions to Clients' problems and have aimed to become famous for their work particular areas through the differentiator of thought leadership. They often do this by conducting issue-based research to position their firm as experts and commentators in a specific field. Nowadays Clients expect their advisors to be leaders in their fields and this is often demonstrated through thought leadership initiatives.

For example, a firm might wish to position itself with large corporates by researching the impact on corporate share prices of mergers in a sector. During the process of interviewing top executives for their views, the firm may build new relationships. By asking the right questions, a firm can take a stance on an issue that yields a high level of media attention and coverage. This leads to Clients and prospects contacting the firm for a copy of the report or for some advice. However, many firms admit to jumping on the bandwagon of other firms' research. This is known as thought followership. Clients are increasingly seeking firms that are innovative and prepared to speak out on topical issues.

Thought Followership

A recent study, 'Follow The Leader', by consultants *Man Bites Dog* suggests that thought *followership* is rife in professional services firms and asks if the 'thinking professions' have run out of ideas. The research revealed that:

- three-quarters (75 per cent) of professional services marketers see thought leadership as the greatest source of differentiation for their firm;

- nine in ten (91 per cent) are forced by partners to cover the same ideas as competitors;

- in 62 per cent of all professional services, 'thought leadership' is in fact 'thought followership'.

THOUGHT LEADERSHIP IS KEY TO PROFESSIONAL SERVICES FIRMS' SUCCESS – A RECENT STUDY

Thought leadership is now the key battleground for professional services firms, according to 91 per cent of professional services marketers. Yet the industry – often heralded as the inventors of ideas-led and issues-based marketing – is being held back by culture and structure, according to 'Follow the Leader', a new in-depth study from strategy and communications consultancy, Man Bites Dog, conducted in October 2013.

Thought Leadership Tops Business Agenda

Three quarters (75 per cent) of professional services marketers see thought leadership as the greatest source of differentiation for their firm, whilst 87 per cent believe that thought leaders are also more likely to become market leaders. Professional services firms are investing heavily in thought leadership, on average 23 per cent of total marketing budgets in the current budget cycle. This is set to grow, with 87 per cent of firms increasing their budgets next year and 29 per cent revising this up significantly. Clients and new business development are driving this investment trend. Around four fifths (82 per cent) of service economy marketers say Clients expect firms to produce insightful content as a matter of course, whilst around three quarters (76 per cent) believe thought-leading content is the key to profitable conversations and establishing deeper long-term relationships.

'Thought Followership' Rife in Professional Services Firms

Despite the critical role of thought leadership in helping firms to stand out, the study reveals an epidemic of thought followership in professional services. 74 per cent of marketers admit their firm tends to 'jump on the bandwagon' rather than set the agenda, and these marketing leaders estimate that 65 per cent of their so-called 'thought leadership' content is in fact 'thought followership'. According to the study, each sector is experiencing its own unique battles. The greatest challenge for law firms is ideas generation with four-fifths (80 per cent) of legal marketers admitting their firms don't provide a nurturing environment for new ideas.

Accountancy marketers experience the greatest level of interference from fee earners compared with other professional services firms, with the vast majority (96 per cent) complaining that partners push them to cover the same topics as everyone else. Management consultancies meanwhile – often regarded as the founders of thought leadership – fail to generate genuinely unique insight, with almost nine in ten (88 per cent) admitting their firm struggles to present a differentiated point of view.

Claire Mason, Managing Director at Man Bites Dog, comments: 'In an increasingly competitive environment, ideas are the only source of differentiation. Put simply, thought leadership is the most effective form of marketing for professional services firms. Yet we are seeing an epidemic of thought followership from the thinking professions. The thing that makes professional services firms stand out from their competitors is the quality of their people and their expertise. But if everyone is saying the same thing, how can Clients tell the difference between them?'

'Talking about the same things as competitors may give firms the comfort factor, but it will do little to drive the profitable conversations fee earners so desperately want. It's time for professional services firms to step off the content treadmill and consider what needs to change at leadership and cultural level to empower marketers to develop ideas that lead.'

The Importance of Having Media-trained Employees

A firm's media relations strategy relies on its ability to access the right journalists in the appropriate media at the right time. If a journalist wants to interview a specialist from the firm, it is important that the specialist has received media training. This means that specialists know how to conduct themselves during interviews. Some firms have received television coverage on an issue, so again their specialists must be aware of the behavioural requirements when appearing on television.

Media training usually puts people through the paces of various media situations, from a simple telephone interview to a filmed appearance. The training involves video recording so that the trainee can make corrections where needed under the tuition of a media specialist.

Putting forward media-trained people to the media is particularly important in a crisis situation, where a firm is receiving the glare of publicity through an incident.

DEALING WITH A CRISIS

A media training firm was asked to train board-level people in a firm to deal with crises. They decided to accommodate the board in a country house.

Delegates arrived for an overnight stay and were expecting a workshop to start on the following day. However, the media training company arranged for a journalist to telephone one of the board members in the early hours of the morning indicating that a serious fraud incident had occurred at their bank.

The board member had no idea what to do in this situation; at breakfast it was revealed that the call had been recorded and was used as part of the training!

HOW A TOP LAW FIRM TRIGGERS CLIENT INTEREST THROUGH MEDIA RELATIONS

When Christian Marroni joined Freshfields Bruckhaus Deringer (Freshfields) in 2008 to take up responsibility for media relations, the firm's media engagement efforts were largely confined to the legal media and to the occasional, (mainly reactive) engagement with national and international broadsheets. In resourcing terms the firm relied on small PR teams based in London and Germany which mainly operated along country lines.

Media Relations Strategy

The overall purpose of Freshfields' media relations activity:

- To protect the firm's global reputation, so a watchful eye is kept on issues that could develop into something more serious.
- To announce corporate information relating to the firm, for example financial results, new partners joining and corporate social responsibility activities.
- To proactively associate the firm with market issues.
- To build the firm's employer brand and tackle any negative connotations (for example lack of diversity or poor work life balance – issues that are so common across the city) that might detract from being recognised as one of the profession's leading employer.
- Using social media as appropriate to reach target audiences directly.

Quality of Content is Key

As Head of Global Media Relations, Christian implemented a strategy aimed at increasing content quality that can trigger pieces in the leading national and international media by developing issue-based research pieces aimed at enhancing the firm's reputation in a particular area and triggering a response from specific Clients and targets.

To increase Freshfields' global presence, a team of PR professionals has been established in London, Paris, Germany, Hong Kong and the US, with agencies in Austria and Italy.

A programme of global thought leadership has been created to help generate media interest around the world. While a lot of content is generated in London with a UK and global audience in mind, not everything that is an issue or thought of in London can work in the media of every market. It's important that the 'centre of gravity' in terms of an organisation's thought leadership development is purposely shifted to other markets as well so that issues that might be more relevant to the US or Asia, but maybe of only secondary importance in Europe, are tackled too.

Freshfields is a commercial law firm that does not do private Client work. Most of the areas it is an expert in do not necessarily yield reams of coverage in the press and given that lawyers are unlikely to be able to ever comment very much on Client matters (which are often newsworthy) and given market sensitivities around many issues, the window of comment opportunity is often narrow. As a result, in order to showcase an expert's insight, it's key to be creative to make a specific corporate issue newsworthy for a broad audience.

In countries where the firm has no direct PR representation, they have improved the skills of local business development teams to deal with their national media. This helps to push out high quality global thought leadership material to gain traction in local markets. For the last three years, Freshfields has held an annual media relations conference in London which is used to share knowledge and up-skill the PR and BD teams. Christian travels to the different supported locations to encourage a continuous programme of media activity.

Attracting Media and Thus Client Attention

'In professional services, and in respect of showcasing an expert's insight, there are really only two types of story that ever feature in the media.

The first is what happens today and will be in the news tomorrow irrespective of what Freshfields or any other organisation does, for example, a major new piece of legislation affecting the regulation of banks. To get a piece of the action the simple objective is to pair an expert with the relevant journalist in a timely way to offer some views.

The second is news content that wouldn't otherwise be written had a professional services organisation not suggested it. This is where quality content is key, so research based material coupled with sharp insight is the end goal to ensure that the material is robust and compelling to persuade the likes of the *Financial Times* to print it.

In developing such content, it's important to align media relations with BD priorities.'

Putting Clients First

'Freshfields uses the media as one of the channels to influence their target audiences, whether Clients or prospects. It aims to seek a position whereby audiences will begin to associate the firm with particular stances on global issues. Given the amount of material reaching corporate general counsel every day Freshfields is in competition with many other law firms. So it aims to position itself as the leading authority on a particular issue to move up the ladder of selection. Freshfields does this by selecting a sector and forming specialist teams with the common interest of elevating the firm's presence globally in that area.'

Measurement of Media Activity

'How best to measure the tangible value of media activity is always a cause for debate, especially for organisations that can't benefit so obviously from improved sales on the back of a feature in the press like a consumer business sometimes can.

As well as looking at the obvious indicators like volume, favourability and how much of its coverage supports its key messages, Freshfields monitors the effect of coverage – how many leads were received, analysing the type and seniority of respondent to see if they are meeting their influencing goals. What we regularly see is that whenever our experts are quoted in leading media on issues that matter to Clients and targets, market participants will approach us, maybe for more information, to discuss an issue or instigate a meeting. On occasion work will directly flow from that opportunity but where it doesn't it's extremely valuable to be able to see that the right people, from the right organisations are being moved to get in touch.'

Innovation

'Freshfields has produced a number of innovative reports to raise its profile. One recent campaign related to global crisis management. The research looked at four particular types of crisis:

- Corporate – e.g. a liquidity issue
- Informational – e.g. a hacking incident
- Behavioural – for example fraud
- Operational – e.g. a product recall

The research covered aspects such as the impact of a major reputational crisis on share price once news of a crisis reached the public domain. It looked at the composition of corporate boards one year after a crisis to see how many board members had kept their jobs. Unsurprisingly, those companies that managed crises well had far less attrition at board level than the companies that fared poorly in crises, but interestingly their ratio was even better than their direct competitors listed on the same exchange but free of a crisis of their own.

A recent survey of global PR agencies sought to establish the impact on corporate reputations on how crises were managed. Social media is now the channel through which crises can become international news within hours!'

Sponsorship

Once a firm has decided its 'go to market' strategy, it has to consider how to best reach its target audiences, whether these are prospective or existing Clients. The increasing use of sponsorship by professional services firms is testament to its effectiveness in raising their profiles and enhancing their reputations. However, for effective sponsorship, different audiences require separate treatment.

Let us imagine that a UK firm decides to segment its Client and prospect base into groups such as:

Group A – Businesses in Leeds with an annual turnover above £100 million.

Group B – General Counsel in the top 50 UK law firms.

Group C – Small to medium-sized business that are acquisitive.

Group D – Those businesses that have a high export focus.

Each of these groups will require different treatment to reach the appropriate decision makers and influencers.

For example, to reach *Group A*, a firm may decide to sponsor of a series of articles about medium-sized companies in a regional newspaper's business section. This may take the form of a series of interviews of CEOs and MDs. Events can be created to invite prospective and existing Clients to further discuss the issues raised in the articles. This might involve a panel of experts including a selection of the firm's partners. The attendees are then followed up to check the level of interest.

To reach the general counsel in *Group B* may require a higher level of sophistication; an example of sponsorship might involve support of a trade journal or piece of research to create a special event of interest. The third group, *Group C*, may find sponsorship of a national mergers and acquisitions conference of interest. *Group D* might be attracted by invitations to overseas business delegations sponsored by a government department.

The decision to sponsor an event, support a cause or an awards ceremony, for example, usually requires considerable planning and may span more than one business period. In some cases a firms aims to be a headline sponsor of an event for several years to raise its profile. This strategy can also be an effective source of competitive differentiation by 'locking out' other firms for a period. The benefit of sponsorship of awards is that there is usually a high exposure for the firm's brand before, during and after the event, and an opportunity for it to demonstrate its breadth of expertise.

USING RESEARCH TO OPEN NEW DOORS

A mid-tier accounting firm wanted to grow its position in the mid-market. It decided to research the historic and projected profitability and growth of companies in this segment, and discovered that many mid-market listed companies were out-performing many of the larger listed companies.

The research, conducted by an independent analyst, was offered exclusively by the PR manager to the business section of a major newspaper, and the list of companies in the top 50 of the research base would be published in the form of an index.

Prior to publication, those companies that would be featured in the published chart were contacted by the accounting firm to advise them of the likelihood of national business press coverage. This raised awareness of the accounting firm. Interviews were sought with board members of these companies and 20 per cent agreed to meet with a marketing manager from the accounting firm. These interviews would feature in a summary report alongside the data.

None of these ten interviewed companies were Clients at the time but they clearly became intrigued by the research and the association of the accounting firm with a highly credible national newspaper. They were also willing to be interviewed to raise their profile. The research and interviews were published in the form of a report and led to further interest around the mid-market. It also was sufficiently interesting to two larger interviewed listed firms that they began to use the accounting firm in an advisory capacity. The campaign was continued for six years and the newly-found Clients have remained loyal.

Issue-Based Marketing Campaigns

As mentioned earlier, an An effective way of positioning a professional services firm with potential allies is to align it with a topical business or public interest issue.

The following case studies illustrate this.

USING ISSUE-BASED RESEARCH TO ENHANCE REPUTATION

A mid-tier accounting firm wanted to build its reputation as a provider of a forensic advisory service in combatting commercial fraud, known as economic crime, in corporate entities. Research showed that if fraud was detected within a large corporation, their general counsel and legal team would recommend the appropriate forensic accountants. Although the accounting firm was relatively successful for its size, it was not attracting such referred work from these large companies. So the firm decided to create an issue-based campaign that would focus on combatting economic crime aimed at alerting top management in corporate entities.

While it was looking at ways to raise its profile with these large entities, a chance meeting occurred between the accountants and some regional fraud investigators. A regional police group was combatting white collar economic crime by creating a forum to encourage the sharing of information between private and public sectors. This results achieved by this forum had come to the attention of a UK government department. The forum was considering the conduct of an economic crime survey among retailers in their region. The accounting firm offered to help with the survey and a draft was created containing around 50 questions. The survey would be printed and it was decided to attract sponsors in addition to the regional fraud forum as this should encourage participation by large retailers. When the government's anti-fraud team was shown the draft document it asked for the survey to be extended to a wider audience than just retailers in a region – it also wanted all UK corporate entities to be surveyed as, according to their data, economic crime was costing £18bn in the UK.

The accounting firm decided to create an economic crime survey that would be conducted among 3,500 companies listed on the UK stock exchange. The survey now had a range of sponsors including a government department and the Confederation of British Industry (CBI) which added to its credibility and response rate. The target audience in the 3,500 FTSE companies were board members at CEO and Finance Director level, as these people were known to influence and recommend the procurement of forensic advisory services from the accounting firm in discussions on fraud issues with their legal colleagues.

The response to the survey was considered significant as it included 10 per cent of FTSE 100 companies, the UK's largest public entities. The data was analysed and by extrapolation and interviews with large companies, the cost of economic crime was quantified at £40bn; £32bn due to identified losses and £8bn required to train people to detect fraud. This figure was considerably higher than previous estimates and astounded a number of commentators. A public relations initiative led to extensive coverage in all of the UK national press and enquiries to the accounting firm.

Each respondent was given a profile showing how it compared with other companies of similar size and industry sector. A report was produced and launched in London to an audience including top listed company bosses. They heard from a panel of economic crime experts and a representative from the government department. Some of these enquiries resulted in a new income stream from large companies which had previously used other, larger accounting firms to investigate fraud. A series of road shows was then held around the UK to promote the report to listed companies. A follow up survey was then conducted with building societies and later with public sector organisations. Both sectors also received excellence media coverage about the fraud issue.

HIGH NET WORTH CAMPAIGN

An accounting firm wanted to forge closer ties with lawyers when dealing with high personal wealth Clients. Many of these Clients had complex business issues, and some had personal issues relating to marital separation and divorce. It was decided to conduct some sensitive market research with high net worth individuals and to include the question of separation and divorce. The findings revealed considerable uncertainty in regard to selection of the appropriate law firm to handle such matters. The report received wide press coverage and a number of specialist law firms contacted the accounting firms offering to help their wealthy Clients. A series of round tables was held nationally each led by a panel including two or more law firms, who explained with examples how they had helped high net worth individuals to resolve their financial affairs. This led to close relationships being developed between the accounting firm and many law firms. A number of high net worth individuals also contacted the accounting firm for more information about their wealth management services.

Memberships of Industry Groups and Networks

Joining selected groups can bring partners closer to their target audiences through networking; nowadays this is becoming an increasingly used approach. By attending sector or issue-based events, it is often possible to meet targets that are otherwise inaccessible.

Many of these groups now meet 'virtually', over the Internet, providing valuable insights into sector issues. The use of 'blogs' and forums to air views is now a global, and daily, phenomenon. These have to be carefully monitored to avoid the possibility of abuse as a firm's reputation is more on the line now than ever before.

SUB-OPTIMISED THOUGHT LEADERSHIP

'Thought leadership is perhaps, ironically, becoming devalued by repetition and by firms not fully working through what it means and what it can do for them. The two main causes I see of firms not gaining potential results from thought leadership are:

- Not thinking through what will really add distinctive value both to them and their businesses.
- Not effectively exploiting the value of the thought leadership and content they generate.

The second can definitely be an issue for firms where the marketing function is stretched and can find it difficult to take a step back and identify all the strategic and tactical opportunities it can provide.'

Robin Dicks, Director, The Thriving Company Limited

The Challenges of Reputation Management

Reputation has explained that in these times of rapid, mobile communications professional services firms need to ensure that they measure the pulse of their Clients and markets through effective research and media relations. News now travels faster than ever before, with social media channels like Facebook, LinkedIn and Twitter often beating the traditional publication route of a press release. Those firms that have a media relations strategy and policy aim to stay abreast of such developments. Professional services firms that have excellent media contacts and media-trained specialists who can face journalists are more likely to be contacted for their expert opinions. Thought leadership is still one of the most effective means of attracting new business, as long as it is fresh, topical and hard-hitting in content.

————

Gaining Reputation

CLIENT MANAGEMENT REVIEW QUESTIONS

To what extent:

1. Do you have a written and communicated media strategy and objectives?

2. Do you use thought leadership to enhance your reputation?

3. Do you have media-trained people who can face the media?

4. Do you have a crisis management process that kicks in when needed?

5. Do you create issue-based campaigns to raise your firm's profile?

6. Are you members of a number of influential networks?

7. Do you have a social media policy that monitors commentary about the firm?

8.   Do you use a media relations agency to complement your internal team?

9.   Do you have a corporate responsibility strategy?

10.   Is your firm involved in social responsibility projects?

11.   Do you track your firm's reputation?

12.   Do you have an updated media contact list with named spokespeople?

These questions also form the basis of the *Reputation* section of your *Client Management Profile*™, which can be found in Chapter 15.

Client Management Model™

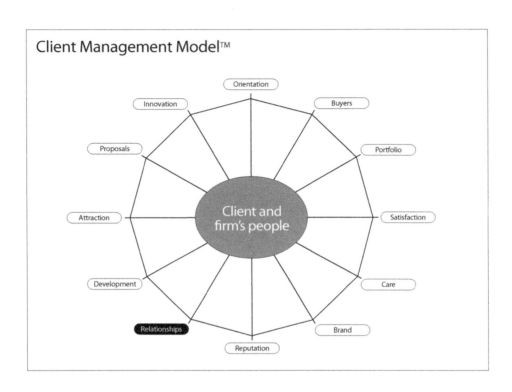

Chapter 8

Relationships:
Client Relationship Development

Synopsis

Relationships, the eighth element of the *Client Management Model*™, explains:

- the aim of relationship development;

- the importance of regular communication;

- Client panels;

- the Client relationship development process;

- types of Client relationship;

- a Relationship Evaluation Process;

- relationship tracking;

- Client segmentation;

- Client data analytics;

- Clients that defect;

- Client Relationship Management (CRM) and systems;

- launching a CRM programme.

THOUGHT STARTERS
- How can you keep Clients interested in your firm?
- What are the communication preferences of your Clients?
- How would you characterise the types of relationship that exist?
- How can you develop stronger Client relationships?
- How should you keep in contact with Clients in-between assignments?
- What is your relationship development process?
- How does CRM operate in your firm?

The Aim of Client Relationship Development

Clients usually have a wide choice of suppliers for professional services. Firms want to become trusted advisers. Clients expect added value during a relationship. Experience shows that those firms that understand the different phases of relationship development are more likely to have a portfolio of loyal, profitable, Clients than those that just view Clients as transactional.

Regular Communication

Clients expect regular communication during their relationship with the supplying firm. One of the most important and least expensive ways of retaining Clients is to keep in touch using a variety of methods:

- sending hardcopy articles that may be of interest – using the personal touch – adding a handwritten note;

- sending emails with links to articles;

- inviting them to a discussion, Client panel, event or exhibition;

- establishing blogs and forums;

- sending them a book that may be of interest;

- asking them to be interviewed for an article;

- asking them to be interviewed and filmed for an internal event;

- newsletters;

- magazines in both hard and digital copy;

- technical bulletins;

- asking for testimonials that can be developed into case studies;

- asking them to help with development of new services.

A CLIENT SPEAKS OUT

A management team agreed to have a guest Client speak to them at dinner during a three-day residential workshop on Client management. This Client was selected since he was very satisfied with their construction work some eight months ago. During his talk about his business, the Client indeed indicated how pleased he was with the project. This drew visible comfort and self-praise from the management team involved around the table.

However, the Client then said: 'What really concerns me is that no-one from your firm has been in touch with me in over six months since that project was completed – and I still have an unspent programme budget worth over £700m.'

This comment created a very different feeling from the top managers seated around the Client!

Client Panels

The use of Client panels is on the increase as firms aim to satisfy Clients beyond provision of advice. Many firms create such panels of satisfied Clients with the aim of:

- improving their services;

- introducing new services;

- welcoming new Clients;

- seeking feedback on working methods;

- seeking referrals;

- seeking ideas for events;

- asking the Client to help with development of new services.

These panels meet regularly to discuss issues of interest to Clients, test innovations in service delivery and generally to keep firms in touch with their markets.

Speaking Engagements

Many firms ask Clients if they would like to speak at a conference, seminar or other event. As stated earlier, it is important to keep in touch with your existing Clients, even when no work is currently being undertaken. Many of these Clients may be seeking solutions to new problems in their business and could be unaware of your range of services.

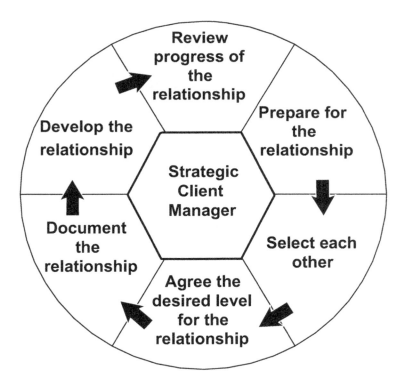

Figure 8.1   The Client Relationship Cycle

The Client Relationship Development Process

One popular process of developing relationships with Clients can be likened to a cycle of Courtship, Engagement and Togetherness. This approach was developed during the author's consulting assignments at *Marketing Improvements Group* and was used successfully with organisations across many markets. For each Client, a manager is usually appointed who is responsible for orchestrating the team through these stages, as shown in Figure 8.1. As will be seen later, this process paves the way to developing higher levels of Client trust. Let's look at the content of each stage.

The cycle follows a series of action steps to take people through the implementation process.

Courtship

PREPARE FOR THE RELATIONSHIP

- Assess the desire within the firm and the Client to have a relationship beyond just transactional.

- Prepare a Strategic Client Plan.

- Raise awareness within the Client.

- Identify and map the decision makers and influencers within the Client.

SELECT EACH OTHER

- Gather information.

- Establish growth potential.

- Select each other with a view to developing a higher level of trust.

Engagement

AGREE THE DESIRED LEVEL FOR THE RELATIONSHIP

- Consider various relationship levels (see types of relationship in Table 8.1).

- Confirm the current level.

- Select desired level.

- Identify the gaps between the current and planned relationship.

DOCUMENT THE RELATIONSHIP

- Share a common starting point and vision.

- Identify the champions in each organisation.

- Set broad objectives.

- Establish success measures.

Togetherness

DEVELOP THE RELATIONSHIP

- Prepare a joint business plan.

- Develop actions.

- Implement actions.

REVIEW PROGRESS OF THE RELATIONSHIP

- Monitor outcomes.

- Review objectives.

- Agree the way forward.

- Celebrate relationship development.

Types of Client Relationship

Given a firm's desire to retain specific Clients and develop relationship strength and longevity, it is useful to review the possible types of relationship that exist and their main characteristics. From experience it is then very useful to segment Clients in this way when reviewing growth plans for the firm. Experience shows that the stronger, multi-service, relationships developed over several years are likely to be more profitable.

Most firms would agree that their aim is to become the Client's trusted adviser, but that some relationships do not move beyond transactional or multi-service. The tipping point occurs when the Client contacts the firm to discuss a new issue. The firm must recognise this unprompted 'Moment of Truth' (see Chapter 5) is it is the key to opening the door to a higher level of trust. Table 8.1 below is a guide that may assist this process. Many firms map their Client portfolio against such relationship characteristics as it serves as the basis for assigning strategic resources to manage Clients.

Table 8.1   Relationship Characteristics

Factors Relationship with Client	Relationship development stage (see Figure 8.1)	Level of trust	Number/type of services supplied	Typical duration (years)	Work scope	Strength of relationship	Client hospitality offered by firm	Satisfaction – Net Promoter Score Range (see Chapter 4)
Transactional.	Courtship.	Low.	One or two basic.	1–2	Basic with one or two experts.	Low: One or two key contacts.	Low.	Mainly Passives and a few Promoters.
Multi-service.	Courtship.	Growing with experts.	Several. Some annuity.	1–5+	Developing with many experts.	Medium: Many key buying contacts.	Medium.	More Promoters.
Loyal.	Engagement.	Growing with firm.	Broad range. Client contacts on new issue.	3+	Projects. Strategic advice sought.	High: Many cross-functional contacts.	Developing.	Mainly Promoters. Provide testimonials.
Trusted.	Engagement.	Trusted business adviser.	Many value added. Regular issue meetings.	3+	Projects Integrated systems.	Very high. Strong networking.	High.	All are Promoters. Some referrals.
Partnership.	Togetherness.	Trusted business adviser.	Broad range. Strategic.	5+	Often complex.	Very high. Collaboration on service development.	Very high.	All are Promoters. Many referrals.
Flagship.	Togetherness.	Trusted business adviser.	Broad range. Strategic.	5+	Often complex.	Highest.	Very high.	All are Promoters.

Relationship Evaluation Process

Given the number of Clients in a firm's portfolio it is useful to be able to rank them in order of priority for strategic planning and Client management. One analytical technique that can be used takes the relationship and other factors and allocates scores and weights to each. An example of this method is shown in Table 8.2 below, where three Clients are evaluated. Each Client total is found by multiplying weight by score.

Table 8.2   Client Relationship Evaluation Matrix

Evaluation criteria	Scoring	Weight	Client A Score	Total A	Client B Score	Total B	Client C Score	Total C
Work scope	one service = 1 multi-service = 3 international = 5	1	5	5	3	3	3	3
Duration	1 point per year engaged	1	4	4	6	6	10	10
Net Promoter	NPS score	2	9	18	8	16	8	16
Buying contacts known	1 per buyer or budget holder	3	5	15	2	6	3	9
Share of Client spend	<10% = 1 11–30% = 2 31–50% = 3 51–75% = 4 >75% = 5	4	3	12	2	8	4	16
Relationship Development stage	Courtship = 1 Engagement = 3 Togetherness = 5	5	5	25	1	5	3	15
	Totals			79		44		69

Relationship Tracking

Most firms classify their most important Clients as Key, Strategic, Premium, and so on. Given the dynamic nature of business and relationships it is useful to review the status of these Clients at least annually or when some trigger causes a change. An example of a trigger is when a Client increases their expenditure or range of services. This would raise the relationship status. Another trigger would be a change of buyer in a Client, or re-organisation, which might lower the relationship status until it develops.

Relationship tracking is the process of regularly reviewing the status of a Client relationship possibly carried out during Client Planning meetings when the multi-disciplinary team discusses business development progress.

Client Segmentation

Many firms are using more sophisticated marketing techniques to target Clients with whom they wish to develop trusted business adviser relationships. One of these is market segmentation, which clusters those groups with similar requirements across sectors and service disciplines. These research-based analyses are often very powerful indicators of buying behaviour and, if followed, can speed up the process of increasing Client expenditure with your firm.

TYPICAL BUSINESS DRIVERS RESEARCHED IN MARKET SEGMENTATION

Influencing factors

- *Service usage* – type, quality, quantity, breadth, depth.

- *Pressure and influences* – cost and management initiatives, changing competition.

- *Buying practices* – fragmented or rationalised supply, use of tenders and bids, adversary or partner.

- *Supplier relationships* – description of how this is perceived, contribution to success of business.

Supplier selection and evaluation factors

- Cost.

- Deliverables.

- Technical support.

- Contact and relationships.

- Information and communication.

- Image and reputation.

- Reliability.

SEGMENTATION BY PURCHASING BEHAVIOUR

A Client supplying plastic materials in various thicknesses and qualities wanted to improve its market position. At present its factories and sales team covered Europe; within each country there were 5–10 sales people, each selling a particular thickness of material for various applications, based on local factory output. Some were selling thin film, coiled material, others sheet and another team were selling strips. Research interviews were conducted with around 100 of their Clients across Europe in various sectors to discover buying preferences. By asking specific questions about buying habits, priorities and preferences, it was possible to create a number of different behavioural segments, each being given a memorable name for internal classification purposes.

- 'Alex Alliance' – these Clients had a preference for forming supplier alliances.
- 'Benjamin Benchmark' – these Clients compared attributes of suppliers with those of other services.
- 'Commodity Kevin' – these Clients put price first, looking for the best deal.
- 'Serge Service' – these Clients put service and delivery first.
- 'Techno Ted' – these Clients put technical expertise at the top of their agenda.

Eventually these types were colour coded for internal reference and planning.

The sales team was then retrained and given a behavioural segment identifier tool so that it could identify the most likely buying preferences, and to sell across the product range, offering a package to suit the buyers' different inclinations, regardless of sector. Market share was considerably increased. The sales team was then restructured to serve specific market sectors, including aerospace, automotive, construction, DIY and packaging.

Source: Marketing Improvements Group.

AN EXAMPLE OF SEGMENTATION

It is often useful to map the potential market for your services and use segmentation to target those Clients that you wish to satisfy.

Segmentation starts with a definition of the problem or issue to be resolved – for example, tax level too high.

We then look at the variables, such as:

- type of organisation – public, private, not for profit;

- location – national, regional, local;

- size by number of employees – up to 500, 500–1,000, 1,000–5,000, 5,000+;

- sector – technology, public, food, transport;

- country – Europe, Africa, Asia, Americas.

Each variable is then mapped so that a route through each variable can be chosen. This is shown in Figures 8.2 and 8.3.

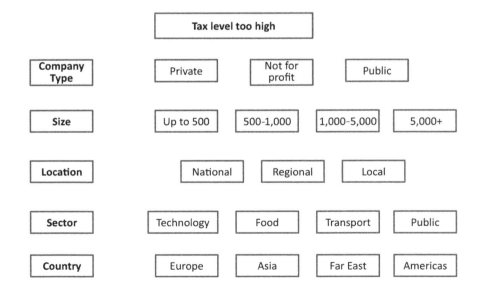

Figure 8.2   First Stage of Market Segmentation

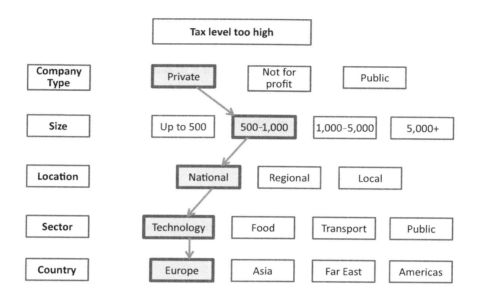

Figure 8.3   Selection Stage of Market Segmentation

By mapping the variables, it is then easy to decide on the areas of focus. In this selection, the firm has decided to review the issue of taxes being too high and then to evaluate the different areas of focus. The route shown in Figure 8.3 shows that the selection comprises: private companies, with 500–1,000 employees in the technology sector, nationally located, in European countries.

Client Data Mining and Data Analytics

This section explains the importance of being able to analyse Client behaviour beyond the routine purchases, analysing your database to establish insights around Client preferences and habits so that communications and campaigns can be better focused.

Current technology enables analysis of Client and prospect data beyond the first level of contact details. Well-known examples of this are in place in the retail sector where stores keep records of Customer purchases and then send out discount coupons for a selection of products already purchased to encourage repurchase. This is known as data mining, using software to sift through thousands of bits of information.

By keeping records of Client activity, such as attendance at seminars, it is possible to predict the likelihood of their attending another seminar. Many professional services firms are investing in data analytics, which is the science of providing inferences from data to make more informed decisions. As traffic through websites and social media increases, so data management and analysis becomes more important in understanding the motivations of Clients and prospects. Given the variety of communication channels available today, many firms now ask Clients to regularly update their contact preferences.

One of the most advanced tools is *Google Analytics*, which can provide reports based on analysis of website traffic and can help to pinpoint the optimum use of digitised content.

Clients that Defect

Here we look at how to spot the likely danger signals of defection through Client satisfaction feedback and media traffic. It's important to watch for press signals about the Client's organisation that may lead to defection. Clients have a choice of whom to use as their suppliers. From time to time, often due to mergers, reorganisation or new people joining, the supplier base is reviewed and some Clients decide to change. There are many other reasons that lead Clients to defect. During Client satisfaction interviews some Clients reveal that they are not totally satisfied; these comments signal the possibility of eventual defection, so it is important to follow up quickly to see if it is possible to salvage the situation.

Clients may also have to rotate suppliers periodically, for example, in audit, due to sector regulations. However, it is important to stay in touch as there may be other work that your firm can carry out. Some Clients may be growing and entering new markets; they may decide to change to a supplier that has greater geographical presence, even if your work has met their current requirements. So it pays to keep aware of developments within the Client organisation and be prepared to deal with such situations. It pays to be alert about any comments related to your firm's response to queries; many companies decide to change if they are not receiving adequate contact from your lead partner.

MOVING CONTACTS

One of your Client contacts Mr A at firm X moves to another company. You may find that the new incumbent Ms B has her own supplier contacts that may not include your firm. Even if you have been in regular contact Mr A, the new situation precludes your firm at present, so you are faced with having to rebuild the relationship with firm X.

However there are things that you can do:

- If you have already developed strong relationships with other people in firm X, they may eventually recommend your firm to Ms B.
- Also, it pays to keep in touch with people that move between companies. Mr A may now be in a position to recommend your firm to his colleagues.

Here are some defection pointers from Client satisfaction interviews:

- Dissatisfaction with services.

- Dissatisfaction with the delivery process.

- Dissatisfaction with the delivery team.

- Projects completed beyond budget.

- Late delivery.

- Lack of access to lead or senior partner.

- Lack of international reach.

- Invoicing detail problems.

- Poor communications.

- Unresponsive to queries.

HOW BIRD & BIRD DEVELOPS ITS CLIENT RELATIONSHIPS

Louise Field is Head of Client Service & Insight at Bird & Bird, a law firm with over 150 years in practice. She joined Bird & Bird in 2009, after eight years at EY, to re-invigorate and manage the firm's key account management and 'Client listening' programmes. These had strong and visible support from the start from CEO David Kerr and the Board, as part of the cultural shift already begun in the firm from 'my Client' to 'our Client'. Regular independent Client feedback helped to explore and confirm opportunities to develop Client relationships and new business. Creating a framework to support and recognise collaborative, team-based key account planning and action encouraged partners to share potential opportunities with their Bird & Bird peers. This shift in mind-set from 'what can I do to develop my practice?' to 'what can I do to develop the firm's Clients?' has driven significant growth opportunities for every part of the business.

Differentiation

By 2011 Bird & Bird had developed a strategic vision of their differentiators in the market, under three 'pillars' of

- deep industry knowledge (sector focus);
- international reach;
- excellence in Client service.

Whilst Partners understood well the first two pillars, it was not yet clear to all what exactly was meant by 'excellence in Client service'. A project team reviewed feedback gathered through the Client Listening Programme and held workshops with international partners and business support staff to find the answer. As it transpired this was already clear to their Clients! The overall feedback was that Bird & Bird are 'surprisingly straightforward' to deal with. They use plain language, have a strong sense of their Clients' businesses, and make their Clients' lives easier. The team harnessed this into a clear and consistent statement that partners now use to communicate the experience of working with Bird & Bird in pitches and relationship meetings.

Communicating the Programme

Communications to Bird & Bird people about the Client listening programme were set up very early in the programme, to share Client insight across the partnership and encourage the ongoing roll-out of interview activity. CEO David Kerr has a regular slot in his monthly report for 'The voice of the Client', containing quotes and anecdotes from Client listening. Quotes are anonymised to protect confidentiality and to retain partners' trust.

Measurement

Bird & Bird's key Client programme uses a range of KPIs to measure success, encompassing increases in spread of work, financial management, relationship breadth and strength and Client development activity. No targets have yet been set for levels of Client satisfaction, as the programme aims first to encourage open and honest dialogue with Clients; experience shows that measuring Client scores discourages partners from nominating Clients who may be less than satisfied (where the need is arguably greatest). The first step has been to report on willingness to participate in Client listening activity.

Evidence (Client Listening Programme)

The interview programme has now been running for several years. By 2012 around 30 interviews per year were being conducted with Clients and prospects from Seoul to San Francisco by senior Marketing and Business Development personnel including Louise Field and Director, Jill Warren. Louise then partnered with an independent Client research consultancy to launch an international on-line Client satisfaction survey, which has been embraced as a valuable complementary offering to ensure that the firm can listen to all Clients.

Louise is also involved in bespoke Client listening projects for specific Clients, interviewing 10 or more stakeholders and reporting back to General Counsel, to review the key messages and agree a way forward to build the relationship.

Evidence (Key Client Programme)

Bird & Bird's key Client programme uses the 'bow tie to diamond' approach to opening up contacts within Clients to embed a relationship with the firm rather than with one partner. The bow tie represents the initial contacts on both sides, opening to a diamond that represents multiple levels of contact between Client and Bird & Bird. To achieve this, the programme encourages regular dialogue with Clients at least quarterly about their business, issues and topics of interest, to generate new introductions. Relationships are mapped and regularly discussed, with partners assigned to developing specific contacts.

Client Relationship Management and CRM systems

Professional services firms aim to build trust with their Clients. This doesn't happen overnight, so it is important to be able to keep track of all contacts and interactions with Clients. However, in some firms this is made difficult through the lack of centralised data.

CRM entails all aspects of interaction that a company has with its Client, whether it is sales- or service-related. It is often thought of as a business strategy that enables businesses to:

- Share Client information within the firm.

- Understand the Client.

- Retain Clients through providing a better Client experience.

- Monitor sales opportunities.

- Attract new Clients.

- Win new Clients and contracts.

- Oncrease profitability.

- Decrease Client management costs.

- Considerable research has shown the benefits of formalising CRM. For example, reducing Client churn by 5 per cent can increase gross profit by up to 85 per cent.

According to Ederer and others,[1] the establishment of effective CRM results in:

- Satisfied Clients bringing in at least three more Clients.

- Regular Clients being less price-sensitive than new Clients.

- Repeat sales increasing as Clients become more satisfied with their suppliers.

- Unhappy Clients communicating their experience to around 10 more potential Clients.

- Client-oriented firms commanding higher fees over poorer performing competitors.

---

1   G. Ederer, L.J. Seiwert and T. Küstenmacher, *The Customer is King: The 1x1 of Customer Orientation*, 2000.

- Lower cost of maintaining Client relationships with CRM in place.

CRM System

A CRM system is a business model for managing a firm's interactions with Clients and non-Clients. It involves technology to organise, automate and synchronise Client data, business development, marketing, Client service and technical support. For a CRM system to be effective, it is important to create and launch a CRM programme that encourages regular use. There are many challenges facing firms wishing to establish a CRM programme:

- Having a clearly stated objective from the start.

- Creating a 'Client first' culture if it is not already in place.

- Obtaining buy-in and support from top management.

- Encouraging people to share Client and prospect information with colleagues.

- Obtaining sufficient investment over time.

- The ability to managing extended sales and business development cycles.

- Managing and maintaining Client data over time.

- Integration of different Client data bases from changes in the organisation such as a merger.

- Integration of social networking and predictive analytics.

- Involvement of the leadership team to manage the change process.

- Working in partnership with a CRM system supplier to ensure specification meets requirements.

It can take several business cycles to establish an effective CRM programme. If a firm has not yet invested in a central Client database, this is a major step in any initiative to focus everyone involved. Many firms still see CRM as providing a central Client name and address list.

However, when fully operative with the support of the board, an effective CRM system enables information to be 'attached' to Clients so that everyone is aware of their status. For example, target Clients can be flagged so that anyone wishing to make contact knows who is responsible for developing the relationship. All meetings to discuss new business opportunities can also be flagged and outcomes can be tracked and classified in terms of discussions, progressions and conversions. CRM thus enables targeting and measurement of the business development team's activities. Data can be analysed by sector, region, service line and individual. A CRM system is also a valuable tool in sending articles, messages, newsletters and other relevant information to specific Clients. This helps to build up trust even when there are no current assignments. Technology enables response levels to be tracked and followed up.

A firm's knowledge about its Clients' business and challenges is clearly a major asset. Your CRM programme should have the functionality to capture, and track the progress of, all activities and information relating to Clients. By creating a central reservoir of information, everyone in the firm can benefit; should an employee leave, the data is still available for newcomers to get up to speed without having to contact the Client for historical or personal information. Many systems have the ability to provide 'taxi' and 'long haul' reports through mobile technology for those people about to meet a Client and need a relationship check. The power of CRM data comes from its analytical potential and ability to measure and track progress of marketing and business development activity across the firm in all areas.

A STRATEGIC, GLOBAL, APPROACH TO CLIENT RELATIONSHIP MANAGEMENT

Diane Nagy is Head of EMEA[1] Client Relationship Management at leading global property adviser DTZ. She has been in post since April 2011; before this she managed their UK CRM programme. Her responsibilities include management of UK CRM and creation and delivery of the EMEA CRM programme. 'This involves identification and development of global and regional Clients across business lines and geographic territories, analysing and increasing revenue targets. CRM is DTZ's strategy for managing its interaction with Clients. The overall goal is to retain, develop and enhance the services provided to Clients and provide colleagues within the firm streamlined internal processes.'

Making CRM Happen

To implement the EMEA Regional CRM Programme, Diane works with multiple Country Leadership, and Business lines. This involves agreeing Client lists, revenues and reviewing performance in line with strategic goals, driving and monitoring the pipeline for the firm. She also leads the Client audit, automated feedback and post decision review (PDR) programme for the firm.

Diane works closely with department heads of Bids, Compliance, Finance, HR Marketing, Quality and Risk to maximise systems and processes to support the CRM programme across the firm, focusing on revenue generation, minimising risk and maximising opportunities. Her role encourages sharing of best practice to support revenue generation and enhancing cross- selling, including targeted marketing campaigns and managing the resources and budget for the EMEA CRM programme.

Client Service Model

'DTZ is using a **Prepare/Engage/Deliver/Enhance** model to describe the Client service cycle. The dedicated business development teams balance time between developing and enhancing the service provided to existing Clients and seeking new ones.

The firm is committed to Client service. Our management team is highly focused on delivering the type and quality of service our Clients require. We have established a standard set of training, procedures, and knowledge-sharing forums to ensure that staff are employing best practices, leveraging internal sector or skill expertise, and providing a high level of service to Clients. DTZ's Group Quality Director, Country Managers, Regional and National Skill Directors are each responsible for training staff, implementing quality procedures and ensuring a high quality of service is delivered by those in their areas of responsibility.'

---

1   Europe, the Middle East and Africa.

Quality Process

In addition, each Client is assigned a senior member of staff to work with them, look after their interests, and ensure that the quality of service they desire is provided and that all DTZ team members are adhering to the firm's procedures. This individual will ensure that DTZ has a clear understanding of our Client's requirements – for both their overall business and the specific project at hand. DTZ will solicit regular Client feedback throughout the project to assess which aspects of our service are meeting or exceeding our Client's expectations or need improvement. DTZ's quality systems comprise:

- Group Quality Director is responsible for managing the firm's quality standards, reporting to the Group Risk & Compliance Director.
- Client satisfaction questionnaires to monitor Clients' satisfaction with quality of service delivered in select countries.
- Quality procedures and other key documents are made available to employees via DTZ intranet site.
- Procedures are designed to capture continual improvements to our quality systems.
- Internal auditing to ensure conformity with requirements and their effectiveness.
- Systematic handling of instructions and assignments, including conflict checks.
- Preparation of project-specific quality plans at the outset of major projects, to be agreed with the Client in advance, and to be operated throughout the project. These include clarification of the standard of work to be delivered to ensure they are fit for purpose and identification of the project timetable, key milestones, details of regular Client meetings and feedback sessions to ensure Client objectives are being met as the project progresses.
- Formal UK complaints procedure, supported by FSA and RICS regulations governing matters likely to affect professional indemnity.

Client Insight

Diane is currently working closely with global counterparts on a Client Insight Programme which will bring together Client feedback and insight globally. Feedback following annual Client audits, surveys, face-to-face interviews and bid reviews will help ensure DTZ exceed Clients' objectives and enable the firm to differentiate itself through world class outstanding service. The programme will include recognition and reward based on Client satisfaction.

Benefits of CRM

There are many benefits of establishing a CRM Programme. These include:

- Enhanced experience for Clients.

- Higher levels of employee engagement with Clients.

- Greater collaboration across the firm.

- Increased business development time to build Client relationships.

- Increased awareness of Client activity and related networks.

- One stop access to Client data and content from laptop, tablet computer or mobile phone.

- Greater insight into Client behaviour.

- Greater awareness of the Client's contacts within the firm.

- Easier integration with content from digital marketing campaigns.

Launching a CRM Programme

For an effective CRM programme, it is essential to have someone at senior level with overall responsibility for its implementation. Before a CRM programme can be put in place, a number of factors have to be considered. These include the following:

- Status of the existing databases that are held around the firm.

- Who is responsible for the maintenance of these databases.

- Review of the extent to which data is shared within the firm.

- Creation of a cross-firm project team to ensure stakeholder involvement.

- Definition of system functionality and deliverables.

- Selection options for a suitable proprietary CRM system.

- Cost-benefit analysis of different options.

- Business case approval at board level.

- Selection of the CRM system.

- Establishment of CRM Project Manager and Team.

- Internal communication and change management process requirements.

- IT support requirements.

- Migration of all data to the new system.

- Pilot testing of the CRM system.

- Roll-out of the system in the form of a programme.

- Selection and training of employees in the use of the system.

- Regular checks that employees are updating the system after every Client interaction.

- Integration with the firm's mobile communication network.

CRM System Functionality

When fully operational, a CRM system should enable a firm to have a record of its Clients and the status of the relationship with each Client. The system has to be accessible by anyone who interacts with a Client so that useful information can be added. Many firms allow CRM system access from mobile technology, so those people who meet Clients do not have to wait until they return to their office to update the Client record. It is important to have embedded within people's behaviour a discipline of regularly updating Client information. CRM systems are usually tailored to a firm's requirements. Apart from the usual Client details such as name, job title, company, address and contact details, it is possible to include other details and activity fields within the Client record to enable a picture of the relationship to emerge. Examples of such details for a Client contact are:

- name of relationship partner within the firm;

- who else in the firm knows this contact;

- how well they know this contact;

- strength of relationship;

- warning alerts.

Examples of activity fields are:

- introductory meeting;

- cross-selling meeting;

- bid or proposal meeting;

- events attended;

- previous job history;

- social media connections;

- purchasing level;

- technical data requests;

- publication requests;

- media coverage.

HOW SAVILLS DEVELOPS ITS CLIENT RELATIONSHIPS

Richard Crook is Head of Business Development & CRM at global property firm Savills. He took up the role after being involved in the merger between Deloitte and Drivers Jonas. Until he joined Savills they had separate functions covering marketing and business development. Richard created a bridge between them by establishing a Client Relationship Management (CRM) team, focusing on firm wide Client initiatives and a bids and pitches team. Savills has two streams of income, one from business to business (B2B), its commercial property arm, and the other business to consumer (B2C), the real estate arm.

A Four-Tier Approach

'Savills has established a key Client management programme structured on four tiers. It started with a pilot group, a mix of key and potentially large B2B Clients. For this first tier they embedded the classical approach to CRM involving: Client account directors, plans, reviews, understanding the Client's business, SWOT analysis, Client feedback on Savills' performance and analysis of income. For the second tier they rolled out the process to cover all Clients earning Savills over £1m in fees. The third tier covered the next 100 Clients by income and the fourth "Fast track 50" tier embraced those Clients where it was important to develop a relationship.

All four tiers had common themes linked to the CRM process and system, and each Client receives a platinum level of service and relationship management irrespective of size of fee.'

Benefits of CRM

'Underpinning the CRM programme are CRM systems which enable greater visibility across the business and ensure Savills teams have a more joined up approach to Client management. The CRM system shows who Clients are, who in the firm knows them, and what work the business has on with them. It also tracks appointments, pitches and some opportunities – classic CRM material. Their systems have an internet style front end and Savills people can pull off using a Google type search facility 'taxi' and 'long haul' reports, each relevant to the time available to update their Client relationship knowledge prior to a meeting. Savills always took CRM seriously, we just brought a more innovative approach to it, and it took around a year to plan and two years to become fully operational. It is still bedding in and may take a few more years for all staff to buy into its benefits' says Crook. 'It is mandatory for anyone about to visit a Client to pull off the appropriate report to be fully informed of the status of the relationship and avoid any confusion with the Client. After a visit the key facts arising are added to the CRM system with a short follow up statement.'

Getting the Best from a CRM System

Any investment of this type will only yield adequate returns if all employees understand the benefits of using it to the firm. In order to ensure that the CRM system is kept in good shape, employees are encouraged through regular internal communications to:

- share contacts with their colleagues by reviewing who is using the data;

- update their contacts regularly;

- add their names to Clients that they know, have met and with whom they have a relationship;

- add new activities as they arise so that people are aware of the relationship development;

- post opportunities on the system, whether new or referral;

- update the opportunities as changes occur, e.g. with sales pipeline status.

Most CRM systems have the capability of generating status and usage reports, which are often accessible remotely from the office. This facility keeps everyone in the picture regarding the Client relationship.

The Challenges of Developing Strong Client Relationships

Relationships warns that Clients have the choice of staying with their suppliers or moving to others that offer more than just quality service. Most Clients expect to be 'managed' by their suppliers and to have someone assigned to oversee and develop the relationship. Fee earners are faced with the dilemma of balancing their current work and maintaining relationships across their Client portfolios. The selection of Client Relationship Managers is a key factor in retaining Clients. Those managers who provide Clients with the added value of business insights and make introductions to other members of the firm are more likely to retain these Clients and grow their firm's revenue stream. CRM programmes can deliver excellent ROI when employees are fully engaged and collaborative.

Client Relationship Development

CLIENT MANAGEMENT REVIEW QUESTIONS

To what extent:

1. Do you keep in touch with Clients even when there is no work with them?

2. Do you use Client panels to understand what Clients expect of our firm?

3. Do you offer speaking opportunities to Clients?

4. Have you segmented your Client base to help manage relationships?

5. Do you have a formal Client relationship development process?

6. Do you regularly monitor the strength of your Client relationships?

7. Do you have a CRM programme?

8. Do you use a CRM system to record interactions with Clients?

9. Do you use CRM system to provide rapid reports on a Client's status?

10. Do your employees update your CRM system after every Client interaction?

These questions also form the basis of the *Relationships* section of your Client Management Profile™, which can be found in Chapter 15.

Client Management Model™

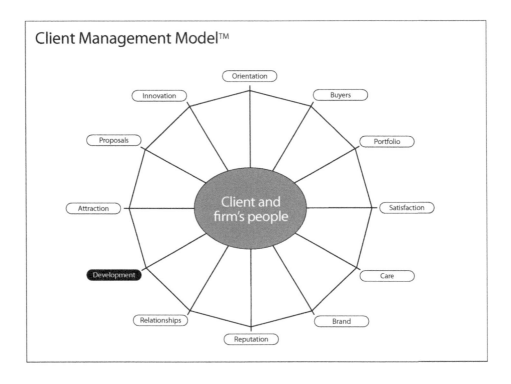

Chapter 9

Development:
Establishing an
Effective Client Business
Development Programme

Synopsis

Development, the ninth element of the *Client Management Model™*, explains:

- the importance of a business development culture;

- prospecting, targeting, contacting, meetings, listening;

- how to structure the BD operation;

- how to establish effective, strategic Client relationships with your firm;

- metrics – sales pipeline measurement;

- strategic Client planning and management;

- aspects of BD planning;

- the importance of leveraging alumni relationships.

THOUGHT STARTERS
- How effective is our business development?
- To what extent is there a business development mind-set across the firm?
- What BD targets should we set?
- What is our sales pipeline worth?
- How well does BD integrate with our marketing and PR activity?

The Growing Importance of Business Development

Best practice business development can be defined as the approach used by a firm's people to identify Client issues and create solutions. It is often said that marketing has the role of analysing markets and targeting strategically important sectors and prospects, thus 'opening doors' for business developers to follow up and 'close' on a commitment from a prospective Client. The business development function and culture are still relatively new to professional services firms but is growing in importance. Some firms have a team that is dedicated to business development. Its purpose is usually to focus sales resources on specific target Clients or prospects. Experience shows that in some professional service sectors there can be a potential 20 per cent 'churn' rate among the Client base. It can take up to 10 productive meetings over an 18-month period to win a new Client. This means that adopting a co-ordinated and sustained approach to business development is essential. The most enlightened firms have stimulated and developed a business development mind-set and collaboration across all Client-facing functions.

Strategic marketing plans are prepared to attract these prospects and Clients through various tactical activities. The leads generated by these marketing activities are then followed up and qualified by business development people. Prior to a meeting with the prospect or the Client, many firms sets up an internal meeting to discuss their potential and agree a plan of action to convert the opportunity into business. The person responsible for business development then helps fee earners to retain and grow business with the Client. As mentioned in earlier chapters, the aim is to develop a portfolio of loyal Clients who consider the firm as its trusted adviser.

As it is not possible to resource a business development programme to cover all of your existing Clients, it is important to have distinct programmes to grow existing Clients and to pursue new Clients. With existing Clients it's best to focus on those that are most likely to yield the highest returns for the time invested. Some firms call these key or strategic Clients.Members of the business development team are expected to be well-versed in consultative selling which involves a detailed analysis of the prospective opportunity prior to contact and preparation of an agreed pursuit plan.

A focused programme requires some form of strategic Client planning and a managed pipeline that shows the flow of opportunities from initial enquiry to conversion to business. Recent research by the UK *Financial Times* revealed that key account planning was considered most important by 68 per cent of managing partners and by 56 per cent of Clients in the professional services sector. When the business development function is operating effectively it stimulates collaboration across the firm to seek out new business opportunities in a planned and managed way.

Prospecting

Your firm may be offered an opportunity to pitch for and win some work at an important prospect. This is the real test of your firm's ability to engage with a Client and build a mutually beneficial working relationship. Many professional services firms would admit that maintaining a Client relationship can be time-consuming, especially during periods of buying inactivity. In the early stages of building the relationship, both the Client and the supplying firm are getting to know each other. There can be many interactions between Client and firm that happen via the internet. Cultural differences and the interplay of working with one another provide development opportunities on both sides. As the Client experience with the firm grows, both parties begin introducing other members of their organisations and this clearly helps to strengthen the relationship and provide an additional income stream for the firm.

Prospecting requires skills in planning, targeting, contacting, listening, questioning and meetings.

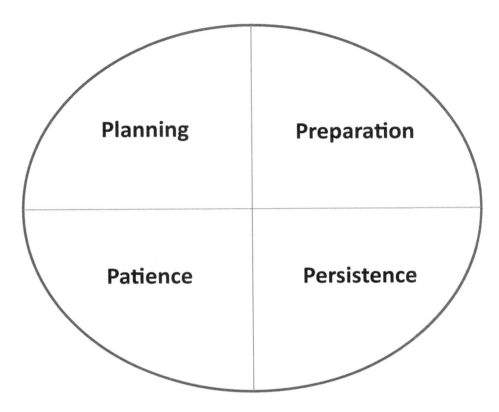

Figure 9.1   The 4 P's of Prospecting

Best prospecting practice needs:

- Planning – knowing which prospects are to be pursued, by whom, when and how.

- Preparation – conducting basic desk research and consulting with colleagues to understand likely business issues.

- Patience – the understanding by all concerned that strong relationships are built over a long time period.

- Persistence – the ability to maintain the interest in all those responsible for attracting and securing prospects.

TARGETING

It is important to select and pursue the appropriate Clients who we suspect have the potential to grow with the firm.

These can be from:

- sectors where we can demonstrate knowledge and expertise;

- specific market segments;

- Clients with growth plans;

- Clients known to spend fees on external consultants;

- Clients who have indicated a high level of satisfaction with our firm.

CONTACTING

We need to assign responsibility for researching, pursuing and contacting these target Clients. If you have a business development function, it usually falls within their remit to set up exploratory meetings with the appropriate partner, director or senior manager. Many potential Clients rely on internet searches about a firm's capabilities prior to making direct contact.

THE IMPORTANCE OF LISTENING AND QUESTIONING

When meeting potential or existing Clients, there is often the temptation to be ready to provide answers and possible solutions too early in the conversation. Patience is crucial at the early stages of developing a relationship. The prospective Client wants to tell you about her/his business and the problems and challenges being faced. The opportunities to serve the Client will increase when the prospect is allowed to continue without interruption. The skills of questioning and listening are critical in establishing Client requirements – we all know how easy is it to get carried away when a prospective Client mentions an issue and we jump in with a solution!

MEETINGS AND CONVERSIONS

Once a meeting date has been agreed, a team of people should be assembled with the right credentials to discuss the likely issues raised by the Client. It is important to stress to your team that the purpose of the first meeting is to listen carefully to the Client, ask incisive questions and take notes. Proposing solutions and selling these to the right people are best left to the follow-up from this meeting. Outcomes from meetings are worth analysing; many firms ask their business development and fee-earning teams to regularly update the CRM system of all meetings.

Some firms even classify these meetings as follows:

- *Conversations* – initial meetings, ongoing discussions, information gathering, but no real progress towards an order.

- *Progressions* – productive meetings that have increased the probability of purchasing.

- *Conversions* – meetings that have led to business.

- *Strategic* – high-level input from the Client often in preparation for additional work.

Such classification enables monitoring and measurement when establishing business development targets.

USING IDEAS TO GENERATE PROFITABLE CONVERSATIONS

Claire Mason is Managing Director of strategy and communications consultancy Man Bites Dog (MBD). Founded in 2005, the consultancy specialises in working with professional services Clients to turn their intangible expertise into Man Bites Dog stories: ideas that generate profitable conversations. The positioning of her firm is very interesting in that it is based on the premise that 'Man Bites Dog' is a more interesting story than 'Dog Bites Man'. The firm became the most award-winning B2B consultancy in the UK within two years of start-up and the now 30-strong team has grown its services from communications and thought leadership to helping Clients develop new propositions, new services and new markets. 'Professional services firms typically struggle to focus, with resources fragmented across sector and practice areas – we help develop propositions to join up that matrix', says Mason.

- 'Professional services firms can no longer differentiate on service, people are waking up to the fact that ideas are the only source of differentiation. We are starting to see the relationship-led sale being enhanced by more scalable ideas-led selling. This is bringing marketing, business development and Client service closer than ever before.'
- Man Bites Dog's Follow The Leader report published in 2014 reveals that Clients are increasingly expecting services firms to provide insight and intelligence as part of their service offer. 'Thought leadership used to be about demonstrating competency, today four out of five Chief Marketing Officers believe that the most important driver of their thought leadership is fulfilling Clients' expectations that firms will be thought leaders and produce insightful content as a matter of course', says Mason. 'Service is a given. Now market intelligence and insight come as standard too.'

Structuring the BD Operation

There are many possibilities in deciding how to structure the BD operation. This partly relates to the strategic focus of the BD resources. If the focus is to seek new Clients, a separate team may be needed from one that develops existing Clients, or a mix of both. The key is to have performance measures that clearly relate to Client acquisition and/or development. In some firms the BD function reports on the same level as marketing, Client care, CRM and bid teams. In others the Relationship Managers report to the Head of BD or Head of Client Service.

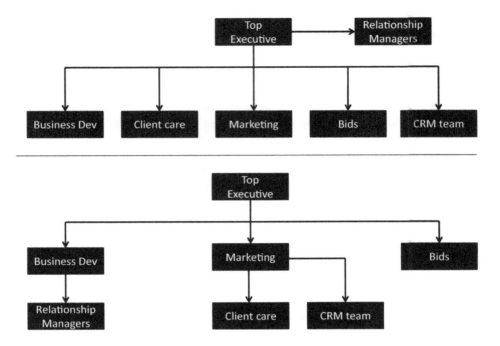

Figure 9.2   Examples of Business Development Organisation Options

CLIENT AND BUSINESS DEVELOPMENT AT GVA

Vikki Bingham is Director and Head of Client and Business Development at GVA, a leading, award-winning UK property adviser with around 900 fee earners. She reports to the CEO and is responsible for a team of 11 business developers covering sectors and service lines, a data team of six people, a bid team of two and a small international team. The firm has 23 business lines which means that her resources must be flexible to accommodate Client needs.

Client Management

The BD team focuses predominantly on existing Clients, but does aim to attract new Clients as well as being involved in bid production with the bid team. Vikki is highly visible around the firm's regional offices to discuss and promote Client development opportunities with local fee-earning teams. GVA has a large and varied Client base, many of whom have developed a relationship lasting over 30 years. During the financial year 2012/2013 the GVA bid win rate was 55 per cent, generating around £13.5m from contracts.

Client Development

The majority of Clients are assigned a fee-earning manager responsible for development. Those Clients that are one-off transactions with little potential to provide further income are not managed in the same way. For the past six years, the firm's top 20 Clients have been largely unchanged and generate about a third of GVA's fees. 'Development requires patience and initially I met with some pockets of resistance when suggesting the sharing of Client information across the firm. It is clear that Client requirements are changing and in a highly competitive market where there is little differentiation in offers between firms; those that have the right approach will have the edge. I also work with our HR director and team to provide Client development skills training.'

Client Satisfaction and Recommendation

GVA takes service quality and Client satisfaction seriously and has in place a continuous Client survey to understand how they are performing against their Client charter and any KPIs set by their Clients. This takes the form of face-to-face or telephone interviews throughout the life of the instruction. During 2013/2013 GVA carried out 150 Client interviews; 27 per cent were very satisfied and 45 per cent would recommend the firm. 'The most recent telephone survey covered 188 Clients of all types. On-line surveys are also in place to handle the volume of responses.'

Recognition

'We have formed a Client Development Group comprising the CEO, two other board members, a business unit head and myself. We discuss the challenges of recognising and rewarding people fairly for their performance with Clients and have some award schemes in place. We still have a way to go.'

Strategic Client Management

In this section we will review aspects of managing selected, potentially lucrative Clients and preparing plans to develop and grow business with them. Many professional services firms have realised the importance of selecting and managing particular Clients – often called Strategic, Premium or Key Clients/ Accounts – to grow business revenue. The practice of having responsibility for one or more key accounts is becoming more widespread. The practice of Strategic Client Management, when effective, can be a major source of business growth and also of competitive differentiation. This is because as relationships develop across organisations, Strategic Client Management can 'lock in' purchasing influencers and decision makers in a 'ziggurat' web of relationships. This often acts as an effective barrier to competitive entry.

Within the professional services sector, there are clearly differences in the approach to managing strategically important Clients between, for example, accountants, chartered surveyors and lawyers. The level of commercialisation and business development varies as the more traditional firms take on a professional sales and marketing approach. In fact, 'selling' is hardly referred to by accountants and law firms; business or Client development have become the acceptable term. Asking professionals to 'sell' raises barriers with some – they are often reluctant to step outside their comfort zone and go beyond providing the service in which they are best skilled. Breaking this inertia is in itself a challenge!

Strategic Client Management aims to break down these barriers to enable collaboration across the firm by stimulating the cross-selling of services to grow the firm's business. In fact, many professional services firms have decided to redefine their propositions from being service-led to that of business advisers. Developing Clients in a professional services firm is a medium to longer-term time investment taking many years to bear fruit; this is often difficult for many partners and managers to take on board, especially if they are measured on annual results and if their performance objectives are changed year on year.

For a Strategic Client Management programme to be effective in its implementation, it is necessary to have the appropriate organisation structure in place, a Client-facing culture and related KPIs. It is critical for success to maintain momentum through consistency in approach and communication to all employees of its benefits to both the firm and its Clients. By measuring Client satisfaction through regular reviews, it is possible over time to raise the performance bar across the firm.

Client (Customer) management had its beginnings in consumer markets. The larger companies realised the growing importance of supermarkets and started to manage these in a different way to smaller independent stores. Equally, supermarkets began to leverage their superior purchasing power over their smaller counterparts. This caused dramatic changes in the way that the supply chain was managed. Consumer companies called this Total Customer Management, a process used to develop key account relationships. There are many elements in the following case study and anecdote that can be applied to professional services firms.

HOW WALMART AND PROCTER & GAMBLE PIONEERED ACCOUNT MANAGEMENT

Historically, the grocery retailing industry was very fragmented and the supplier-retailer relationship was transactional and often very adversarial. In the early 1980s, Procter and Gamble (P&G) a major US multi-national, was process-driven with 12 product divisions operating almost autonomously. As a manufacturer with leading brands, its strategy had been to rely on advertising focus to attract consumers to buy rather than working closely with retailers. In the late 1980s the retail industry was consolidating and manufacturer's sales were static. During this period, Walmart, a major US retailer decided to take the initiative with P&G.

Walmart had lengthy discussions with P&G to suggest an improved business relationship. This would replace the more adversarial situation that typically existed between retailers and manufacturers. The approach was the forerunner of account management using cross-functional teams on both sides, so that information could be shared and joint business plans created with agreed measurement of key performance parameters.

After a pilot study, the account team approach was rolled out across all P&G divisions. Customers were classified based on size and strategic importance. P&G created a number of teams to manage major Customers, market channels and geography. Within P&G, Walmart, Sears and Tesco each had a separate account team. P&G was now committed to go to its Customers with one face, rather than through many supplying divisions. The approach had the full support of the P&G board. It was soon realised that both manufacturer and suppliers would benefit from closer working relationships.

As consumers and retailers became more sophisticated, it was clear to P&G that they had to manage their business globally and exploit the growing usage and capability of information technology. P&G created a Customer business development strategy which focused on the 80 per cent of its business that came from major Customers, working with them as key accounts to build market share and profitable sales.

P&G established account team leaders, whose skills were likened to 'entrepreneurial politicians'. The leaders were expected to:

- Contribute to and implement the joint strategy.
- Understand how to find common ground with the Customer.
- Know the key people within the Customer organisation.
- Seek out new business opportunities.
- Create added value initiatives.
- Know what to feedback to the P&G board – what works and what is not working.
- Monitor the level of trust being developed on both sides.

Key Performance Indicators were established covering sales growth, market share by Customer and cost/sales.

Over time P&G created internal cross-functional support teams to drive out unnecessary costs, improve logistics and spread the approach to its global operations. Customer satisfaction surveys were conducted to fully understand the key drivers that operated in the various markets and channels.

The ultimate trust in the relationship developed when P&G and Walmart management agreed to share stock data: access to Walmart inventories. An enterprise solution was developed enabling faster response to out of stock situations.

THE IMPORTANCE OF DEVELOPING TRUST

Some years ago a major European health care products manufacturer decided to establish key account teams to manage major retail outlets such as Carrefour and Tesco. One of the delegates in a negotiation workshop showed his colleagues a checklist which he had been given by one of the buyers in these outlets who wanted a close relationship. His company had a reputation for an adversarial stance which clearly showed how they wanted to treat their suppliers. The checklist indicated how to be tough when negotiating prices and not to accept the first price offered. It also stated that the supplier should not be trusted under any circumstances.

The Developing Role of the Client Manager in Professional Services

Within international professional services firms, the role of the Client Manager is still developing, where responsibility is given for global Clients and/or sectors. Some firms call the role Strategic Client Manager. Experience has shown that having such a focus on the development of specific Clients leads to improved business results.

When selecting Clients for strategic investment and treatment, it is useful to review their level of satisfaction with your firm. 'Satisfied' Clients are those giving average scores when surveyed; the firm is likely to retain that Client at a certain gross margin level. 'Delighted' Clients are usually buying many services and this usually results in higher than average margins. 'Enchanted'

Clients are real advocates of your firm and generate higher margins. These are usually those with the highest *Net Promoter Scores*.

Other strategic Client selection factors include whether the Client is in a sector where your firm has an excellent reputation, the potential income expected over the next 5–10 years and related gross margin potential.

A strategic Client manager, or partner, usually leads a team, comprised of those specialists who can be made available to provide solutions for Clients across the service range. If your firm is considering investment in strategic Clients, it will require managers who are responsible for a small portfolio of Clients. Here is an example of the desired attributes of such a role.

Role Description for a Strategic Client Manager in a Professional Services Firm[1]

- Responsible for the achievement of a broadening of the firm's offering in the Client, requiring visible and dynamic activity; it is effectively a general management role.

- Unable to hide. It is clearly apparent who is in charge of co-ordinating activities across the firm. It is therefore a high-risk role.

- Limited in direct authority. This varies according to the Strategic Client Manager's position, but it is usually necessary to negotiate for resources and support from a wide network of people inside and outside the firm.

- Expected to cut across normal organisational boundaries and Clients and needs to be unconventional in approach; dealing with resistance or opposition is very demanding.

- Often working in new areas for the firm – new technology, new markets or new approaches to old situations. The unknown and unpredictable will often be feared by many in the mainstream of the firm's organisation. Credibility in the Manager role starts at a low level and may need to be built up.

---

1   Source: from one of the author's past roles.

OVERALL ROLE: A RELATIONSHIP BUILDER

- Responsibility for profitable revenue maximisation and growth of a portfolio of selected Clients (strategic/key accounts) across the firm.

- Co-ordination and tailoring of the firm's total offering to key accounts through Client knowledge, DMU analysis, Client surveys and Client account planning.

- Facilitation of multi-level, multi-functional contact to achieve the appropriate level of relationship with Clients over an agreed time period.

- Championing the Client management approach within the firm.

- Communicating Client interest in the firm's approach within the firm.

- Regular communication of results achieved through review meetings.

- Management of stakeholders and the performance of individuals not reporting directly to the Strategic Account Manager.

TYPICAL COMPETENCES

- Team leadership ability.

- Sufficient knowledge of the firm's overall competences to be able to *increase work scope* when opportunities arise and sell the benefits of the firm's solution.

- Interpreter of Client's culture, values, needs and priorities.

- The ability to develop, communicate and implement a succinct Client account plan.

- Diplomacy and other political skills to assess the readiness of parties to work together.

- Negotiator for resources to ensure the best available account team is established.

- Consultant on business issues affecting the relationship.

- Information broker, including of understanding of open-book working.

- The ability to locate areas of added value to increase Client's and firm's margins (and firm's cash flow/profile).

- The ability to make things happen without constant reference to head office.

SKILLS OF THE STRATEGIC CLIENT MANAGER

- The ability to assess the current stage of a Client relationship and select appropriate approach and account team members.

- Understanding the potential level and scope of the relationship which could be developed and agreeing with the Client the stages of taking this forward.

- The ability to understand the Client's business to identify the areas where the firm can add value.

- Presentation of a differentiated offer, justifying it to match the Client's objectives.

- Agreeing how increased value to the Client translates into improved profitability for the firm.

- Developing specific account teams and plans.

Strategic Client Managers are expected to prepare and present plans to develop relationships and business with their Clients. In the following tool box there is an example of the format for a plan and a bidding/proposal process, followed by a specimen plan.

FORMAT OF A STRATEGIC CLIENT PLAN
- Executive summary.
- Client profile.
- Income history.
- Market analysis.
- Competitive comparison.
- Strengths, Weaknesses, Opportunities and Threats analysis of Client situation.
- Assumptions for the future.
- Objectives.
- Strategies.
- Action programme.
- Client reviews.

Strategic Client plans must be signed off at senior level and should cover:

- Executive summary of why the Client is selected for relationship development.
- Business issues faced by the Client related to the firm.
- Critical success factors to win business with the Client, including necessary strategic alliances with third party influencers.
- Client profile, including an analysis of the decision making unit and needs / priorities of its key members.
- Details of the firm's recommended offering, including clear statements of how the firm will be differentiated from its competitors.
- Strategic Client Manager's expectations of support needed from various management levels (Board downwards) in the firm.

Strategic Client Planning Process for Major Purchases

When proposing or bidding for major assignments, it is vital to plan and prepare accordingly, with sufficient attention to detail to ensure a good probability of success. One process adopted by many firms has 10 steps. These are as follows:

1.   Select opportunities.

2.   Pre-contact analysis.

3.   Gain commitment of the decision maker.

4.   Identify and gain agreement on needs.

5.   Develop a solution.

6.   Cost-justify the solution.

7.   Obtain agreement.

8.   Prepare proposal.

9.   Present and close.

10.   Build a continuing business relationship.

I   SELECT OPPORTUNITIES

We must have some idea of whether the prospect or Client is ready or likely to purchase our services. As resources are finite, we should evaluate whether the time and effort in preparing a proposal is worth investing in. It is also worth prioritising this opportunity with others in our remit – should this one be pushed back to allow more probable opportunities to be captured?

2   PRE-CONTACT ANALYSIS

At this stage we check for any possible gaps in our knowledge about the Client's business and industry sector. If we discover any gaps, we need to secure additional data accordingly and know where to find it. At this point we should also be assessing the primary concerns and likely requirements of the Client.

3   GAIN COMMITMENT OF THE DECISION MAKER

At this point we need to check whether we know the DMU (key decision makers and influencers) and who is the person most likely to sign an order of the size to be proposed. If we have some knowledge of the DMU, are we aware of each person's key interest and concerns? At this stage the Client can be 'qualified' in the sense that funds are known to be available, we have the attention of the key decision maker and an agreed upon need. We also need to establish whether the Client is committed to buying our services given that there is an acceptance that our solution works. There may be specific requirements that the Client may be willing to reveal through a short survey.

4   IDENTIFY AND GAIN AGREEMENT ON NEEDS

We are now in a position to check that we fully understand the Client's specific needs and requirements. We have also established how important the solution is to the Client and that it is likely to work. Given this position, we now prepare to gather factors to cost-justify the sale. We prepare solutions that are cost-justifiable and consider whether these still meet the Client's needs. These can be tested with the DMU to ensure that we are still on track and that we have full Client involvement and support. We also need to establish whether our solutions will cause any dissatisfaction with existing procedures and systems.

5   DEVELOP A SOLUTION

We need to establish that our solutions agree with the needs and requirements of the Client. We should clarify that the needs identified carry top priority with Client management. We have to identify and tailor the appropriate services that match the Client's specific needs. We have the cost data and have prepared our cost-justification. We are now ready to test the desire of the Client to move forward.

6   COST-JUSTIFY THE SOLUTION

We should identify the probable impact areas of our solution on the Client's operations; these may require changes to the way the Client works. We need to be ready to determine the tangible value of these projected changes along with non-tangible values of the solution we are proposing.

7   OBTAIN AGREEMENT

At this stage we check whether the DMU and influencers have agreed with the solution and cost-justification. We should identify likely objections or disagreements with the solution and be prepared to resolve them if they arise.

8   PREPARE PROPOSAL

We should know at this stage who is likely to review the proposal, both internally and in the Client's organisation. We need to select the most appropriate proposal or bid approach – for example, has the Client specified how the proposal/bid should be submitted? Is it going to be formally presented? A final check should also be made to ensure that everything in the proposal has the agreement of each person in the Client DMU. One technique that works quite effectively is to prepare a proposal for each DMU member, highlighting the areas of most concern to them.

9   PRESENT AND CLOSE

We should check that timing is appropriate for presenting the proposal. We should establish who on the Client side is likely to attend the proposal session and whether they will ask questions as the proposal unfolds or at the end. We then arrange a suitable date, time and venue to suit the Client. During the presentation we should re-check with the Client that the solution still meets the Client's needs and requirements as these may have changed in the interim. It is worth attempting to close on a commitment from the Client and to counter all objections. If there is agreement, the assignment has been won and will have been worth the necessary painstaking effort.

10   BUILD A CONTINUING BUSINESS RELATIONSHIP

It is important to track the progress of such a major assignment and to monitor the implementation of the solution to assure Client satisfaction. We can measure and report the actual results and also check for any new requirements. As we move through the implementation stage, we should ensure that we are trying to integrate our firm with the Client's processes.

The above strategic Client Planning Process is displayed as a checklist template in Appendix 4.

EXAMPLE OF A STRATEGIC CLIENT PLAN

Confidential

- Executive summary.
- Client profile.
- Income history.
- Market analysis.
- Competitive comparison.
- Strengths, Weaknesses, Opportunities and Threats analysis of Client situation.
- Assumptions for the future.
- Objectives.
- Strategies.
- Action programme.
- Client reviews.

Executive Summary

ABC Corporation has been a Client of our firm since June, 2011. We have acted in an advisory capacity earning fees of around £250,000 per year. Recent changes in the corporation's strategy have highlighted opportunities for our firm to provide other services with a potential annual fee income of well over £2m. This plan sets out these opportunities and how we plan to leverage our credentials to gain new business during the next year.

Client Profile

ABC was formed from the merger of A and BC companies in 2008. At that time it had an annual turnover of £2bn, supplying agricultural equipment throughout Europe. In 2013 its turnover had risen to £5bn and a further merger with Japan's DE Corporation in the Far East is now in progress. This merger will allow equipment manufacture in two strategic locations to serve world markets. ABC is structured to serve European markets, and has recognised the growth opportunities in China and other eastern markets. It is looking to establish a new hub in Asia within two years.

Income History

2011 – £247,000

2012 – £302,000

2013 – £342,000

Market Analysis

ABC occupies a strong position in the European agricultural supplies sector, ranking only second in its specialist category to CATT Inc. It has a small presence outside Europe, but has resisted the temptation to enter the highly competitive US market which is dominated by KKM Inc. It estimates the value of the Asian market to be around £30bn alone by 2015. DE has a turnover of £4bn in this market.

Competitive Comparison

Overall market size – estimated at around £40bn in 2013, rising to £60bn by 2016.

ABC *– £5bn, around 12% share of global market.*

CATT *– £8bn, market leader in Europe, 20% share globally.*

DE *– £4bn in Far East, 10% share globally.*

KKM *– £20bn in USA and South American markets, 50% share globally.*

Others *– Around 10 suppliers make up the balance of £3bn globally.*

Table 9.1   SWOT of Client Situation

Strengths	Weaknesses	Opportunities	Threats
Product quality	No coverage in Asia	Growth in Asia	Opposition from KKM
After sales service	High manufacturing costs	Merger with DE	Rising labour costs in Europe
Sector knowhow	Little exposure to Asian culture	Establish new base in China	Local competition in new markets
Strong Client relationships	Few Clients outside Europe	Client relationship development	Farming practices in Asia unknown to ABC
Strong financial base	Declining market in Europe	Links with KKM	DE merges with KKM

Assumptions for the Future

We anticipate being called upon to bid for the merger due diligence if ABC's talks with DE continue positively. We believe that we are in pole position.

There could also be advisory work with setting up of licence agreements.

Objectives
- Ensure that our strong relationships with the CEO and CFO of ABC continue.
- Secure the M&A fees of around £1.5m attributable to a merger with DE during 2014.
- Bid for licence fee advisory work when appropriate.

Strategies

Enlarge our ABC Client team to include specialist advisory associates in the USA, Japan and China.

Action Programmes

- Relationship partner to contact ABC's CEO in January to establish strategy meeting by March 2014.
- Head of M&A to visit associates in Japan for preparatory discussions about merger when cleared with ABC.
- Analyst to map the decision making teams in ABC and DE with the help of ABC's CFO, our 'coach' in ABC.
- Advisory teams to be briefed about opportunities and bid preparation.

Client Reviews

The most recent Client satisfaction report shows a high loyalty score from ABC, so we can expect to increase our share of their expenditure on advisory work in the coming years. Our Client satisfaction score has been at 9 or 10 (Promoter)in the past two years. Ensure that next review precedes the forthcoming merger.

The Importance of Leveraging Alumni Relationships

Here we define alumni as people who used to be employed by the firm and have now moved on. Employees can leave a firm for many reasons, for example:

- restructuring;

- offer of a better job elsewhere;

- another family member has an opportunity abroad;

- setting up a new business;

- career development;

- health issues;

- retirement;

- to take up voluntary work.

All of these past employees are alumni of the firm; many move into similar roles in another firm, while some go into industry rather than continue in the professional service sector. There is considerable 'churn' in the professional service sector, so the key factor for any firm is to have a process and mechanism for keeping in touch with their alumni, recognising the sensitivities that go with such contact. After all, many alumni could become loyal Clients if they were well-disposed towards the firm that they left; other alumni may be the source of valuable referrals.

So clearly alumni are a potential source of fee revenue. Many alumni take up senior positions and non-executive directorships. For example, let us suppose that you have identified 5,000 alumni. If you were able to convert just five per cent into Clients, through targeted communications and events, imagine the financial benefits for your firm. We can analyse and segment our alumni database so that we are sensitive to their likely interests and requirements. As an example, we are likely to treat those alumni who left due to restructuring differently from those who have retired. Contact with alumni can take many forms, for example:

- Dedicated alumni area in a firm's website.

- Events.

- Webinars.

- Training days.

- Technical updates.

- Online forums.

- Industry discussion panels.

- Newsletters.

- Referral requests.

- Speaking opportunities.

- Supporting bids to prospective Clients.

For an example of a plan to leverage alumni, see the case study later in this chapter.

EXAMPLE OF A BUSINESS DEVELOPMENT PLAN

Objectives for the Coming Year

- Generate £3m of leads from target prospective Clients resulting in at least £1m of new business.
- Achieve at least 60% *Net Promoter Score* for Client satisfaction. Current level is 50%.
- Increase the current 20% conversion rate from meetings to fees to 25%.
- Increase % cross-selling meetings from current 30% to 40%.
- Develop Strategic Client Plans for at least 80% of our 50 top tier Clients.
- Develop Client plans for 30% of our 100 mid-tier Clients.
- Use our sector credentials to penetrate selected growth sectors of logistics and technology.
- Develop awareness of our firm in the public sector to achieve at least 20% increase in recognition over last year.
- Increase our business with international Clients by 10%.
- Invite alumni to all events throughout the year and aim to develop at least 10 new Clients.

In 2014 our overall aim will be to retain and grow our existing Client portfolio. We will continue to pursue a Client-centric mind-set across the firm and focus on developing stronger, multi-level relationships with our Clients. In particular we will map all 50 top tier Clients' decision making units to ensure that we can build relationships at many levels within our top Clients. Given Client satisfaction feedback from 2013, we need to demonstrate a better understanding of our Clients' businesses. We will therefore devote more field visit time to arranging for partners to attend strategic business meetings with current Clients. We will also raise awareness of our service line offerings and propositions in those Clients where only one service line is currently sold.

Clients First

To ensure that we become more Client-centric, we will work with the marketing and internal communications teams to implement a programme which features Client stories, case studies and examples of where our teams made a difference to Clients. We will continue to add information on our successes to the central database of Client testimonials. Our Client Panel will meet monthly to discuss our Client satisfaction results and strategic Client plans progress. The group will now include partners from each service line and growth sector leaders.

Sales Pipeline

Our new business pipeline currently has 200 prospective, researched Client targets from which we plan to generate fee income in excess of our £1m target. These targets will have scheduled meetings, the outcomes of which will be monitored for conversations, strategic discussions, progressions and conversions. All such activity will be recorded within a week of the meeting on our CRM system by members of the business development team. Any significant changes will be flagged immediately to the appropriate partners for action.

External Communications, Campaigns and Events

We have briefed our public relations agency so that they can generate suitable material and media coverage in our two growth sectors. These activities will support specific marketing campaigns events targeted at prospective Clients. The attendees will be encouraged to interact with current Clients and alumni at these events so that they can understand more about our culture and how our firm does business. A new series of activities will aim to raise awareness of our firm in the public sector.

International Clients

2013 was a successful year with Clients operating beyond our shores. We would anticipate a further £250,000 of new business in 2014 from these Clients. In particular, we will pursue Clients that have cross-boundary issues requiring solutions, liaising with the relevant global account manager.

Client Satisfaction

In 2013 our *Net Promoter Score* was 50%, resulting from 60% Promoters and 10% Detractors. We will aim to reduce the Detractor component by following up all such Clients scoring between 0 and 6 on the Net Promoter question, with a goal of achieving a reduction in Detractors to 5% and an increase in Promoters to at least 65% over the next year. This would increase the NPS to 60%.

Challenges for the Year Ahead

Strategic Client management – we need to increase the focus on producing realistic action plans for our 50 top tier Clients and start to develop such plans for mid-tier Clients. To do this in the coming year we will provide an ongoing series of practical workshops where attendees bring their Client data for discussion and sharing with colleagues to generate new ideas. By the end of a workshop each mid-tier Client team will have produced a draft Client plan.

Reward – we will provide financial incentives across the business development team once a level of 85% of new business is generated.

Service line training – we will continue or monthly briefings that cover our service line offerings, how these are communicated, key messages and points of differentiation.

Campaign briefings – *our marketing campaigns helped us to raise brand awareness last year by 5% among prospective Clients, and also positioned us favourably in our growth sectors. We will continue our regular campaign briefings to ensure that our business development team and partners are all 'on message'. We would expect to generate over 500 prospect meetings from leads generated through these campaigns.*

Sponsorship – *we will continue our sponsorship of the national business awards in the technology sector and will seek for a similar high profile opportunity in the logistics sector. We will also continue to support a worthy national cause this year.*

CLIENT SERVICES AT KNIGHT FRANK

Philip Gardner is Head of Client Services at Knight Frank, leaders in the commercial and residential property market. Previously head of BD in a Dubai property firm, he joined Knight Frank five years ago as Business Generation Co-ordinator. He is now responsible to the three heads of the residential business for a business generation team of 10 UK based Client Managers that are organised by service line; Country, London and Lettings. This team develops business with existing Clients and seeks to re-establish contact with Clients that Knight Frank have lost touch with. His team is due to be expanded to include Applicant Management. In addition to managing his team Philip also has an advisory and training role that spans the firm and also advises on IT support.

'We prefer to use the term Client Services rather than Business Development in our firm as we wish to downplay the selling aspect of the role. Knight Frank is dominated by its commercial and residential service lines and Philip's team spans the whole of the residential business thus acting as co-ordinators when cross-selling opportunities arise both in commercial and residential service lines. There are plans to explore further opportunities with the firm's commercial Clients using a similar model in the near future. Key Clients include private Clients dealing with assets usually worth £1m+ and private banks including Barclays Wealth, Julius Baer, UBS, which are managed by a regional team that covers the UK.'

Client feedback is sought after each transaction using e-mail and a standard form. This is the only formal mechanism Knight Frank uses to understand the level of Client satisfaction. Philip admits that the firm has so many Clients that it is not possible to stay in touch with all of them on a regular basis. 'We have built up a large, loyal Client base that come to us when they need advice or have a potential transaction to be managed, and they know that they can count on us for excellent service.'

'All of the Knight Frank Client-facing teams are fee earners and have targets and performance measures. Remuneration is linked directly to Client fee income and each person is accountable for their Clients, so the firm doesn't have a specific Client care function. The firm has three CRM systems on the residential side of the business, one transactional system for sales, one for lettings and the other a contact management system.'

Sales Pipeline Management

Most business development teams operate some form of process to keep track of enquiries and conversion to business. One of the most important business development performance metrics is the sales pipeline. Many firms now operate a pipeline, or 'sales funnel', where target Clients feature at the top, becoming active sales leads that are converted into opportunities. These then become prospective Clients and some become new Clients. This tool acts as an effective driver and focus for the business development activities.

Figure 9.3   Sales Funnel

Figure 9.3 shows an example of a sales pipeline or 'funnel'. By recording and measuring the volume and value of potential Clients at each stage, it is possible to determine the operating ratios between the various levels. We can calculate the required number of target Clients from this information. For example, if our historic data shows that:

- we gain one new Client commitment, worth on average £30,000, for every three proposals or bids. Ratio 1:3;

- we need three prospects to achieve one proposal or bid. Ratio 1:3;

- we need five qualified leads to achieve one prospect. Ratio 1:5;

- we need seven enquiries to obtain one qualified lead. Ratio 1:7.

So, to calculate how many enquiries are required to achieve one new Client, we multiply $7 \times 5 \times 3 \times 3 = 315$, giving a pipeline target potential value of over £9 million (315 x £30,000). Over time we can aim to improve the individual ratios and thus the overall conversion rate. Pipeline ratios form useful key performance indicators for the BD team. It is considered good practice to monitor and report these on a monthly basis.

Adding Referrals to the Sales Pipeline

Once a sales funnel is accepted as the key metric for monitoring sales progress, it can be extended to include referrals from loyal Clients, as shown in Figure 9.4. This extension helps to remind the business development team of the value to the firm of having a steady stream of referral business.

Adding Testimonials to the Funnel

As stated earlier, loyal Client testimonials are often used to attract new Clients through the production of case studies or stories about how the firm solved a problem for the Client. By extending the funnel again, we can include and thus monitor the rate of conversion of loyal Clients to testimonials, as shown in Figure 9.5.

Figure 9.4   Sales Funnel Extended to Include Referrals

Figure 9.5   Funnel Extended to Include Testimonials

The Importance of Client Service Plans

The recent *Client Care Survey* research revealed that professional services firms have differing views on the number of Clients that they consider as 'Key', as shown in Table 9.2. Depending on a firm's size and resources, it is not possible for all Clients to have this strategic status. It is also interesting to note that only around 25 per cent of firms stated that all of their key Clients had a formal service plan as shown in Table 9.3.

Table 9.2   How Many Clients are Considered as Key?

Over 50 Clients	24.7% of respondents
41–50 Clients	13.8%
31–40 Clients	5.4%
21–30 Clients	14.7%
11–20 Clients	22.8%
1–10 Clients	15.9%
None	2.7%

Source: Client Care Survey 2013.

Table 9.3   Proportion of Key Clients with a Formal Service Plan

All Clients have a formal service plan	24.2% of respondents
A majority	13.2%
Around half	12.6%
A minority	33.3%
None	13.8%
Unsure	2.9%

Source: Client Care Survey 2013.

ALUMNI AS A REFERRAL SOURCE

A large law firm had no formal strategic plan to leverage its alumni relationships. The head of business development believed that this represented an untapped opportunity to leverage its large, growing alumni base. Here is the BD report.

Executive Summary

We have an opportunity to add around £2m in annual fees by leveraging our growing alumni base. Responsibility for alumni development is required to organise a more formal approach to this potential revenue source.

A New Revenue Stream

The return on investment is expected to be relatively high as the target audience is already generally well-disposed towards our firm compared with prospects. It is clear that maintaining contact with alumni is not only an important part of goodwill towards previous employees but can also lead to a valuable revenue stream if carefully managed. If we converted just 5 per cent of potential relationships into fees this could amount to over £2 million per year based on current average fees per Client.

Stakeholder Review

It is recommended that key stakeholders convene to review the options regarding our alumni, whether partners or non-partners. Our database reveals that we have over 5,000 alumni, including over 500 ex-partners. Many are now heading the legal departments of large corporate entities. At present we have no national business strategy or programme regarding our alumni. Over the past few years a quarterly newsletter has been issued and sent to partner alumni. There have been a number of local relationship building events and dinners for non-partner alumni.

To improve alumni relations is likely to require assigned responsibilities and appropriate resourcing and budget if it is to progress towards developing a revenue stream. A focused effort is needed – returns are such that revenue from gaining one new Client will pay for the investment. It is suggested that the leveraging be led by marketing/BD with a steering group to prepare and implement the strategy nationally.

Possible Areas for Action

We have a dedicated space in our web site for alumni; this needs to be updated to encourage Client testimonials and referrals. There are some alumni databases held within regional offices that should feature on our CRM system.

We need to look at the various possibilities leading to a more formalised approach to alumni. In many professional services firms, alumni are managed as part of a business development effort. We have recently discovered untapped potential in LinkedIn and have identified the locations of 2,000 alumni that are still in employment.

Business Development Needs Focus and Metrics to be Successful

Development explains how many firms have invested in a dedicated BD team to manage new Client opportunities and grow business with existing Clients. BD requires focus on selected targets, pursuit, and conversion to business. However, unless there is some form of performance measurement process in place, BD will not be effective enough to pay its way. The key indicators of performance come from the establishment of a sales development pipeline with appropriate tracking of all qualified opportunities. A successful BD team is one that regularly exceeds its targets and whose leadership constantly raise the bar to keep everyone on their toes. The team also retains and develops existing Clients as part of its remit. When BD and marketing teams work in harmony, they form one of the most powerful business growth resources in a firm. BD really stands for Client Development and when most effective stimulates a collaboration mind-set across the firm to seek out and work together to win new business opportunities.

———

Business Development

CLIENT MANAGEMENT REVIEW QUESTIONS

To what extent does your firm:

1. Have a dedicated business development (BD) team?

2. Set targets for Client acquisition?

3. Set targets for conversion of sales leads into business?

4. Appoint managers to oversee key Client relationships?

5. Create strategic service plans for key Clients?

6. Share its strategic service plans with Clients?

7. Leverage its alumni to gain new business opportunities?

8.   Produce BD plans for each business area?

9.   Use a sales pipeline to monitor and report BD progress?

10.   Have a pipeline that includes targets for referrals and testimonials?

11.   Have sales targets that are linked to the strategic business plans?

12.   Reward BD performance?

13.   Encourage BD to work with marketing to provide an integrated approach to market?

14.   Have BD employees that are Client-facing?

15.   Have an active referral network and strategy?

These questions also form the basis of the *Development* section of your *Client Management Profile*™, which can be found in Chapter 15.

Client Management Model™

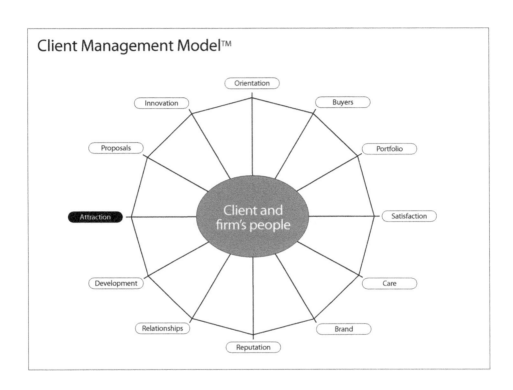

Chapter 10

Attraction:
Attracting New Clients

Synopsis

Attraction, the tenth element of the *Client Management Model*™, explains:

- how to grow your Client base strategically and profitably;

- using testimonials to attract Clients;

- the importance of having a website that is more than just a shop window on your firm;

- creating Client-researched content that is easy to find, dynamic and retains interest;

- tracking, and acting on, Client interaction;

- the power of referrals to attract new Clients;

- attracting Clients through effective campaigns – how to manage the stakeholders and activities to ensure success;

- attracting Client interest through events – how carefully targeted events can enhance the firm's reputation in a sector, location or service by focusing on Client interest.

THOUGHT STARTERS
- How do you attract new Clients?
- Where should you focus your resources?
- Which Clients should you target?
- Which Clients can you approach for referrals?
- Which Clients might be willing to give us a testimonial?
- Which events are the most effective?

Growing the Client Base Strategically and Profitably

THE POWER OF REFERRALS IN ATTRACTING NEW CLIENTS

Converting referrals from existing Clients is one of the strongest, most successful and cost-effective ways of growing your business. Referrals can come in many forms and can be used in many powerful ways:

- *Those referrals that we don't know about* – one of our very satisfied Clients mentions our firm in conversation to a peer. When the person referred makes contact with our firm, we should ask them how they heard about us – they may divulge their source.

- *Those referrals that we stimulate* – we ask our very satisfied Clients if they know of any other organisations that might benefit from our services.

As stated earlier, we can put a value on referral business through Client satisfaction measurement.

TRACKING PROSPECTIVE AND PAST CLIENTS

Creating a database of prospective, target Clients is very important – ideally a centralised database – storing contact details of potential Clients, their interests and preferences, their attendance at events, dinners and responses to various campaigns. This database (usually a CRM system) can be the same one that is used to store Client information, using the appropriate classification of non-Client or prospect. Ideally, your database should give one view of the Client, so that anyone searching for that Client will find everything in one place: from meetings, to transactions and payments, to attendance at events and so on.

We should also keep a check on those Clients that engaged our firm for one piece of work and then, for some reason, have 'gone cold', or even defected to another supplier. We should try to determine why this has occurred. Sometimes a short telephone call moves matters forward and renews the contact.

PROSPECTIVE CLIENT PREFERENCES

In these days of information overload, rapid communication and multiple channels of contact, it is vitally important to determine the things that non-Clients are interested in – by asking them – this avoids them being bombarded with too much irrelevant information.

RAISING AWARENESS IN NON-CLIENTS ABOUT YOUR FIRM

A well-known advertising acronym often used when attracting new Clients is to create 'AIDA' – **A**ttention, **I**nterest, **D**esire, and **A**ction.

There are many proven ways of attracting attention and interest in your firm – your investment can vary from:

- *Advertising* – in appropriate media channels, with copies in reception areas and conference rooms.

- *Articles* – placing these in appropriate media channels and reception areas.

- *Awards* – putting Clients forward for accreditation.

- *Conference speaking* – inviting a prospect to speak at a conference.

- *Contacts from previous employers* – when you recruit new people, they may be able and willing to alert their past Clients to your firm.

- *Digital media channels* – many non-Clients search for suppliers through websites, blogs and social media.

- *Direct marketing* – sending collateral via post or email.

- *Events* – arranging events that mix Clients with non-Clients.

- *Exhibits* – taking a stand/booth at a trade or recruitment fair; contacts made can be followed up.

- *Face to face contact* – organising a meeting to discuss a specific issue.

- *Interviewing* – asking visitors at an event if they would agree to a short interview, possibly videoed, seeking feedback about the content. This can then be followed up.

- *Magazines* – aimed at specific audiences.

- *Podcasts* – providing Clients and prospects links to audio material.

- *Promotional merchandise* – products carrying the firm's brand.

- *Seeking referrals* – asking loyal Clients to recommend others to use the firm.

- *Sending information that may interest target Clients* – newsletters are quite popular here.

- *Telephone contact* – the least costly – organising campaigns with a specific message known to be of likely interest to a non-Client.

- *Webinars* – seminars held via a website that can be attended via an email invitation.

- *Website* – the shop window into the firm with compelling content and easy navigation.

PREFERENCE MANAGEMENT

Some years ago a colleague in an accounting firm mentioned that one of his potential Clients revealed that he had received over 40 items in one month from a competing accounting firm! He said that most of the items were a waste of time – the firm could have improved likely response to these stimuli if only they had asked about his preferences.

The Power of Client Testimonials in Attracting New Business

Many firms ask existing, very satisfied, loyal Clients if they would be prepared give a quote, a testimonial and/or agree to be involved in a video case study interview/article for publication. These can then be used, with permission, in bids, case studies featured in your website, articles in magazines and internally for developing your people's awareness in seeking such materials. These can then be used selectively to attract new Clients.

Producing Client Case Studies

It is important to decide which Clients are likely to provide the most interesting and relevant case material. In planning to create a bank of case material, ideally its selection criteria should align with the firm's marketing strategy – which sectors, geographical regions and transactions would be appropriate. It is important to secure stakeholder support at board level to ensure that the effort in creating and publishing the material is going to pay off. The most effective case studies are often in story format, making interesting reading and just touching on your firm's competences and how these helped meet the Client's needs. The benefits to Clients can range from external publicity about their company/organisation to appearing at a conference or seminar, thus raising their profile. If your firm has sufficient resources, it is possible to produce case studies internally; however, there are many specialist agencies that can produce case studies covering one or more countries.

HOW TO PRODUCE A SERIES OF CLIENT CASE STUDIES: A SUGGESTED APPROACH

Step 1: Set Objectives for the Project

- Decide how many case studies are required in first year, for example, one per month.
- Decide how case studies are likely to be used and by whom.
- Decide which sectors/geographical regions will be targeted during pilot stage and roll out.
- Agree a budget for the first full year of activity (start-up and maintenance costs).
- Agree who will sponsor (board level partner) and lead (senior manager) the project team.
- Decide who will conduct and write up Client interviews (internal and/ or agency).
- Establish a small project team (ideally cross-functional).
- Agree how case studies will be stored and accessed.
- Choose pilot sector(s) to kick off the programme.

Step 2: Decide the Client Selection Criteria

For example, you could choose Clients that:

- are well known in their marketplace;
- are likely to provide an interesting and compelling story;
- are leaders in their industry/sector;
- have a strong brand name;
- are growing faster than the average in their field;
- have an international presence;
- have an interesting and charismatic leader;
- have a high *Net Promoter Score* in the latest Client satisfaction survey;
- use a number of different services provided by your firm.

Step 3: Seek Out Suitable Clients

- Communicate programme details, including anticipated benefits to the firm and participating Clients to all partners and managers.
- Ask your partners and managers to submit names of Clients that fit most of the selection criteria.

Step 4: Select External Agency (or Use Internal Resources if Available)

- Prepare the brief and ask several specialist agencies to pitch.
- Conduct interviews and short-list candidates.
- Select the agency with best fit to firm's goals.
- Ask the agency to present its process to the project team.
- The agency prepares a set of interview questions for approval.
- Agree possible publication media (website/blogs/printed material, videos).

Step 5 – Create a Client Case Study Template to Send to the Relationship Partner/Manager for Discussion

Usually prepared with or by the agency, this sets out:

- Client contact details;
- which selection criteria are met;
- challenges faced by the Client;
- services provided by the firm;
- benefits cited by Client (e.g. from the Client satisfaction report);
- whether corporate clearance is needed at the Client (which is often the situation with larger companies).

Step 6: Seek Client Agreement to Participate

- Ask the relationship partner/manager if they wish to seek Client agreement or whether the agency can do this.
- Contact the Client.
- If the Client agrees, agency sets dates to discuss the Client with the firm's service team, followed by the Client interview. The agency may interview several people at the Client.

Step 7: Interviews

- The agency interview service team to establish background on the Client.
- The agency contacts the Client to schedule interview(s) (filming may be requested if appropriate).
- The agency conducts and writes up the interview.
- The agency sends the interview copy to the relationship partner/manager for review and comment.

Step 8: Client Feedback

- The agency sends notes/video (if appropriate) to the Client for review and approval.
- The agency requests photographs from the Client for publication alongside the case material.
- Client approval.

Step 9: Case Study Produced

- The agency prepares case study in agreed format.
- The case study is sent to the firm for approval.
- The case study is sent to the Client, explaining likely usage, for approval.
- The case study is approved by the Client and published.

Step 10: Monitoring and Communication of Case Study Usage and Outcomes

- If possible, try to evaluate the additional revenue accruing from the use of case studies in pitch and business development activities.
- Communicate successes internally.

Step 11: Thank the Participating Clients and the internal team

Of course, case studies do have a finite life, and this is usually one or two years, so it is important to refresh the bank of material regularly. Many firms have a central reservoir of case material, which is accessible to all who are involved in bid preparation. Any usage of material is noted to avoid over-use. Some firms create space in their website to showcase Client comments, and many use such material to support bids for new work.

Websites that Attract Interest

Most professional services firms have invested in creating a website to showcase their firm and convey messages to target audiences. It is interesting to look at the various sites and make comparisons. An effective website makes it easy for the visitor to find what they seek quickly. Characteristics of effective websites are as follows:

- Useful, original and compelling content that benefits the reader – content is king.

- Ease of navigation – user-friendly simplicity is key and a good experience gives visitors an insight to your firm's culture.

- Interactive – people want an enjoyable experience, enabling the sharing of information through blogs, forums, etc.

- Simple, professional, design – clear fonts, careful use of colour, with a mix of multimedia like images, graphics, video and text to convey messages.

- Speed – most people are short of time, so your webpage should load in seconds to avoid losing visitors.

- Links – creating relevant, active links is important as search engines will pick these up. Links can be added to directories in Google, LinkedIn and Yahoo.

- Management – websites require constant vigilance – any link that fails to open will deter a visitor, content needs regular refreshing, and enquiries need to be tracked and followed up. Most website owners have a dedicated manager and some have a supporting digitally focused team.

Advertising and Digital Media Channels

In recent years the restrictions on advertising by the professions have been relaxed. In today's dynamic markets, an investment in media advertising is likely to be substantial. Such activity is therefore usually reserved for specific situations, for example:

- supporting a marketing campaign;

- promoting a change of positioning of the firm;

- raising the firm's profile in a particular sector or geographical area;

- announcing a merger or acquisition;

- recruitment.

Many firms are now advertising in digital media, such as websites, using 'banner' ads that are far less costly than those in the national press. The benefit of using the web and social media is the ability to elicit and track response. When people open a webpage, it is possible to track how long they spend on the site and which pages are viewed. This is a far more effective use of funds.

Articles and Magazines

The placement of articles in the national, regional or trade press is still considered an effective way of attracting interest from prospective Clients. Some firms aim to create a series of articles and offering these exclusively to a particular journal or newspaper. These can raise the profile of the firm, show its particular expertise and generate new sales leads for follow-up. Articles can also be featured in websites with links to other material for those wishing to seek out more information.

Many firms publish magazines filled with articles of interest to specific audiences. These can feature interviews with well-known business figures, entrepreneurs, Clients and targets. Magazines also enable firms to display something about their culture. These are becoming digital in format, enabling access and navigation to relevant materials via mobile technology.

Conferences and Other Events

Professional services firms often participate in conferences and seminars to raise their profile and attract new Clients. Some firms invite loyal Clients to speak on a topical issue or to join a speaker panel. This form of relationship building can also be extended to target Clients who may be willing to participate. Many firms wishing to raise their profile in the regions may establish a series of seminars in the firm of a road show that can involve local Clients and targets. Webinars are becoming popular, enabling audiences to attend seminars without leaving their desks.

Direct Marketing and Podcasts

In past years direct mail was considered an effective way of attracting interest from targets through the provision of a response mechanism. This technique has been almost superseded by the use of email with attachments or links to website pages. The power of electronic media is the ability to track every click and measure the time spent on webpages, and so this has become a popular contact method. Given the increasing volume of email traffic, the use of podcasts has grown. These enable people to listen to articles, talks and so on through computers and mobile devices.

Power and Influence of Clients

According to research in 2013 by *B2B International*, the four most trusted information sources for purchasers of services are:

1. word of mouth (84 per cent);

2. business development person (69 per cent);

3. webinar (69 per cent);

4. printed material (66 per cent).

HOW SAVILLS ATTRACTS NEW CLIENTS

Richard Crook, Savills' Head of Business Development & CRM, says 'Savills considers its bids and pitches team to be "best in class" and therefore, due to its strong reputation, expects to receive its fair share of requests for proposals or bids. All major bids are handled by a central team that tailors the Savills pitch to the Client's brand, their language and objectives. Savills has a 65 per cent success rate with such bids.

Savills also puts in a lot of effort in promoting its brand in its two markets. It is seen as premium and aspirational by Clients, who want to be seen to be using the best firm. Savills brand is associated with the people that endorse it.

Clients are also attracted by Savills world class thought leadership research, providing a series of published articles, briefing papers and seminars. Most of these are electronic in format but some major work is still published in hard copy.

Given the real appetite for property and the trends in the two markets, Savills is often sought after to comment in the media which further builds its reputation as a market leader.'

The Challenge of Attracting New Clients

Attraction discusses the fact that most professional services firms are aware that it is far more cost-effective to grow their business by developing existing Client relationships and cross-selling new services to these Clients. However, to develop the firm strategically, especially in new areas of activity, requires resources devoted to acquiring new business.

Attracting new Clients takes time, effort and patience. It also needs a dedicated budget and adequate resources. It is important to set targets for new business, broken down as far as possible by practice area, sector, location and even partner/manager if appropriate. Existing, loyal Clients can help to attract new ones by providing referrals and allowing the publication of testimonials, both of which can be stimulated by a proactive BD team.

Attracting New Clients

CLIENT MANAGEMENT REVIEW QUESTIONS

To what extent:

1. Do you stimulate referrals to attract new Clients?

2. Do you track target Client preferences and activities?

3. Do you have a specific programme/campaign to attract new business?

4. Do you use Client testimonials to attract the interest of target Clients?

5. Do you use your website to attract new Clients?

6. Do you monitor the rate of Client acquisition each month?

7. Do you leverage your alumni to gain referrals?

8. Does your business development team have new business targets?

9. Do you know the conversion rate of leads to new Clients?

10. Do you regularly seek publishing opportunities to attract new Clients?

These questions also form the basis of the *Attraction* section of your Client Management Profile™, which can be found in Chapter 15.

Client Management Model™

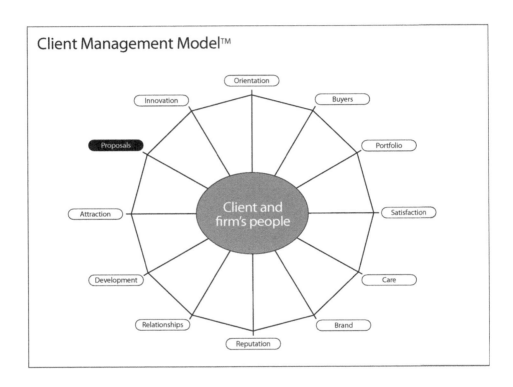

Chapter 11

Proposals:
Developing Winning
Client Proposals and Bids

Synopsis

Proposals, the eleventh element of the *Client Management Model*™, explains:

- the elements of winning proposals and bids;

- the bid management process;

- how to ensure that proposals and bids are appropriately structured;

- bid evaluation;

- Features, Advantages, Benefits and Evidence;

- managing the bid team.

THOUGHT STARTERS
- How should you manage large-value bids?
- Do you seek Client references to support bids?
- How do you decide if a bid is worth preparing?
- What is your bid conversion rate?
- What feedback do you seek after bidding?

Winning Proposals and Bids

A steady stream of requests for proposals and bids is essential to the lifeblood of a firm. Most firms have limited resources to handle the various enquiries that come in from Clients and prospects, so it pays to have a way of evaluating requests for proposals, formal bids and invitations to tender. Enlightened firms have established strict qualification criteria to ensure that they focus their resources on the right opportunities. Winning proposals and bids are those that:

- show an understanding of a Client's business and its issues and challenges;

- show an understanding of the Client's issues, situation and requirements;

- show an understanding of the Client's motivations and drivers;

- know how important the situation is for the Client;

- indicate a knowledge of the decision makers/influencers within the Client;

- identify bid-critical relationships;

- provide a creative solution that meets or exceeds the Client's requirements;

- provide value-rich content that differentiates the firm;

- clearly state the reasons to buy – benefits and risks to the Client in terms of outcomes;

- have a clear idea of the timescale of the solution;

- have an understanding of how the Client makes purchasing decisions;

- have an understanding of how they choose between suppliers;

- have an idea of budgetary constraints;

- demonstrate with evidence that they have the people, competences and processes to implement the solution effectively;

- are communicated effectively with a focus on the Client rather than the firm.

Proposal and Bid Content

The best proposals and bids are those that respond to the Client's requirements and give reasons to buy. This may seem obvious, but many submissions fall short in this area and concentrate far too much space on the abilities of the firm! The careful use of features, advantages, benefits and evidence is considered best practice and can provide powerful reasons to buy.

Many proposals, bids and other marketing communications often focus more on showcasing the features of a firm rather than how it can meet Clients' requirements. Not all supplier proposals provide Clients with any, or sufficient, evidence of their abilities, but just state how large they are. Some proposals merely state a price without offering any reasons to buy; these are really basic quotations like the ones you might receive from a local tradesman.

In a proposal or bid, it's important to distinguish between features (what the firm has and does), advantages (what the firm has and does that exceeds others), benefits (outcomes for the Client) and evidence (proof of delivery). For example, a powerful use of evidence is in the form of testimonials and case studies featuring Client comments. An exercise on features, advantages, benefits and evidence can be found later in this chapter.

Experience has shown that in conversations with, and in writing to, Clients, account managers often heavily emphasise the features and advantages of their firm rather than focusing on outcomes for the Client. If you would like to review your understanding of the differences between features, advantages, benefits and evidence, try the exercise featured later in this chapter.

Responding to Proposals and Bids: A Step-by-Step Process

A request for proposal (RFP) is an inquiry made to potential suppliers to submit a proposal, often through a formal bidding process, by an organisation interested in procuring a service. RFPs are usually submitted before formal procurement and the process allows the risks and benefits to be identified clearly. The RFP presents preliminary requirements for the service and will expect a particular structure and format. Similar, less formal requests include a request for a quotation and a request for information.

Figure 11.1   The Bid Management Process

This section describes a step-by-step process for preparing an effective bid. Figure 11.1 shows an outline of the process using the funnel analogy.

I   BID OR NO BID?

Right at the outset, it is important to decide whether this proposal/bid is worth the likely preparatory effort. So it pays to check early on if the opportunity has a strategic fit with your firm's goals. Will the success in this bid move your firm closer to its strategic goals by focus sectors/geographical locations/ type of work sought? Many organisations are interlinked with others.

Your firm may already be engaged by such an organisation, so it pays to check if there is any conflict of interest with other engagements, for example, working with a competing organisation. It is also important to have a minimum level for responding to bids. As an example, a firm may decide that for its central bid team to respond, a bid has to be worth at least £100,000; a regional bid may have a value of at least £50,000 and so on.

It makes sense to consider what your chances are of winning. Has your firm any history of bid success/failure with this Client? All proposals/bids take time and resources to prepare. If you prepare a bid, will the estimated cost to bid outweigh the fee/profitability benefit to your firm? Many large organisations submit requests to existing and other suppliers, even if you are already engaged for some work. It pays to consider how this bid might impact your relationship with the Client. A bid evaluation process is described later in this chapter. After consideration, you may decide to decline this opportunity; it could be that the Client is not of a size that is appropriate for your firm to serve. There could also be a conflict of interest.

2   BACKGROUND RESEARCH ON THE CLIENT

It is important to show your Clients that you understand their business and current/likely issues to be faced in their operating arena. Ensure that your team collect relevant information about the potential Client. For example, what press coverage have they had recently? What issues does this reveal for this Client? What revenue and profitability data is available?

It is clearly very useful if you are able to meet with the Client to scope their requirements in advance of submitting a formal response. This will enable an understanding of why the request has been sent, who is involved in making decisions and so on.

3   SOURCES OF YOUR CREDENTIALS

- Referrals from similar Clients (i.e. size, sector).

- Awards relevant to the situation.

- Current Clients.

- Reference case studies.

- Sector-specific credentials.

- Service line-specific credentials.

- Published articles.

4   VALUE TO YOUR FIRM

Estimate the likely projected fee income worth over time, e.g., £50,000 a year over next five years. There may be potential for recurring business. Having a well-known Client may enhance your reputation.

5   SELECTING YOUR BID TEAM

It is vital for a successful response to choose the right people, with the right credentials, who are available and are likely to get on well with the Client and operate within their culture. It is a bonus if the team selected have worked well together on other similar assignments. Ensure that the team size is appropriate to the Client's requirements. Involve external specialists if relevant. Depending on the bid's scope, a bid team typically consists of the following people and roles:

Bid manager – to manage the project, co-ordinate the stakeholders and assess overall value to the firm.

Client manager – to discuss the strength of relationship and DMU analysis.

Technical experts – to assess the required capabilities to service the Client.

Legal expert – to assess risk.

BD – potential sales opportunities across the firm.

Relationship/other partners – to assess whether there are any reputational issues/conflicts with the potential Client.

External specialist – if required to increase the chance of bid success.

6   MEETING THE CLIENT TO UNDERSTAND THEIR REQUIREMENTS

If possible, try to arrange for the Client to meet selected members of your proposed bid team in advance of a formal submission. This will help to develop the relationship, gain useful information about the commercial issues and enable the Client to have a feel for your firm and its culture. By asking appropriate questions, your team will demonstrate how interested they are to work with the Client. It may also be possible to seek and test the Client's early interest in possible solutions. It is also important to identify the bid-critical relationships that may need developing. It is worth finding out how the Client feels about the increasing use of technology in meetings, for example is it acceptable to use tablet computers, smart devices?

7   THE CLIENT'S REQUIREMENTS AND PROCESSES – 10 KEY QUESTIONS TO BE ANSWERED

- What does the Client want?

- What are the key business issues faced by the Client?

- Who are the key decision makers?

- What cultural issues are important?

- How does the Client decide between suppliers?

- What process is used to make the purchasing decision?

- Who in our firm should prepare and deliver the response?

- What is the timescale?

- What is the budget?

- Who are the key stakeholders?

The more answers you have to the above questions, the more likelihood there is of delivering a successful proposal.

8   BID EVALUATION

In deciding whether or not to proceed with a bid, many firms have a formal evaluation process that gives a weighting to particular questions and then requires a scoring by the bid team.Here is an evaluation approach. The evaluation criteria are divided into sections: opportunity/competition/relationship/value to our firm.

Opportunity

- Do we know what the Client really wants?

- Does the Client know what they want?

Competition

- Can we compete on price alone?

- Do we know the Client's decision-making process?

- How does the Client choose between suppliers?

- Do we have the capability to do the work?

Relationship

- What is the strength of our relationship with the Client?

- Is there a conflict of interest (e.g. employees owning shares in the company may preclude bidding)?

Value to our firm

- Does the work fit our firm's strategy?

- Is the relationship likely to be profitable?

- Can we recover our bid costs?

- Is there any recurring business (e.g. audit)? Can we also sell advisory or other services?

- Company size – is the Client too big or too small for our firm?

- Would the Client's brand add value to the firm?

- Is it a fast-growing, dynamic business?

Each of the above 15 statements is then weighted in order of importance to the firm. So, for example, 'Does the work fit our firm's strategy?' may receive the highest weighting of 15.

Reviewing the bid criteria

The criteria can be reviewed and refined over time as the evaluation process develops. It may be necessary to modify the criteria for specific bid situations.

An example of a bid evaluation chart is shown in Table 11.1.

Table 11.1   Bid Evaluation Chart

Evaluation criteria	Weighting	Score out of 10	Total
Opportunity			
Do we know what the Client really wants?	3	7	21
Does the Client know what they want?	2	6	12
Competition			
Can we compete on price alone?	5	8	40
Do we know the Client's decision-making process?	4	7	28
How does the Client choose between suppliers?	7	4	28
Do we have the capability to do the work?	1	7	7
Relationship			
What is the strength of our relationship with the Client?	14	7	98
Is there a conflict of interest?	8	2	16
Value to our firm			
Does the work fit our firm's strategy (sectors, international, etc.)?	15	9	135
Is the relationship likely to be profitable?	13	7	91
Can we recover our bid costs?	10	6	60
Is there any recurring business?	11	7	77
Company size – is the Client too big or too small for our firm?	6	8	48
Would the Client brand add value to the firm?	5	7	35
Is it a fast growing, dynamic, business?	9	7	63
Bid (> 600)/no-bid total			759

Source: Dave Chadda, Bid Specialist.

In Table 11.1, the statements have been weighted in priority order from 1 to 15. Each criterion has then been scored by the bid team out of a maximum of 10 points. The total column is the multiple of weight and score to give a weighted total. The overall weighted score is 759 and is considered acceptable in this instance as the minimum bid/no-bid total is 600. The maximum possible score is 1,500.

If a bid evaluation points to a no-bid, it is possible that one or more team members may feel that the Client is worth bidding for and may challenge a no-bid decision. In this case there needs to be a process in place to enable these bids to be discussed at a higher level. Some firms establish a *Bid Escalation Board* to review such bid situations. Bid criteria should be regularly reviewed based on results and amended to sharpen the process so that the criteria and weightings that resulted in the highest level of wins are retained.

9   THE PROPOSAL DOCUMENT

Client-focused content is key

It is important to decide on how each element of your proposal or bid response will impress the Client; however, the impression needs to be on the right factors that relate to the Client's requirements rather than impressing them with your credentials!

Show that you understand their requirements

It is important for those involved in preparing the response to read the RFP very carefully to ensure that the proposal content follows the 'route map' usually provided in the RFP.

Summarise

An executive summary is usually required. This should clearly show an understanding of the Client's requirements, state the value and outcomes of the proposed solution. Any clear points of differentiation should be evident. It is useful to include the Client's brand name/logo if available to personalise the presentation.

Use charts, graphics, tables, credentials

For clarity, it is important to provide these to complement the text.

Developing your value proposition (see also Chapter 6)

Value-rich content will be read by the Client. Proposals that are tailored for their audience with clearly beneficial outcomes are more likely to win than general ones. If you understand how the Client buys and have been able to map the different decision makers and influencers, you can produce a more bespoke proposal. Clients views on value differ, so these should be sought where possible by testing your ideas with the Client. In terms of value, some Clients may be seeking cost benefits; others may need compliance, legal or technical advice. An accompanying letter should clearly re-state the value proposition – what benefits the Client gains by adopting your solution.

10   PRESENTING YOUR PROPOSAL

Most proposals require a formal presentation if short-listed. If your firm is fortunate enough to be short-listed, you will need to prepare and rehearse your presentation to the Client if one is required. It is useful to find out who is likely to attend on the Client side so that you can consider those elements that are important to each audience member. You will probably be given a time slot and duration. Ensure that your presentation team reflects who will manage and do the work, focusing on the benefits to, and outcomes for, the Client of your solution rather than too many facts about your firm. When opportunities arise to propose and present solutions to Clients' issues and problems, many professional services firms begin their presentation with an introduction to their firm, their competences and then their proposed approach. But is this format appropriate and relevant?

11   DECLINING TO RESPOND TO A RFP

If your go/no-go analysis results in a 'no' decision, you will need to communicate this to the Client in such a way that the door is always open to future RFPs. Many firms do this within hours of deciding not to proceed with a response to a RFP. A quick phone call to the Client, rather than an email, to explain your decision may also lead to other opportunities to help the Client at a later date.

12   MONITORING AND CELEBRATING THE SUCCESS RATE OF PROPOSALS AND BIDS

It is important to keep track of factors relating to bids, such as time, cost and success rate. It's also good to celebrate the achievements over time, especially when large wins are gained. Large wins are often communicated internally to boost employee morale.

PRESENTING THE BENEFITS

A Client asked three companies to present their proposals over a three hour period. Each was allowed 45 minutes and 15 minutes for questions. The first two presentations took more of the allotted time than expected, leaving the third company only 30 minutes. The first two presentations over-ran and had so many facts about the suppliers but were short on benefits. The Client apologised and asked the third team if they could present in around 30 minutes! When the final presentation came, the benefits and outcomes were stated well within the time left and that supplier won the bid contest.

Features, Advantages, Benefits and Evidence

Many proposals and bids fail to distinguish between the attributes of a firm and what these mean to the Client. Far too many bid submissions concentrate on the firm, its history and its competences. The most successful bids are those that show an understanding of the Client's requirements and state how the firm's solution will provide tangible Client benefits.

If you would like to test your understanding of the differences between features, advantages, benefits and evidence, try the following exercise attributed to *Marketing Improvements Group*.

FEATURE, ADVANTAGE, BENEFIT, EVIDENCE EXERCISE

Indicate with a circle around the appropriate letter which of the following statements made by account managers in presenting their ideas to a prospective Client. For suggested answers, see Appendix 3.

We have specialists with long-term practical experience working with many Clients in your sector.	F...A...B...E
Our expertise allows us to create services that meet all of your requirements.	F...A...B...E
You've said that you want our service to be delivered more quickly. Here is how we can do that by changes we've made.	F...A...B...E
We advise our Clients on their asset holdings.	F...A...B...E
Our Client service team will ensure that delivery arrives correctly and on time.	F... A...B...E
We have an international reputation in the marketplace. This case study shows how we helped a global company achieve better results.	F...A...B...E
If you want to upgrade your quality as your Clients are demanding, our new system will help considerably.	F...A...B...E
If you want advice on how to further improve your quality, we can give you that advice to ensure optimum performance.	F...A...B...E
Using the methods we are proposing will ensure that your staff can understand how and where improvements are possible.	F...A...B...E
You said that timely information on your orders is a major concern. We can provide you with state-of-the-art technology responses.	F...A...B...E

Source: Marketing Improvements Group.

HOW TO ESTABLISH AN EFFECTIVE BID TEAM

Anne Blackie is Head of Bids & Client Care at business advisers Grant Thornton UK LLP. When Anne joined the bid team in 2007 there were three senior managers, two bid managers and one executive, to support the firm's significant bids. Recognising that different markets and sectors had different procurement methods, Anne split the team into public sector and corporates. 'The tendering approaches are so different that it made sense to reflect this in the structuring of the bid team.' The team is now ten strong with a matrix structure covering service lines and investment sectors. 'It's flexible enough to cover the major bids that we are asked to take part in. As part of the advisory service we provide to the firm we ensure that bids are strategically aligned to the firm's key markets when deciding whether to bid. Depending on the size and complexity of the bid, a senior manager or manager will work with the bidding team. They will be involved at all stages of the process from the bid/no bid decision to the de-brief at the end of the process so that lessons are captured and acted upon.'

Motivating People in Remote Locations

'Two of the members of the bid team are located in the regions. We have a strong team ethos and everyone is very supportive of each other. If someone needs extra help they will usually ring someone else in the team for support.'

How to Deal with International Bids

'If it is decided to proceed with a bid with international requirements, we very quickly reach out to partners in those countries where the Client has a requirement. One of the advantages of a firm of our size is that more often than not, someone on the bidding team, be it a partner, director or manager, will have worked with someone in the other jurisdiction. If not the firm's International Business Centre is asked to locate suitable partner contacts. The key is establishing a team as quickly as possible and certainly within 48 hours.'

Identifying Bid-Critical Relationships

'We identify and map out the known decision makers and influencers in the Client to ensure that we have no gaps. We identify the strength of each relationship. Careful DMU analysis is important.'

Managing the Bid Process

'For every "go" decision we work on project management principles, establishing key tasks and a timeline, following a staged process including a bid-evaluation. And we always follow up bids to establish why we won or lost to ensure we are enhancing our approach.'

Well-managed Bids and Proposals Help to Grow the Business

Proposals shows the importance of managing bids and proposals. Having an effective and robust bid management process is considered best practice by the leading professional services firms. Once firms reach a certain size, they often decide to create a dedicated bid team to manage the larger, and often more complex, opportunities that may arise. Given the importance of winning tenders and major assignments, considerable investment is usually made in preparing bids. A bid evaluation process that maps the situation against strict criteria is important to enable decisions to be made on whether to respond to, or decline, a bid opportunity. Showing an understanding of Client needs and stressing the benefits of a solution are key elements of a winning bid.

Proposals and Bids

CLIENT MANAGEMENT REVIEW QUESTIONS

To what extent:

1. Do you have a formal bid evaluation process for large-value opportunities?

2. Do you operate a minimum value policy before working on a bid?

3. Do you have a dedicated team responsible for managing large bids?

4. Do you understand the difference between features, advantages and benefits?

5. Do you know your bid success rate and regularly take action to improve it?

6. Do you always seek feedback from prospective Clients when losing a bid?

7. Do you always aim to meet with a prospective Client prior to bid submission?

8. Do you always include a clear value proposition in bids and proposals?

9.   Do you always include a time plan with bids and proposals?

10.   Do you always include a risk assessment with bids and proposals?

These questions also form the basis of the *Proposals* section of your *Client Management Profile*™, which can be found in Chapter 15.

Client Management Model™

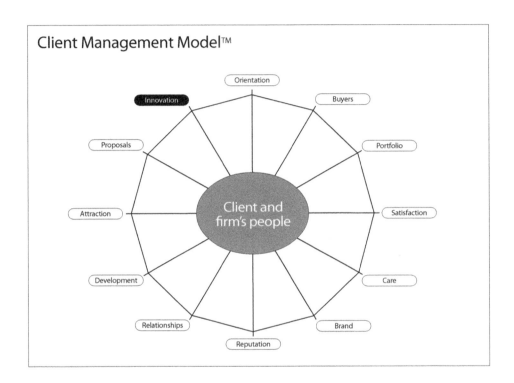

Chapter 12
Innovation:
Innovations that Impact Clients

Synopsis

Innovation, the twelfth element of the *Client Management Model*™, explains:

- the importance of innovation by professional services firms;

- innovations that characterise the most enlightened of today's professional services firms;

- the importance of having a project management capability in professional services firms;

- innovative mergers;

- current practices in corporate responsibility and partner development;

- innovative service development.

THOUGHT STARTERS
- How can we encourage innovation in our firm?
- How do we capture innovation in our employees?
- What innovations have we introduced for Clients?
- Which innovations are the most lucrative?

Most Clients expect their suppliers to be innovative and to demonstrate examples of their creativity when bidding for new work. This section covers the following areas of innovation seen in many firms:

- Project management.

- Mergers.

- Corporate social responsibility.

- Services developed with Clients.

Project Management

In recent years there have been many surveys on the extent of project management in professional services firms. As assignments and matters become more complex, the number of activities increases. Effective project management can significantly improve quality and reduce the overall time, and thus cost, to complete such assignments. Having project management disciplines and competences in place is now becoming a key requirement when Clients select firms. It is worth reviewing what this means in today's business environment. The elements of project management are as follows:

- Clear definition of the project in terms of outcomes.

- Clear overall project management responsibility.

- Project scoping.

- The project breakdown structure – showing the key building blocks.

- The tasks within the project breakdown structure.

- Task scheduling.

- Task time duration.

- Task responsibility.

- Team management.

- Budgetary control.

- Identification and management of key stakeholders.

- The 'critical path' timeline.

- Understanding those elements on the 'critical path'.

- Dealing with changes in project scope.

- Dealing with project 'creep'.

- Risk management.

- Communications management.

Those firms using Client project management effectively can expect increased assignment efficiency, improved communications across and between organisations, added value and more rewarding Client relationships. Although often understated by Clients and prospects, a clear demonstration of project management skills can often be a differentiating factor when selecting a firm. Many RFPs now ask detailed questions about the level of project management skill that exists in the supplying organisation. Clients that see benefits from the time savings that can accrue through the application of project management processes by its suppliers are likely to buy further services.

When assigned complex work, many firms assign a project manager at the outset. There are many supporting technologies to enable the process to be carried out consistently. Most proposals use timelines in the form of bar charts to show prospects and Clients how the assignment will be managed over time. However, the use of critical path network planning enables a clearer understanding of those tasks that are the most important to complete on time. Any tasks on the critical path that run late will affect the overall project completion time accordingly. Network planning also clearly shows dependencies between tasks.

With costs under pressure, it is possible to assign tasks with specific codes to enable improved budgetary control and transparency over the project's duration.

In international assignments across many borders, project management is an essential part of the Client management process. Many Clients use project management techniques and processes in their own businesses, so it is not surprising that they may demand evidence of such skills of their suppliers. One of the key elements is project scope, as it is not unusual for stakeholder requirements to change – often known as project 'creep' – without proper communication of the consequences in terms of the three variables of quality, cost and time.

Innovative Mergers

The consolidation in the professional services market is experiencing more unusual mergers to disrupt the market. An example is the innovative merger of partnership Drivers Jonas and the real estate arm of accountants Deloitte in 2010.

Clients and Corporate Social Responsibility

Over recent years, many professional services firms have realised the importance and benefits of corporate social responsibility (CSR or CR) – how the firm behaves in its localities. Sponsoring good causes is now a part of many professional services firms' corporate strategy as local presence increases.

Many firms have created innovative CSR policies and programmes to engage local people and schools and to support national charities. These include providing reading tuition in local schools, charity fundraising and related activities. Some firms provide short internships for aspiring accountants or lawyers. Some CSR initiatives can significantly raise a firm's profile in the community and beyond. Some Clients will resonate positively with CSR initiatives, especially if they too are involved in similar programmes.

CSR Programmes

Successful CSR programmes have objectives covering such factors as:

- brand;

- commercial benefits;

- competitive advantage;

- employee engagement;

- environmental considerations;

- reputation;

- stakeholder management;

- strategic advantage.

The question arises as to who should take responsibility for a firm's CSR activities. The driving force behind CSR programmes often starts in one part of the firm – for example, it is often the responsibility of the human resources department. This appears logical since the people aspect of CSR is clearly a key component. Given the potential for the external exposure and commercial outcomes from CSR activities, marketing and branding often guide the programme, so it is logical for a marketing input. Other firms expect the managing partner to play an important role. The most effective CSR programmes are usually those which are managed by cross-functional teams within a firm.

As with any other resourced activity, effective CSR requires key performance indicators or success measures to be put in place. These can cover such factors as:

- altruistic outcomes for the firm and individuals;

- the amount of time given to CSR activities;

- carbon footprint change over time;

- commercial outcomes;

- employee engagement and satisfaction;

- the level of employee participation;

- reputational benefits.

It is important to clarify the aims of a CSR programme so that everyone knows how to play their part. As with any initiative, the introduction of a CSR programme has significant challenges and requires careful thought and planning. Whoever is charged with the creation of a CSR programme will need to obtain management support from the outset. In many firms, CSR is considered important enough to be part of the firm's strategy. It will require funding and measurable objectives. Effective and regular internal communication is a vital part of employee engagement. Many firms forge strategic alliances with charities over a period and focus their fundraising in support of CSR activities. Some firms create a dedicated intranet site for CSR and also feature their activities for all to see on their website. As firms reach out into their communities, opportunities to sponsor local projects emerge, raising the firm's profile. National firms also use CSR to raise their profile.

EXAMPLE OF A SUCCESSFUL CSR PROGRAMME

An accounting firm created a CSR programme; a small multi-disciplinary team was formed to suggest, select and manage the activities.

These ranged from:

- local initiatives with schools;
- national fundraising schemes in partnership with national charities;
- local fundraising involving office teams;
- sponsorship of local task forces;
- taking on students with an interest in the firm's activities.

Each of the firm's offices had progress charts showing the results of fundraising and over time, targets were set. As a result, the firm was nominated for its CSR activities and achieved considerable recognition in the media.

Many Clients and prospects may be involved in CSR programmes. Evidence of these may arise when pitching for new work. The fact that both parties may have strong, and similar, CSR beliefs could be a deciding factor when firms are selected as suppliers.

REPORTING CSR ACTIVITIES

A CSR forum now exists which supports recent changes implemented by the International Integrated Reporting Council (IIRC). This requires organisations to measure and report on environmental and social, as well as the financial impact of their business. The IIRC is a global coalition of regulators, investors, companies, standard-setters, the accounting profession and non-governmental organisations (NGOs). Together, this coalition shares the view that communication about value creation should be the next step in the evolution of corporate reporting.

Innovative Service Development

The following case study explains how a law firm has developed innovative services, many with Client involvement.

PUTTING CLIENTS FIRST IS IN OUR DNA[1]

'The traditional image of the lawyer as an old-fashioned adviser is being rapidly consigned to history as the market for legal services undergoes a transformation' says Neville Eisenberg, Managing Partner, Berwin Leighton Paisner.

'The combination of Client demand for better value for money, technological advances and deregulation has created an environment where the best lawyers are innovating in order to provide legal advice in different ways.'

'Clients' needs are at the heart of any creative solutions and many of the best solutions in modern legal services are being developed together with Clients. For many lawyers, collaborating with Clients in designing new ways of delivering legal services is, in itself, an innovative approach.'

'A wide range of new approaches is emerging. At BLP, where we have put innovation at the heart of our Client service delivery models, we have developed a number of market-leading services. For example, these include flexible resourcing alternatives through our Lawyers on Demand (LoD) business. LoD now offers virtual transaction teams – groups of lawyers who work remotely and come together for defined projects.'

'We have developed an Integrated Dispute Resolution service which brings

---

1   First published in the March edition of Business Reporter's Innovation Supplement for the UK *Sunday Telegraph*. Reproduced with permission.

together a unique set of services designed to support Clients at all stages of dispute resolution. While this service is specifically for dispute resolution, the firm as a whole has adopted new ways of delivering legal advice using virtual techniques, making complex advice accessible to executives with limited time.'

'Innovation isn't always about inventing new things. At BLP, we encourage our people to think in innovative ways. It's become part of our DNA.'

Other Innovations Used by Professional Services Firms

ATTRACTING PROSPECTIVE CLIENTS AT EVENTS

An *Economist* conference about an important business issue was sponsored by a large accounting firm. Invitations were sent out by the journal and the accounting firm to over 3,000 people, resulting in an attendance of around 500 delegates for the full-day event. There were a number of breaks between the high-level presentations and it was decided to select delegates to be interviewed and filmed for about five minutes each about the event, why they had chosen it and their key business issues.

A queue soon formed as other delegates became curious about the filming. By the end of the day, the accounting firm had interviewed 20 delegates, all prospective Clients. Each interview was followed up post-event by contacting the interviewee for a short meeting. As a result, a number of new relationships developed, leading to new business.

CREATING CLIENT INTEREST THROUGH THOUGHT LEADERSHIP

It takes considerable effort to attract the interest of prospective Clients of professional services firms. An increasing approach is to create new research on a topical issue that encourages prospect participation. The results from the research can then be used to attract further interest in the form of an executive summary and full report. Events can be held on the back of the research findings, leading to small group discussions with target prospects.

CREATING INTEREST THROUGH SPONSORSHIP

Another credible approach is to sponsor a series of press articles and provide interview candidates who can eventually become Clients. If the firm has a strategy to work with start-up businesses, it could sponsor an exhibition for entrepreneurs or appear at a sponsored conference.

CREATING UNUSUAL SOCIAL EVENTS

One law firm mentioned a successful event held at a specialist winery where Clients and prospects could mingle and taste various wines from all over the world. The aim of the event was to demonstrate the global reach of the law firm and partners from member firms attended to speak with visitors.

CREATING UNEXPECTED PARTICIPATION AT A SEMINAR

An accounting firm wanted to highlight its focus on the technology sector, so it conducted some research about research and development tax credits among its target audience and invited them to a seminar to hear the results.

However, the delegates did not expect to participate in a case study which was conducted by four technology specialists from the firm and a friendly law firm. This involved delegates being split into four groups, each aiming to solve a problem relating to protection of intellectual property.

Each group elected a spokesperson who presented a brief summary of the group's solution. These presentations were judged by an independent panel formed from Clients.

The feedback was very positive as most delegates just expected presentations of the research findings. The case study really livened up the proceedings and the seminar was repeated in the following year in another sector with similar results.

Innovative Proposals

Clients expect innovation from their suppliers, even in proposals. An example of how some firms do this is in the way that proposals are tailored to the audience. For example, the documentation can be ordered to suit the specific reader, so the financial data and cost-benefit analysis would be in a section marked for the CFO and so on.

Innovative Contact Strategies

Global firms have an opportunity to provide responses to Client queries around the clock through the application of mobile technology. Many firms are investigating the possibility of providing 24/7 contact, showing the strength and accessibility of their network.

CREATING A SCENARIO ACTED OUT BY CLIENTS AND PROSPECTS

An accounting firm launched a report on white collar fraud and ran a series of road shows around the UK to share the results with interested parties from private, public and not-for-profit organisations. It was decided to produce a profiling tool to help people with responsibility for fraud prevention to benchmark their approach against their peers.

A case study was created featuring a board meeting where the CEO had received a tip off from a local journalist that fraudulent activity was occurring in the company. Five delegates were selected at the start of the road show to read a brief relating to their particular role on the board. They would act their parts after lunch.

After the lunch break, a time when interest levels usually wane, the case study was announced and members of the audience were asked to observe and make notes as the board meeting occurred. This activity aroused considerable interest. One half of the audience was given guidelines relating to the profiling tool, the other half were not.

After the board meeting it became clear that those in the audience who were briefed had a better idea of the key issues and this led to the acceptance of the profiling tool.

HOW SAVILLS USES INNOVATION

In addition to its CRM approach, mentioned earlier, Savills has embraced things like:

- augmented reality – a virtual fly-through of a scheme depicting various environmental aspects and views of well-known landmarks;
- 3D printing of a building rather than the traditional modelling;
- joint service line offerings;
- providing a Client extranet facility to share financial and other data.

Richard Crook – Savills

Innovative Firms Attract Clients

Innovation explains how professional services firms must continually find new, innovative ways of doing things for their Clients. Clients increasingly expect this. By its very nature, innovation brings out the creative nature in people and those firms who engage their talent in this way will always be sought after by Clients.

Innovations that Impact Clients

CLIENT MANAGEMENT REVIEW QUESTIONS

To what extent:

1.   Do you try to create innovative Client solutions wherever possible?

2.   Do you have a process for evaluating innovative ideas in your firm?

3.   Do you have regular discussions about new approaches and ideas?

4.   Do you reward innovative ideas that lead to new business?

5.   Do you encourage and train your employees to be more innovative?

6.   Do you regularly ask your Clients if they feel that your firm is innovative?

7.   Has the firm won awards for innovative Client service?

8.   Do you regularly introduce new services for your Clients?

9.   Is innovation part of your firm's culture?

10.   Has your firm won awards for innovative marketing campaigns?

These questions also form the basis of the *Innovation* section of your *Client Management Profile*™, which can be found in Chapter 15.

Chapter 13

The Impact on Clients of Mergers among Firms

Synopsis

This chapter sets out the challenges, opportunities and pitfalls of mergers and acquisitions between firms and their impacts on Clients.

THOUGHT STARTERS
- If you are considering a merger with a firm, what will be the impact on your Clients?
- What is your firm's development strategy?
- Do you want to grow organically or by acquisition?

Market Consolidation

Today's professional services firms operate in highly competitive markets. Consolidation, particularly in the accounting and legal sectors, is becoming more frequent. The most important assets are your people, so any merger or acquisition is going to impact on them, followed closely by the Clients of both firms.

Many issues are faced when considering a merger and they require considerable attention for a successful result. Careful due diligence is paramount to avoid problems later on. A period of pre-merger courtship is advisable, as the ongoing process can be difficult, expensive and risky. The aspect of knowledge transfer between firms and how this will be captured and used is at the heart of any change.

Many other questions arise, for example: if your firm is committed to a growth strategy, will there be a good strategic and organisational fit with the other firm? What impact will the change have on our Client base? Clearly, the more differences that exist between firms, the harder the implementation will be. Another aspect relating to people is that mergers and acquisitions can often lead to conflicting organisational behaviours, leading to confusion among Clients.

Benefits to Clients

For Clients, a merger may mean an enhanced service line offering providing more depth and experience. It may also mean that the Client is geographically closer to its supplier Mergers can benefit the firms involved in many ways. They may improve their geographical coverage – larger firms often merge to consolidate or improve country positions, while others look for regional gains. Mergers and acquisitions can often address any strengths and weaknesses that exist in professional staff credentials. Other factors, no less important, are the possibilities of increased specialisation, fee billings and intellectual property.

HOW PENNINGTONS' STRATEGIC ACQUISITIONS STRENGTHEN ITS OPERATIONS

Law firm Penningtons merged with Manches in October 2013. Rolland Keane is the Business Development Director of the merged firm Penningtons Manches LLP and sits on its board. He is therefore involved in decisions relating to strategic growth and was part of the acquisition team.

Prior to that time Penningtons had been expanding with the acquisition of Dawsons and Wedlake Saint in 2011, as well as opening offices in Cambridge and Guildford in Spring 2012.

Strategic Fit

'Penningtons has an organised strategic planning process which flexes with the dynamics of an ever-changing marketplace in achieving its aspirations in the accelerating legal sector' says Keane. 'Traditionally a London and South East England based firm Penningtons has had a strong commitment to increasing its London presence to facilitate greater access to international Clients. When Penningtons seeks a partner firm it tends to focus on international ambition and sector fit rather than legal discipline or geographical gaps. That said, the merger worked well in the regions; Penningtons' base in Cambridge complemented Manches in Oxford. Both firms can now take advantage of the technology and life sciences university spin-outs requiring legal advice. The merger strengthens their presence in the Thames Valley technology corridor with offices in Basingstoke, Oxford, Reading and Surrey. Penningtons' strength in Private Client work also neatly fitted with Manches' strength in Family practice.'

Cultural Fit

'Penningtons seeks potential partner firms with a similar culture and vision to their own. It was important to ratify this selection factor during the relatively short courtship of Manches. Given the compatibility of sector focus and complementary practices, cultural fit was of key importance. To assess this it's important to meet people in the target firm. Although culture is an historical legacy and difficult to define, it is hard to hide and can be felt even when visiting different offices. The luxury of having more time available would make assessing the cultural fit easier but in this case it worked well. In its search for a suitable partner firm Penningtons was careful to discount some firms along the way. This was due to factors such as the degree of transparency of information, how equity was shared and how the firms were managed and their working methods.'

A Short Courtship

'Penningtons and Manches had been in discussions about a possible merger earlier in 2013; there was more synergy in the relationship than both parties had initially expected. Penningtons was interested in merging as equal partners from the outset. However, due to Manches' declining financial situation, it was necessary to structure the deal in a particular way and move quickly to ensure protection of the wellbeing of the legacy Manches Clients and business.'

Impact on Clients

'Penningtons was keen to seek a firm with similar characteristics and type of Client base to its own and had already established that there was a good match. Mergers can unsettle Clients, so it's important to ensure a smooth transition when firms merge by appropriate communications and visits that reassure Clients about service quality and benefits of the enlarged firm. As mentioned earlier, Penningtons' Private Client practice will now be able to work alongside Manches Family practice and vice versa to offer a more holistic and joined-up service. To date the merged firm has not seen any noticeable Client attrition.'

Penningtons is proud of its Client satisfaction record. As Business Development Director, Rolland Keane is involved in around 30 face-to-face Client reviews annually along with his colleagues. 'We have a key account management process in place and we have the mechanism to get frequent feedback from even the smallest fee level Clients. Qualitative and qualitative Client feedback slots into our appraisal system, ensuring a culture of Client focus. Unlike some firms, Penningtons partners have always embraced the feedback process and it is evident that legacy Manches partners hold a similar view.'

Responsibilities in the Merged Firm

Clearly any merger requires structural decisions to be made where similar roles exist. Penningtons Manches understands the need for compromise as in any good marriage, so most of the time it has been possible for the enlarged firm to find suitable candidates to manage the relationship in jointly held Client and lead practice groups.'

Rolland Keane expects the next few years to be even more dynamic than the past five years which have seen a rapid consolidation of firms in the sector.

KEY FACTORS WHEN CONTEMPLATING A MERGER

Allan Evans is partner at accountants BDO with responsibility for marketing and sales (including industries) and also sits on their Global Leadership team to ensure consistency in marketing, brand and Client service across the 148 countries in which it has member firms.

When discussing mergers, Allan observes that firms in the professional services sector are led by very entrepreneurial leaders and conversations about consolidation in their market are a constant backdrop, particularly given the current market dynamics.

'If two firms see an opportunity to grow and improve their Client proposition by merger or acquisition they will begin a dialogue rather than rely solely on organic growth which can be a slower burn. Consolidation is an expansive rather than a defensive strategy for like-minded firms.'

Allan feels that the key factors in considering merging are:

- The chemistry between the key partners – can they visualise the combined firm?
- The need for strategic assessment reviewing the Client portfolios – is there too much overlap or are gaps filled if merged?
- Will the merger extend the market reach of the combined firm?
- Will the merger mean giving up some work due to conflict of interest/ legal reasons?
- If the two firms operate in different markets what risks and pricing issues are likely?
- Cultural matches are important, as it is in this area that mergers can often fail.

The impact of innovative mergers on Clients is described in Chapter 14.

Well-managed Mergers Can Improve a Firm's Market Position

Mergers explains that if a merger is to succeed, any likely pitfalls must be considered early on in the process and plans should be made to avoid these. It is important to understand the culture of your firm and how it is likely to relate to the newly created firm. If a merger is planned, it is important to secure the support and understanding of your partners and senior management through regular communications about the merger process. Although mergers require a great deal of internal reflection and activity, the effect on Clients must not be forgotten. It is highly likely that over time there will be changes to the team serving the Client and, if at partner level, will affect the relationships on both sides. For a successful merger, it is vital to focus on whether it will improve your firm, its market standing and Client perceptions.

The Impact of Mergers

CLIENT MANAGEMENT REVIEW QUESTIONS

To what extent does your firm:

1.   Have a development strategy?

2.   Consider the impact on Clients when considering a merger or acquisition?

3.   Have a formal set of selection criteria when seeking a merger or acquisition partner?

4.   Look for cultural fit when considering a merger or acquisition?

5.   Consider growth through merger or acquisition above organic growth?

6.   Have international Clients that expect the firm to have a more global outlook?

Chapter 14

The Way Ahead for Clients of Professional Services Firms

Synopsis

Based partly on discussions with leaders of professional services firms, this chapter reviews what Clients can expect of enlightened firms: consolidation of the sector, market development, competition regulation and technological advances, The impact of globalisation. The growth of digitised content marketing. The impact on Clients of a well-managed firm.

THOUGHT STARTERS
- What is happening in your sector?
- How can you leverage the latest technology?
- Where should you focus your Client and firm development?

The Enlightened Firm

The enlightened firm may exhibit many of the following characteristics:

- Highly engaged people that make a difference to Client relationships.

- High use of mobile technology, providing a rapid response capability.

- Client-friendly processes.

- Paperless business transactions.

- Shared databases with Clients.

- Online secure portals for Clients.

- 24/7 access for Clients.

- Accountancy and law firm partnerships.

- Integrated marketing, business development and PR utilising social media channels.

- Secondments between a firms and its Clients.

- Automated processes, such as auditing, purchasing and tax computations.

- Programmes supporting the well-being of employees.

- Services development with Clients.

- Development in emerging economies.

THE CHALLENGES IN ESTABLISHING EFFECTIVE CLIENT MANAGEMENT

'On-going and effective Client management can only be achieved if the Client management teams remain sensitive to the changing pressures being experienced by their Clients, adopting a pro-active approach to Client service. For example, in an economic downturn, Clients' requirements rapidly change. Funding becomes a key concern alongside cost cutting measures to reduce overheads, rapidly followed by the first rounds of redundancies and restructurings, triggering a requirement for debt capital, refinancing and employment advice amongst other things. Anticipating Client requirements is the key to providing effective Client management and exceptional Client service. Sharing knowledge and best practice amongst industry professionals and offering Clients innovative, efficient and pro-active support will deepen relationships and carry them through a difficult period.'

Ashley Nicholls, Founder, The Recruitment Site Limited

Sector Consolidation

As already mentioned in Chapter 13, there is considerable appetite among professional services firms for mergers and acquisitions enabling them to grow their operations. Consolidation is particularly prevalent in larger accounting firms wishing to grow their member networks and mid-sized law firms, especially those aiming to fill regional gaps in coverage of their services.

Occasionally, cross-sector mergers occur. An interesting recent, innovative development was the merger in 2010 between real estate firm Drivers Jonas and business advisers Deloitte. The merger created one of the largest real estate businesses in Europe, with a group of around 700 partners and staff. In what was a new model in the real estate advisory market, the merger has revolutionised how property services are provided and has significantly differentiated the resultant offering from competitors. What is really interesting is the dual impacts created by the merger of two strong brands. For the two firms, the merger enhanced their market power and for their joint Clients launched an enhanced, differentiated offering.

Market Development Impact on Clients in Emerging Markets

Many professional services firms have enlarged their global presence and revenues by attracting and recruiting new members to their networks. Historically these have occurred in the developed economies. More recently, such firms have begun to investigate opportunities in the two groups of emerging economies, known as 'BRIC' and 'MINT'. These acronyms were coined by British economist Terence James (Jim) O'Neill, previously Chairman of Goldman Sachs Asset Management. 'BRIC' stands for Brazil, Russia, India and China, which were cited by Jim O'Neill around 14 years ago as the fastest growing economies. These slowed from high double-digit growth at the turn of the century to single-digit growth more recently. In 2013 the 'MINT' group – Mexico, Indonesia, Nigeria and Turkey – have been put forward by O'Neill as the next fastest growing group, each with double-digit growth. So it makes sense for the more enlightened firms to seek partnerships and joint ventures in these emerging economies.

Clearly firms have to weigh the opportunities and risks offered by these emerging economies. There is plenty of evidence of corruption and poor human rights in many of these countries; however, all have growing middle-income groups and Clients looking for advice from established firms. Such Clients could become the global Clients of the future.

Clients Working with Their Advisors to Develop New Services

Many firms work with their Clients to develop new services; for example, a law firm decided to create for its top 50 Clients a portal via subscription with secure access, enabling the search of any documentation relating to matters completed or in progress. Clients were involved at the inception and worked alongside the law firm's specialists to develop a user-friendly site. This portal was extended to 50 Clients after piloting with five Clients to iron out any issues. It has now become standard for all Clients who want the added-value, chargeable service.

Competitor Regulation Impact on Clients

In the UK, the *Competition Commission*[1] exists to regulate practices to avoid unfair market dominance. In the past few years it has been indicating a need for auditor rotation in the accountancy sector to reduce the dominance of the big four firms in the large corporate market. The introduction of such a directive will alter the way that accounting firms operate. It will lower the barriers to entry for the mid-tier firms who have the capability to deal with the complexities of the larger corporations that usually select the larger accounting firms. The *Competition Commission* cited the following lack of competition in UK listed companies market:

FTSE 100 firms:

- 31 per cent had the same auditor for more than 20 years.

- 67 per cent had the same auditor for more than 10 years.

FTSE 250 firms:

- 20 per cent had the same auditor for more than 20 years.

---

1   The Competition Commission became the Competition and Markets Authority in April 2014.

- 52 per cent had the same auditor for more than 10 years.

In February 2013 the Competition Commission published its full provisional report into the audit market, after an earlier summary, and concluded that the audit market was not serving shareholders well enough. Its 297-page report concluded that a lack of visibility on audit quality was having a negative impact on competition and was putting companies off changing auditors more frequently.

The Use of Technology to Target Clients

Enlightened firms will increasingly realise the power of the data they hold and the legitimate use through analytical methods to segment their Client base for specific service offerings. Data analytics enables a firm to drill down through its Client or prospect information to reveal business opportunities. For example, let us suppose we analyse the 3,000 prospects in our database. Over the past year, through various marketing campaigns and activities:

- 3,000 were offered invitations to events;

- 2,500 were sent technical literature relevant to their situation;

- 1,300 attended events;

- 1,200 attended webinars;

- 400 attended meetings with a partner of the firm;

- 150 purchased for the first time.

By using data analytics, we can discover whether there are any patterns or triggers leading to purchase. As an example, our analysis shows that:

- our conversion rate was 150/3,000, i.e. 5 per cent;

- 60 per cent of purchasers attended at least two events and had a subsequent meeting with a partner;

- 25 per cent of purchasers received technical literature and had a subsequent meeting with a partner;

- 15 per cent of purchasers had a variety of triggers.

From this analysis we can conclude that it would seem logical to follow up multiple-event attendees and requests for technical information with a meeting involving a partner. This is a fairly simplistic example, but data analytics can provide even deeper insights into purchasing behaviour.

Using Social Media Channels to Build Client Relationships

Social media includes blogs, Facebook, Google+, LinkedIn and Twitter. Many of these channels are being exploited in a variety of ways by organisations wishing to keep in regular contact with their Clients. Professional services firms have been traditionally slow in picking up on new trends; however, they ignore social media at their peril! These channels, along with other digital platforms, should form an integral part of any marketing campaign. In many instances these channels can be the first Moment of Truth for a prospective Client.

Firms researched recently in the *Client Care Survey* indicated that they use social media to:

- engage Clients on a regular basis;

- build Client relationships;

- attract new Clients;

- contact alumni;

- publicise articles.

Many firms also use LinkedIn to better understand individuals within a Client, as a majority of people create a personal profile in this channel.

SOCIAL CRM: A VIEW FROM IBM[1]

Welcome to the age of Social CRM, a different way of thinking about Customer relationship management that focuses on using social media to enhance Customer engagement. How prepared are companies to make this shift? Despite widespread adoption of social media, for most, Social CRM is still in its early stages, execution is patchy and concerns about ROI remain. To fully exploit the power of social media to connect with Customers, organizations need to move beyond isolated projects to integrated programs and, ultimately, a Social CRM strategy.

[1] From Social Media to Social CRM: Reinventing the Customer Relationship – a report published in 2011 by IBM Institute for Business Value.

Social CRM in Professional Services

Social CRM reflects the growing, community-based environment. Most professional services firms are still reviewing the potential benefits of embracing the power of social media. The consumer and service sectors are well ahead in this area. Characteristically, most firms have entered this new area with caution. They are naturally risk-averse and are aware that their reputation is on the line on a daily basis in the social media arena. However, as indicated by IBM's research, firms need to move rapidly from having often isolated social media activities and projects into programmes that are integrated with marketing, business development and media relations. Enlightened firms will now be creating a Social CRM strategy that augments their existing Client relationship management processes. In the recent *Client Care Survey* around 57 per cent of respondents said that their firm was using social media to build Client relationships, as shown in Table. 14.1. The control of relationships is shifting through social media channels to the Client.

The Increasingly Mobile Client

The increasing power and mobile use of technology enables Clients to be contacted on the move. Clients can do their research into a supplier via their mobile phone or laptop and have the required data in seconds. Those firms that harness the latest technology will have the greatest impact in their markets as Clients increasingly expect rapid responses.

Social Media Channel Usage

The usage of social media channels is on the increase and varied across firms surveyed, as shown in Table 14.1. As shown by the *Client Care* research, the greatest use of social media by the firm as a whole is to publicise articles (77.2 per cent), followed by attracting new Clients (65.8 per cent) and building Client relationships (57.1 per cent).

Table 14.1   Uses of Social Media Channels

	To build Client relationships	To attract new Clients	To contact alumni	To publicise articles	Not used	Unsure
Firm as a whole	57.1%	65.8%	33.7%	77.2%	6.0%	2.7%
Individual departments	49.5%	52.2%	16.8%	56.5%	22.3%	7.1%
Individual partners	64.1%	53.3%	19.0%	52.7%	10.9%	9.8%

Source: Client Care Survey 2013.

Just over 64 per cent of individual partners use social media to build Client relationships. The type of social media channel used varied, as shown in Table 14.2.

Table 14.2   Type of Social Media Channel Used

	Frequently	Occasionally	Never	Unsure
LinkedIn	69.1%	28.2%	2.8%	0.0%
Twitter	43.1%	37.6%	18.8%	0.6%
Blogs	24.9%	32.6%	38.1%	4.4%
Facebook	8.8%	28.2%	57.5%	5.5%
Google+	7.2%	18.2%	59.1%	15.5%
YouTube	1.7%	35.%	54.7%	8.3%

Source: Client Care Survey 2013.

The most used social media channel was LinkedIn, with just over 69 per cent using it frequently and a further 28 per cent using it occasionally. This was followed by Twitter. The growing use of blogs is enabling firms to send specific messages to tightly selected audiences based on their preferences.

The Growth of Digitised Content Marketing

Enlightened firms keep in regular contact with their Clients and prospects to determine what type of content is of interest to them and their preferences for content distribution. It is important to understand that some Clients prefer to receive their information by email, others in hard copy and others through digitised content in articles, magazines and social networks.

The majority of today's busy Clients want information fast and to meet their requirements, and to be ideally accessed through technology. The advantage of using digital channels and content to provide such information is that it can reach audiences much more rapidly, cost-effectively and accurately than traditional methods. Many firms have established knowledge hubs for Clients to access. A prospective time-poor Client visiting a firm's website can now discover whether the firm could solve their business problem and can enter into dialogue with an expert during the same interaction.

Results from digital marketing campaigns can be measured down to a very high level of detail. It is relatively easy to know how many visits were made to an area on a website page and which were the most visited in a period. The use of analytics enables firms to discover the routes taken by Clients when following content. Digitised content aimed at specific targets can generate high-quality sales leads compared to other methods. Another benefit of having digitised content is the ability to share it with others rapidly.

THE IMPACT ON CLIENTS OF A WELL-MANAGED FIRM

Richard Chaplin, Founder of the Managing Partners' Forum, explains how delivering the impression of a well-managed firm impacts the frontline, Clients and firm profitability.

'All too often, people talk about firms as though they were principals, as in "the firm will do X …". The reality is that it is always the people at a firm – whether leaders, management team members or frontline employees – who are the actors. Most frontline employees see Client needs in terms of personal deliverables – technical insights and expertise, attentive service, strong reputation, a close relationship and acute awareness of Client issues. Suggest "firm management" as a possible Client need, and it tends to receive a very low ranking.'

'Yet the FT/MPF Study into Effective Client-adviser Relationships[1] indicated that, when selecting an adviser, the majority of Clients view the impression of being a well-managed firm as an essential pre-condition. The conclusion was that being seen as a well-managed firm matters, but that it is only actionable if two further questions can be answered: "What surrogates do Clients use in arriving at the impression?" and "How can management best demonstrate its direct contribution to the Client experience?" Preliminary evidence suggests that the main surrogate is "frontline behaviours" and that management should focus on delivering "consistency".'

'How does management encourage its people to change behaviours? Conventional wisdom suggests that: stars are best left alone; losers are best counselled out; and converting "low-energy" people into "high-energy" people increases profitability and Client engagement. This requires the CEO to:

- Agree on collective priorities from strategic plans and Board discussions; commit publicly to progress a few items; distil these into specific personal goals; and then share them with everyone. This earns the right to reciprocity.
- Engage in a messy process to distil, agree and share everyone's personal goals. Progress must be recorded in a way that can be transparently tracked.
- Provide regular praise and reward for participants, and reprimand for those that opt out.
- Watch as energy levels rise as people break barriers, forge relationships and uncover hidden knowledge.

An energetic workplace may lead to greater engagement but does not automatically result in consistency as people are human so make mistakes. This

---

1   2012 Report: *Financial Times*/Managing Partners' Forum Study into Effective Client-Adviser Relationships.

risk is dramatically reduced once firm management establishes a direct channel with its peers at Clients, for example by publishing an independent report into the extent that firm management is delivering its contribution to the Client experience. Annual reports and accounts serve this purpose at most Clients.'

'Now imagine a world where pricing and procurement experts conclude the commercial arrangements and a resourcing unit allocates people to jobs. This too is reality at smart firms. The outcome is that just three frontline performance indicators matter: Client satisfaction; upward feedback from the team; and financial variances against budget. Once these structural changes are in place, leaders at Clients are more willing to take the risk that their counterparts at firms fail to deliver the behaviours and consistency that underpin single-sourced profitable long-term contracts. The sting is that everyone living the values of a well-managed firm cannot be faked. If management does not have the requisite authority, don't expect your firm to grow.'

Richard Chaplin, Managing Partners' Forum

An Innovative Merger of Law Firms

King & Wood Mallesons (KWM) was a market leader in the Asia Pacific region. When SJBerwin, a member of the 'silver circle' of law firms, was looking to expand its operations, it joined forces with KWM to become one of the largest global law firms, and the first headquartered in Asia. This merger also provides SJBerwin's European Clients with a gateway into China. This positioning gives the merged firms a strong differentiating proposition for its global and European Clients. It also gives KWM's Clients unparalleled access to Europe.

THE TRUE GLOBALISATION OF A LEADING COMMERCIAL PROPERTY FIRM

Dr Charles Doyle is the first global Chief Marketing Officer of market leading commercial real estate firm JLL (previously Jones Lang LaSalle) and also heads their 350-strong global research team. Speaking about the significance of his strategic appointment, Doyle says that 'These days, our Clients are either global or else they are local but affected by global forces, and they demand global servicing, or access to a global platform – so they have to be managed accordingly. Now, in addition to having the resources to manage our international Clients, all of our functions are becoming globalised – marketing, finance, HR, IT and so on – as well as many of our core services – it is a sign of how the commercial property market is developing. JLL is a public company listed on the New York Stock Exchange, and as such is run very differently to partner-owned private firms.'

Research as a Differentiator

'JLL is a truly global brand with wholly owned operations in the majority of the countries; this is a key differentiator and guarantees a seamless service to its global Clients. Most of our business comes from the mature economies and large cities worldwide. 'We leverage our 350-strong leading commercial real estate capability as an added value benefit to our Clients. This capability helps our Clients to understand local, regional and global property markets and enables investors to make comparisons between property and other asset classes. It is also a prime asset in JLL's global brand development.'

Managing Client Relationships

'Deep Client relationships, many over 25 years in length, have developed through four factors: our expertise, track record, our research and personal relationships – all of which help us to leverage our local and global strength. Some of our Clients have specific local requirements that could be met by local suppliers in certain regions, but the strength of our brand is a major differentiator.'

'All Clients are allocated a relationship manager, and succession is in place in case of moves and transfers of staff. Apart from nurturing existing Client relationships, the business development team also look for new opportunities to assist Clients in specific sectors and locations; other teams look to attract new Clients and pitch for new instructions with investors, institutions and corporates. JLL has a growing group of marketers investigating new opportunity sectors and market segments. Leads are generated from on-line sources such as blogs, websites, commercial trading platforms and social media. There is a move to trade in real estate space on-line – and this requires a different approach that leverages technology. Many Clients are expecting the provision of specific and customised portals so that they can access market data from us directly.'

'Another important source of leads is through our alumni, in fact around 30 per cent of our new business in mature markets such as the UK comes from this source. They often stay in the real estate industry and become loyal advocates of our firm.'

'One of the benefits of being a public company is that Clients are perceived as belonging to the whole firm, not to a particular private partnership individual partner – as is often the case in private professional services firms. Client service is seen as part of JLL's culture and seems to seep through its every pore. In some private firms, Clients are often 'carved up' and made to fit into the partnerships' internal structures. We adopt a different approach; the firm is structured around its Clients, both by geography and by industry sector, so there is less confusion both inside the firm and, more importantly, in the Client relationship.'

The JLL Brand

In March 2014 the Jones Lang LaSalle name was simplified and 'modernised' to JLL. Doyle states the main reasons for this decision are: the growing use of the Internet with its associated shorter attention spans and spatial limitations, globalisation, visibility, pronunciation and culture. 'We are in a global world of short names and symbols that have become more important than remembering long lists of Western founders' names. Many of the large accounting firms have taken this route in the past ten years and no doubt other professions will follow.'

Innovative Services

Making its extensive research available to its Clients is considered to be an innovation that differentiates JLL from the competition. The firm has developed a series of innovative web-based applications that can be accessed through mobile devices. Web-based property marketing is increasing. Another innovation relates to running sustainable buildings using high-tech, intelligent, tools; hence the 'intelligent' building. There continues to be innovation about how workplace environments are monitored and managed.

Creation of Tailored Networks for Clients

Professional services firms often need to reach board-level executives to increase the buying opportunities that may arise. This has led some firms to create 'Clubs' and forums for specific functions, for example, a Finance Directors' Forum, a CEO Club, a General Counsel Group and so on. This process may develop into new initiatives around lifestyle, for example, a Classic Car Forum which only allows CEOs, Managing Directors and Managing Partners to be members. The increasing power of social networking will allow such groups to thrive more quickly than traditional approaches.

THE GLOBAL VISION OF DLA PIPER

Sir Nigel Knowles is Co-CEO and Managing Partner of global law firm DLA Piper. 'Leading and managing a large firm is not that different to running a smaller one. You have to have a vision – ours is to be the leading global business law firm. You have to have clear values – ours relate to caring for our people, our Clients and the communities within which we operate. We believe that an important source of competitive advantage lies in our organisational alignment: each office is aligned with our core values, and each office naturally embraces the local culture, as it is run by people from that country. For example, our office in Germany is run by a German with staff that know the local scene, the decision makers and influencers, and the business multipliers.'

Sharing of Clients

Sir Nigel has been Managing Partner for around 19 years and along the way from the 90-person firm formed in Sheffield there has been a lot of evolutionary decision making to arrive at today's global entity. 'DLA Piper now operates out of 77 offices in 32 countries, and during this evolution we have had to encourage people to change their behaviour in terms of sharing Clients between practice groups and between countries. These behaviours are suitably rewarded. So the average Client profile is very different from the earlier days. We target the largest players in their sector on a global, national and local basis. We still treasure our strong local Clients, but we are also striving to serve the largest organisations around the world with world class services. We can do this because we are located where global companies are, and often where they want to be.'

Trusted Adviser

Sir Nigel spends at least 30 per cent of his time meeting with key Clients. 'What DLA Piper wants to do is to deliver consistent, high quality work and develop a trusted business adviser relationship with Clients. In this way we can become much closer to Clients and act as a confidant and a friend because we understand their sector or their industry.'

Metrics

'DLA Piper subscribes to the benchmarking system "Acritas" which factors in Client awareness, favourability, expertise, value proposition, relationship and commercial savvy. This is how we know where we stand competitively. We do carry out Client reviews, but we prefer not to have a regimented review mechanism to monitor Client satisfaction because we believe that Client feedback can be gained opportunistically when Clients are contacted or are in touch with the firm.'

Managing Key Clients

'Key Clients are assigned an executive sponsor who oversees the relationship and is usually a partner not associated with the Client. For global Clients the executive sponsor brings together the relevant partners for regular conference calls to co-ordinate Client-related actions. This enables sharing of information and best practice.' Sir Nigel speaks of having to manage internal Client relationships when dealing with new opportunities in a country not yet covered by an office. This is an added dimension that challenges the firm.

'During the recent financial crisis, when law firm panels and legal service cost were trimmed back considerably, DLA Piper was able to provide a full range of services to match those of the largest law firms on a global basis, so now the firm is well placed to service its larger, global Clients.'

Challenges Ahead

This chapter has shown that professional services firms face challenging times ahead, as by their very nature they are dealing with a more dynamic, highly connected marketplace than in the past. Mid-sized firms are rapidly catching up their larger peers, either through merger, acquisition or organic growth. The consolidation of smaller firms in certain sectors is increasing as the battleground gets tougher. Globalisation is increasing as Clients move beyond their shores or are affected by new competitors. Those firms that are Client-oriented, have highly engaged employees, are technologically savvy and follow best practice in Client management are more likely to succeed in this ever-changing environment.

The Way Ahead

CLIENT MANAGEMENT REVIEW QUESTIONS

To what extent does your firm:

1. Use technology to target new Clients?

2. Embrace new technology to enhance its relationship with Clients?

3. Provide 24/7 access to its Clients?

4. Use social media channels to increase contact with Clients and prospects?

5.   Develop new services by involving Clients?

6.   Understand how a well-managed firm impacts on Clients?

7.   Create specific groups of Clients by job title to enhance its Client reach?

8.   Develop new services using the latest technology?

Chapter 15

The *Client Management Profile*™

This chapter enables you to produce your own profile of Client management effectiveness.

On the following 12 pages are a series of statements. Allocate a score to each statement, based on your level of agreement, until all sections are completed. These scores are then used to create your *Client Management Profile*™ which can be found after the 12 pages.

Scoring Guide

If you *strongly agree*, score 8–10 points. If you feel that there is no room for improvement, score 10. Otherwise select 8 or 9 if you strongly agree.

If you *agree*, score 6–7 points.

If you *disagree*, score 4–5 points.

If you *strongly* disagree, score 1–3 points.

I Developing a Culture of Client Orientation

TO WHAT EXTENT DO YOU AGREE WITH THE FOLLOWING STATEMENTS?

Rate out of 10

1.   Our firm is Client-centric.   ☐

2.   We can access total income, split by practice area, from a Client.   ☐

3.   I can locate the firm's top 10 Clients at the press of a button.
(by income/sector/revenue)   ☐

4.   Our employees are highly engaged and exhibit a Client first behaviour.   ☐

5.   We know our Clients' expectations.   ☐

6.   Our processes are designed to be Client-friendly.   ☐

7.   Client-centricity is part of our firm's DNA.   ☐

8.   Client service features in the firms' values.   ☐

9.   Employees' objectives relate to Clients.   ☐

10.   Key Performance Indicators relate to performance with Clients.   ☐

11.   Client matters are discussed regularly at board level.   ☐

12.   We regularly meet with Clients outside of work periods.   ☐

Total Orientation score

This total score is now transferred to the *Orientation* section of your *Client Management Profile*™.

2   How Clients Buy Professional Services

TO WHAT EXTENT DO YOU AGREE WITH THE FOLLOWING STATEMENTS?

Rate out of 10

1.   We explore and record each Client's buying process.   ☐

2.   We explore and record each Client's buying motivations.   ☐

3.   We regularly use DMU analysis to determine buying influences.   ☐

4.   We classify buyers with the BACPOD (or similar) tool.   ☐

5.   We map contacts in the Client's organisation alongside ours.   ☐

6.   We know how much business comes from referrals.   ☐

7.   Our appraisal process rates our performance with Clients.   ☐

8.   We regularly discuss Client buying habits and trends.   ☐

9.   Our firm develops its employees' competences related to Clients.   ☐

10.   Our firm regularly benchmarks itself against its competitors.   ☐

Total Buyers score

This total score is now transferred to the *Buyers* section of your *Client Management Profile*™.

3   Managing the Client Portfolio

TO WHAT EXTENT DO YOU AGREE WITH THE FOLLOWING STATEMENTS?

Rate out of 10

1.   We have classified our Client portfolio into strategic groups.

2.   Our method of classifying Clients is regularly reviewed.

3.   We review our KPIs to see how these are managed over the Client mix.

4.   We know the penetration level of our top 10 Clients.

5.   We know and report internally our gross margins per sector.

6.   We know and report our income growth per sector and service line.

7.   We use data analytics to improve our knowledge about Client preferences.

8.   We create service and development plans for top Clients.

9.   We have allocated Client Service Partners/Managers to our key Clients.

10.   Our key Clients have an allocated marketing budget.

Total Portfolio score

This total score is now transferred to the *Portfolio* section of your *Client Management Profile*™.

4   Client Satisfaction and Loyalty

TO WHAT EXTENT DO YOU AGREE WITH THE FOLLOWING STATEMENTS?

Rate out of 10

1.   We regularly benchmark our firm's service against competitors.

2.   We have identified each Client's requirements and preferences.

3.   We regularly identify service performance gaps.

4.   We have created a performance/service matrix for groups of Clients.

5.   We monitor Client effort in dealing with our firm.

6.   We set targets for Client satisfaction.

7.   We use the *Net Promoter Score* with all Clients.

8.   We regularly review Client satisfaction surveys at board level.

9.   We regularly update our Client satisfaction targets.

10.   We know our *Net Promoter Score* by sector.

11.   We know our *Net Promoter Score* by service line/practice area.

12.   We know the referral value of our Promoter Clients.

Total Satisfaction score

This total score is now transferred to the *Satisfaction* section of your *Client Management Profile*™.

5   The Role of Client Care

TO WHAT EXTENT DO YOU AGREE WITH THE FOLLOWING STATEMENTS?

Rate out of 10

1. We have a published Client Care policy.

2. We regularly discuss examples of Client Touch Points.

3. We use Moments of Truth to discuss Client care behaviour.

4. We discuss the Client journey and experience internally.

5. We discuss the Client experience with our Clients.

6. We have a written Client charter.

7. Our Client charter is published internally.

8. Our Client charter is displayed on our website.

9. We train all our employees in the elements of Client care and service.

10. We involve Clients in developing our Client care approach.

Total Care score

This total score is now transferred to the *Care* section of your *Client Management Profile*™.

6   Brand, Differentiation and Positioning and their Impact on Clients

TO WHAT EXTENT DO YOU AGREE WITH THE FOLLOWING STATEMENTS?

Rate out of 10

1.   Our employees' behaviour reflects our brand values.   ☐

2.   Our brand promise is clearly stated in all of our published communications.   ☐

3.   We regularly survey unprompted recognition of our brand with non-Clients.   ☐

4.   Our branding is consistently applied in all communications and signage.   ☐

5.   We regularly audit whether our branding is consistently applied.   ☐

6.   We clearly communicate what differentiates our firm from competitors.   ☐

7.   We have clearly defined positioning and value propositions.   ☐

8.   Our brand promise is regularly reviewed with Clients.   ☐

9.   Our brand values are clearly communicated to all our employees.   ☐

10.   Our brand values are clearly communicated to audiences outside our firm.   ☐

Total Brand score

This total score is now transferred to the *Brand* section of your *Client Management Profile*™.

7   Gaining Reputation with Clients

TO WHAT EXTENT DO YOU AGREE WITH THE FOLLOWING STATEMENTS?

Rate out of 10

1. We have a written and communicated media strategy and objectives. ☐

2. We create and use thought leadership to enhance our reputation. ☐

3. We have media-trained people who can face the media. ☐

4. We have a crisis management process that kicks in when needed. ☐

5. We create issue-based campaigns to raise our firm's profile. ☐

6. We are members of a number of influential networks. ☐

7. We have a social media policy that monitors commentary about the firm. ☐

8. We use a media relations/PR agency to complement our internal team. ☐

9. We have a corporate responsibility strategy. ☐

10. Our firm is involved in social responsibility projects. ☐

11. We regularly track our firm's reputation. ☐

12. We a regularly updated media contact list with named spokespeople. ☐

Total Reputation score

This total score is now transferred to the *Reputation* section of your *Client Management Profile*™.

8   Client Relationship Development

TO WHAT EXTENT DO YOU AGREE WITH THE FOLLOWING STATEMENTS?

Rate out of 10

1.   We keep in touch with Clients, even when there is no work with them.

2.   We use Client panels to understand what Clients expect of our firm.

3.   We offer public speaking opportunities to Clients.

4.   We have segmented our Client base to help us to manage relationships.

5.   We have a formal Client relationship development process.

6.   We regularly review the strength of our Client relationships.

7.   We have an ongoing CRM programme.

8.   We use a CRM system to record interactions with Clients.

9.   We use a CRM system to provide rapid reports on a Client's status.

10.   Our employees update our CRM system after every Client interaction.

Total Relationships score

This total score is now transferred to the *Relationships* section of your *Client Management Profile*™.

9   Establishing an Effective Client Business Development Programme

TO WHAT EXTENT DO YOU AGREE WITH THE FOLLOWING STATEMENTS?

Rate out of 10

1.   We have a team dedicated to BD.

2.   We set targets for Client acquisition.

3.   We set targets for conversion of sales leads into business.

4.   We have appointed managers to oversee key Client relationships.

5.   We create strategic service plans for key Clients.

6.   We share our strategic service plans with Clients.

7.   We leverage our alumni relationships to gain new business opportunities.

8.   BD plans are produced for each practice area.

9.   We use a sales pipeline to monitor and report BD progress.

10. Our sales pipeline includes targets for referrals and testimonials.

11. Our sales targets are linked to the strategic business unit plans.

12. BD features in our performance management plans.

13. Our BD team works with marketing to provide an integrated approach to market.

14.   Our BD employees are Client-facing.   ☐

15.   We have an active referral network and strategy.   ☐

Total Development score

This total score is now transferred to the *Development* section of your *Client Management Profile*™.

10   Attracting New Clients

TO WHAT EXTENT DO YOU AGREE WITH THE FOLLOWING STATEMENTS?

Rate out of 10

1.   We stimulate referrals to attract new Clients.

2.   We track target Client preferences and activities.

3.   We have a specific programme/campaign to attract new business.

4.   We use Client testimonials to attract the interest of target Clients.

5.   We use our web site and social media to attract new Clients.

6.   We monitor the rate of Client acquisition each month.

7.   We leverage our alumni to gain referrals.

8.   Our business development team has new business targets.

9.   We know the conversion rate of leads to new Clients.

10.   We regularly seek publishing opportunities to attract new Clients.

Total Attraction score

This total score is now transferred to the *Attraction* section of your *Client Management Profile*™.

11   Developing Winning Client Proposals and Bids

TO WHAT EXTENT DO YOU AGREE WITH THE FOLLOWING STATEMENTS?

Rate out of 10

1. We have a formal bid evaluation process for large-value opportunities.

2. We operate a minimum value policy before working on a bid.

3. We have a dedicated team responsible for managing large bids.

4. We understand the difference between features, advantages and benefits.

5. We know our bid success rate and regularly take action to improve it.

6. We always seek feedback from prospective Clients when losing a bid.

7. We always aim to meet with a prospective Client prior to bid submission.

8. We always include a clear value proposition in bids and proposals.

9. We always include a time plan with bids and proposals.

10. We always include a risk assessment with bids and proposals.

Total Proposals score

This total score is now transferred to the *Proposals* section of your *Client Management Profile*™.

12   INNOVATION

TO WHAT EXTENT DO YOU AGREE WITH THE FOLLOWING STATEMENTS?

Rate out of 10

1.   We try to create innovative Client solutions wherever possible.

2.   We have a process for evaluating innovative ideas in our firm.

3.   We have regular discussions about new approaches and ideas.

4.   We reward innovative ideas that lead to new business.

5.   We encourage and train our employees to be more innovative.

6.   We regularly ask our Clients if they feel that we are innovative.

7.   We have won awards for innovative Client service.

8.   We regularly introduce new services for our Clients.

9.   Innovation is part of our firm's culture.

10.   We have won awards for innovative marketing campaigns.

Total Innovation score

This total score is now transferred to the *Innovation* section of your *Client Management Profile*™.

The *Client Management Profile*™ Summary Scores Chart

You can now create your own profile to determine your level of Client Management Effectiveness:

1.   Transfer your chapter scores to the chart below.

2.   Calculate and insert your total overall score.

3.   Transfer your chapter scores onto the profile template on the next page.

4.   You can now easily compare your results with best practice (a score of 10 in each question).

5.   A guide to your level of performance is given after the profile chart.

Table 15.1   Your Total Score

Chapter	Client Profile Category	Your Score	Maximum
1	Orientation		120
2	Buyer		100
3	Portfolio		100
4	Satisfaction		120
5	Care		100
6	Brand		100
7	Reputation		120
8	Relationship		100
9	Development		150
10	Attraction		100
11	Proposals		100
12	Innovation		100

Guide to Overall Profile Scoring

The total possible score is *1,310*, based on adding each category score.

Here is a guide to the performance related to the score:

1,000–1,310	An *excellent* level of Client management effectiveness
800–999	A *good* level of effectiveness
500–799	An *average* level of effectiveness
300–499	A *low* level of effectiveness
0–299	A *poor* level of effectiveness

Taking Remedial Action

To decide whether further action is needed, it is recommended that you go back to each profile category and seek out those questions where your score is around 5 or less. Then review the chapter for ideas to improve performance in that area.

The *Client Management Profile*™

To create your profile, transfer your scores from the profile table to the chart below, then join up the points on each element to form your profile.

You have the author's permission to make a copy of your profile.

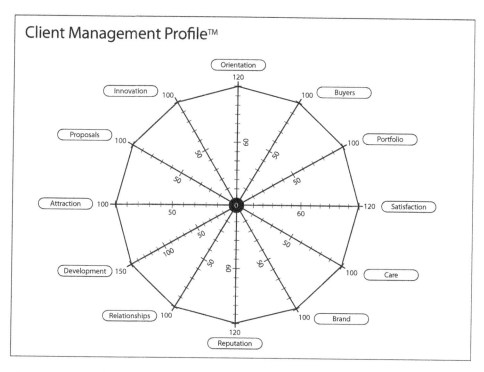

Figure 15.1   The *Client Management Profile*™

The *Client Management Index*™

To calculate the *Client Management Index*™ related to your Profile, simply take your score and divide it by 1,310, the maximum possible score.

So, for example, if your total score is 900, your *Client Management Index*™ is 900/1,310 = 0.69.

This is an indicator of overall Client Management Effectiveness of 69 per cent.

It is also possible to calculate your *Client Management Index*™ for each element of the model by taking the score and dividing it by the maximum for that element. For example, if your *Brand* score was 83 out of a possible 100, your *Client Management Index*™ for Brand is 0.83, an effectiveness level of 83 per cent.

A More In-depth Profile Analysis

If you found this profile interesting and would like a more in-depth analysis of your firm's Client management effectiveness, please contact the author.

A REQUEST FROM THE AUTHOR

As part of my continued interest and research into Client management, it would be appreciated if you would send me by email a copy of your profile summary scores along with your name, job title and firm name. This information will be treated with confidentiality and any reproduction will be anonymised.

Please send a copy of your details and scores to: *jack.berkovi@btopenworld.com*

Thank you.

Appendix 1

How Clients Think and Feel

This exercise is from Chapter 2.

How Clients think and feel – the sequence most favoured is C, H, A, F, D, B, E, G.

Ref	Statement	Suggested order
A	That idea will help to develop our business.	3
B	I am not certain whether they can be consistent.	6
C	They are concerned about our company's performance. Normally suppliers are only interested in getting more business from us.	1
D	Let's hope their support team understands the details.	5
E	I need to have a revised timetable.	7
F	I hope that they can explain how this will work.	4
G	On balance, I think that we will give them a chance.	8
H	It's interesting that they asked those questions, it happens to be a critical issue for us.	2

C They are concerned about our company's performance. Normally suppliers are only interested in getting more business from us.

H It's interesting that they asked those questions, it happens to be a critical issue for us.

The sales person has asked questions and has started to build a rapport.

Statements C and H show that the Client feels important and deserves respect.

A That idea will help to develop our business.

F I hope that they can explain how this will work.

The salesperson has presented ideas.

Statements A and F show that the Client is interested in the supplier's ideas and how they might help.

D   Let's hope their support team understands the details.

B   I am not certain whether they can be consistent.

The salesperson has to understand obstacles to progress.

Statements D and B indicate Client's concerns.

E   I need to have a revised timetable.

G   On balance, I think that we will give them a chance.

The salesperson has handled objections and moved to closure.

Statements E and G indicate a desire and a commitment to buy.

Buyer Profiling

Discovering and Mapping Client Motivations

PART 1: INSTRUCTIONS

Consider significant people (that could make or influence the buying decision) that you met at your most recent Client meetings. Rate each individual against each of the statements below using the following designation:

A   Not really true of him/her

B   Sometimes true of him/her

C   Often true of him/her

D   Always true of him/her

Name of person being profiled _____

Client _____

Job title _____

Statements

1   Likes to set realistic challenges and get things done.   A B C D

2   Tends to be non-assertive and warm.   A B C D

3   Enjoys a good debate and likes competing with people.   A B C D

4   Is concerned about how others regard him/her.   A B C D

5   Is systematic in his/her approach to tasks.   A B C D

6   Is business-like and likes dealings to be to the point.   A B C D

7   Is visibly disturbed by indifference and avoids cool or cold people.   A B C D

8   Likes to take the lead in situations.   A B C D

9   Likes to have a high profile at work.   A B C D

10   Is concerned that others see him/her as effective at work.   A B C D

11   Is cautious about changes which will affect him/her.   A B C D

12   Takes great pride in a completed task.   A B C D

13   Is good at taking risks.   A B C D

14   Quickly forms an opinion and persuades others of its correctness.   A B C D

15   Is concerned about the status he/she has.   A B C D

16   Will begin conversations with a non-business discussion.   A B C D

17   Is actively concerned about the happiness of others at work.   A B C D

18   Tends to set targets which can be comfortably met.   A B C D

19   Tends to react to others opinions rather than initiate them himself/herself.   A B C D

20   Will volunteer for leading positions.   A B C D

21   Takes every opportunity to present ideas to management himself/herself.   A B C D

22   Actively plans his/her own development and progression.   A B C D

23   Looks forward to performance reviews.   A B C D

24   Actively seeks the company of other people.   A B C D

25   Waits until he/she knows people well before introducing his/her ideas.   A B C D

26	Avoids conflict with others if possible.	A B C D
27	Works hard to keep the conversation going and dislikes silence.	A B C D
28	Enjoys recognition publicly for what he/she has done successfully.	A B C D
29	Likes to act as a representative or spokesperson for a group.	A B C D
30	Tends to play safe when making decisions.	A B C D
31	Is concerned about the organisation's financial soundness.	A B C D
32	Likes to set measurable targets.	A B C D
33	Does not work well under close supervision.	A B C D
34	Works hard to create warm personal relationships.	A B C D
35	Lacks self-confidence.	A B C D
36	Tends to dominate conversations with his/her own views.	A B C D
37	Prefers to work in group situations.	A B C D
38	Enjoys new learning situations.	A B C D
39	Reacts badly to criticism.	A B C D
40	Shows sympathy to those who are less fortunate.	A B C D

Part 2: Instructions

IDENTIFYING MOTIVATIONAL FACTORS

Transfer the rating letter given in the questionnaire (A, B, C or D) for each statement to the chart below.

Assign points to each rating (A, B, C, D) at the following values:

A 1   B 4   C 6   D 10

The resulting scores will provide a profile of the person's motivations.

Profiling Buyer Motivations

Table A2.1   Profiling Buyer Motivations Score Chart

ACHIEVEMENT			INFLUENCE			AFFILIATION			SECURITY		
Question	Rating	Value	Question	Rating	Value	Question	Rating	Value	Question	Rating	Value
1			3			2			4		
5			8			7			10		
6			9			16			11		
12			14			17			18		
13			15			24			19		
22			20			26			25		
23			21			27			30		
32			28			34			31		
33			29			37			35		
38			36			40			39		
	Total			Total			Total			Total	

Table A2.2   Example of a Completed Profile of a Buyer

ACHIEVEMENT			INFLUENCE			AFFILIATION			SECURITY		
Question	Rating	Value	Question	Rating	Value	Question	Rating	Value	Question	Rating	Value
1	A	1	3	C	6	2	D	10	4	A	1
5	B	4	8	C	6	7	C	6	10	A	1
6	D	10	9	B	4	16	C	6	11	B	4
12	A	1	14	A	1	17	B	4	18	C	6
13	B	4	15	B	4	24	A	1	19	A	1
22	C	6	20	C	6	26	A	1	25	B	4
23	B	4	21	C	6	27	A	1	30	A	1
32	B	4	28	C	6	34	A	1	31	B	4
33	B	4	29	D	10	37	C	6	35	A	1
38	A	1	36	B	4	40	B	4	39	A	1
	Total	39		Total	53		Total	40		Total	24

So this buyer's highest score is for Influence, followed by Affiliation and Achievement.

Feature, Advantage, Benefit, Evidence Exercise

Suggested Answers

The circle around the appropriate letter shows which of the following statements made by account managers are **Features**, **Advantages**, **Benefits** or **Evidence**.

1 We have specialists with long-term practical experience working with many Clients in your sector.   (F.).....A.......B.......E

      *A **Feature**. A fact about your specialists.*

2 Our expertise allows us to create products that meet all of your requirements.   F.....(A.).....B.......E

      *An **Advantage**. Tells the Client what they can get because of our expertise.*

3 You've said that you want our service to be delivered more quickly. Here is how we can do that by changes we've made.   F.......A.....(.B.).....E

      You've said that you want ...' The Client has expressed a need.

      'Here's how we can achieve that ...' Gives the solution that you propose.

      *A **Benefit**.*

4 We advise our Clients on their asset holdings.   (F.).....A.......B.......E

*A **Feature**. What you do.*

5   Our Client service team will ensure that delivery arrives
correctly and on time.
This is why you have your Client service team, so that
things happen on time.   F.....(A.).....B.......E

*An **Advantage**.*

6   We have an international reputation in the marketplace.
This case study shows how we helped a global
company achieve better results.   F.......A.......B.....(.E)

Evidence.

7   If you want to upgrade your quality as your Clients
are demanding, our new system will help considerably.   F.....(A.).....B.......E

*An **Advantage**. You are saying 'because we have this process, you can
improve your quality'.*

8   If you want advice on how to further improve your
quality, we can give you that advice to ensure
optimum performance.   F.......A.....(B.).....E

'So you want advice …' The Client has expressed a clear Need.

*A **Benefit** statement.*

9   Using the methods we are proposing will ensure
that your staff can understand how and where
improvements are possible.   F.....(A.).....B.......E

*An **Advantage**. What we think you will be able to do because of
the method we are proposing.*

10   You said that timely information on your orders is a
major concern. We can provide you with state-of-the-
art technology responses.   F.....(A.).....B.......E

'You said that timely information is a major concern.' The Client has made a strong problem statement, not a need. An **Advantage** and not a Benefit.

Appendix 4
Strategic Client Planning Checklist

This checklist may help to verify the overall application of detailed planning to a specific Client. On a step-by-step basis, it helps to determine whether certain actions have been completed.

Step 1: Select Opportunities

- Is this Client likely to make a major purchase of my services?

- Is the potential revenue from a sale to this Client worth the investment of my time and effort?

- Is my work with this Client more likely to result in a major sale than other potential Clients in my portfolio?

Step 2: Pre-contact Analysis

- Do I already know what I need to know about this Client's business and industry sector?

- Do I need additional information about the Client's business and industry sector?

- Have I identified where I can get the additional information I need?

- Have I identified some of this Client's primary concerns and possible areas of need?

Step 3: Gain the Commitment of the Decision Maker

- Have I identified the decision maker – the individual authorised to sign an order of the size I am likely to propose?

- Have I identified this Client's key interest or concern?

- Is this Client qualified – are the funds available and do I have the attention of the decision maker to an area of agreed-upon need?

- Is there a commitment that if the solution meets their identified needs and requirements, they will seriously consider buying my product or services?

- Has the decision maker made a commitment to a survey to ascertain specific needs?

Step 4: Identify and Gain Agreement on Needs

- Have I identified the Client's specific needs and requirements?

- Does the Client place an appropriate amount of importance on resolving the need or requirement?

- Do my services offer probable solutions to these needs and requirements?

- Have I gathered the relevant cost factors that will enable me to justify the sale?

- Is the solution I am likely to propose probably cost-justifiable?

- In cost-justifying my possible solutions, have key members of the Client's organisation agreed to the needs and are they likely to support the probable solutions?

- Will the probable solution cause dissatisfaction with existing procedures?

- Has the Client been actively involved in the identification of need and the development of a probable solution?

Step 5: Develop a Solution

- Do I have solutions to agree upon needs that meet the requirements of the Client?

- Have I identified needs that carry top priority with Client management?

- Have I identified the appropriate services?

- Do I have the cost-relevant information I need to cost-justify the solution?

- Is my solution likely to cause the decision maker to take positive action?

Step 6: Cost-Justify Solution

- Have I identified the probable impact areas of my solution?

- Have I identified the changes that these areas affect as a result of implementing the solution?

- Have I identified the extent of these projected changes?

- Have I determined the tangible value of these projected changes?

- Have I identified the non-tangible value of the solutions I am proposing?

Step 7: Obtain Agreement

- Has everyone who will influence the decision to buy agreed with the solution and the cost-justification?

- Have I identified objections or disagreements?

- Have I resolved the objections or disagreements?

Step 8: Prepare Proposal

- Have I identified who will review the proposal?

- Have I selected the most appropriate proposal approach?

- Has everything that is included in the proposal been reviewed and agreed to by each person who will influence the decision?

Step 9: Present and Close

- Is the timing appropriate for presenting the proposal?

- Have I presented the proposal?

- Did I obtain formal agreement that the solution meets the Client's needs and requirements?

- Did I try to close the sale during the presentation?

- Have I countered all objections?

Step 10: Build a Continuing Business Relationship

- Have I monitored the implementation of the solution to assure Client satisfaction?

- Have I measured and reported the actual results from implementation?

- Am I doing everything I can do to identify new requirements?

- Am I taking action to make myself an integral part of the Client's business planning process?

Appendix 5

Client Care Survey 2013

An online survey was conducted by the author and was completed during summer 2013 by 232 participants from professional services firms across the globe. The majority of respondents were members of the *International Managing Partners' Forum* and *Professional Marketing Forum*.

The survey covered a wide variety of questions on Client management and care, and revealed that there is still room for improvement in these areas for many firms. A number of participants provided quotes which are shown at the front section of this book. As a result of the survey, many firms agreed to be interviewed on related topics and their input is featured throughout this book. Where a response is used in this book, the Table number is stated. Respondent profiles are shown after the list of questions.

The *Client Management Model*™ was developed from the survey.

CLIENT CARE SURVEY 2013 QUESTIONS

1. Please advise the capacity in which you are responding to this survey (see respondent profiles).

2. In respect of which section of your firm are you responding?

3. How many people work at the selected section of your firm?

4. How much time on average is spent weekly by the management team at the selected section of your firm with those in equivalent management positions at Clients (i.e. CEO to CEO, FD to FD, etc.)?

5. How does your firm use social media channels (Twitter, LinkedIn, blogs, etc.)? (Table 14.1)

6.   Which social media channels are used by the selected section of your firm to stay in touch with Clients? (Table 14.2)

7.   How many of the Clients of the selected section of your firm are formally treated as 'key'? (Table 9.1)

8.   What proportion of key Clients have a formal service plan? (Table 9.2)

9.   What criteria are used to decide which key Clients do not have a formal service plan?

10.   For what proportion of key Clients do you create business development plans to grow revenues?

11.   What targets are set for Client satisfaction? (Table 4.3)

12.   What proportion of key Clients receive satisfaction reviews? (Table 4.5)

13.   What proportion of non-key Clients have a formal service plan?

14.   What criteria are used to decide which non-key Clients have a formal service plan?

15.   For what proportion of non-key Clients do you create business development plans to grow revenues?

16.   In which areas are formal Client satisfaction targets set for non-key Clients?

17.   What proportion of the non-key Clients receive satisfaction reviews?

18.   How do you compare the level of Client satisfaction at the selected section of your firm with those of equivalent sections at other firms? (Table 4.1)

19.   Approximately how many post-transaction Client satisfaction reviews by channel are *currently* carried out annually by the selected section of your firm? (Table 4.8)

20. Approximately how many post-transaction Client satisfaction reviews by channel do you believe *should* be carried out annually by the selected section of your firm? (Table 4.9)

21. Who at the selected section of your firm receives formal reports based on data from Client satisfaction reviews? (Table 4.4)

22. How many post-transaction Client satisfaction reviews are formally acted on by management at the selected section of your firm? (Table 4.6)

23. How many post-transaction Client satisfaction reviews are formally discussed with Clients?

24. Who follows up commitments made as part of Client satisfaction reviews? (Table 4.7)

25. How does your firm's approach to Client care feature on your firm's website?

26. Do you have a formalised welcome programme for new Clients?

27. Do you have a CRM (Client Relationship Management) process which involves all partners?

28. Do you have a central Client database?

29. How is your central Client database used?

30. Do you provide a Client portal accessible via a secure extranet website?

31. Does your firm have a formal Client service charter?

32. Where is the charter displayed?

33. What sales/marketing collateral is available in your reception area?

34. Do you ask Clients for testimonials?

35. How are Client testimonials used?

36.   Is an external agency used to source Client testimonials?

37.   Does your firm formally reward perceived excellence in Client service?

38.   What form of reward is involved?

39.   Does your firm enter externally organised awards for excellent Client care?

40.   Has your firm won any such awards in the past two years?

41.   If so, which awards have been won?

42.   Which social media channels are used to stay in touch with alumni?

43.   How often do you send personalised communications to your alumni?

Table A5.1   Response Profiles

Respondents	Response
Managing partner/CEO	24.8%
Other board member	12.0%
Other management team member (finance, HR, etc.)	15.7%
Practice group leader	5.4%
In-house marketing expert	42.1%

Type of firm	Response
Global firm	24.5%
Global network/association of independent firms	4.3%
Zonal firm (transatlantic, EMEIA, etc.)	2.7%
Firm based in a national capital	14.1%
National firm (multi-site national presence)	21.8%
Regional firm (multi-site)	21.2%
Regional firm (single site)	11.4%

Sectors	Response
Law	51.1%
Accountancy	17.9%
Property Consultancy	9.2%
Marketing Services	4.9%
Management Consultancy	4.3%
Engineering and Technical Consultancy	2.7%
Patent Attorneys	2.2%
Construction Consultancy	1.6%
Architects/Town Planners	1.6%
Financial Services	1.1%
HR and Recruitment Consultancy	1.1%
Information and Research	1.1%
Insurance	0.5%
Barristers	0.5%

References

The Balanced Scorecard, attributed to Drs Kaplan and Norton.

Ederer, Seiwert and Küstenmacher, *The Customer is King: The 1x1 of Customer Orientation*. Gabel, Offenbach, 2000.

SAVE – Motorola Inc.

Effective Client-Adviser Relationships 2012 report – *Financial Times*, Managing Partners' Forum and Meridian West.

Sustaining High Performance. The Strategic Transformation of a Customer-Focused Learning Organization, Delray Beach, St Lucie Press, Haines & McCoy, Florida, 1995.

The *Net Promoter Score* is attributed to Fred Reichheld, introduced in his *Harvard Business Review* article 'One Number You Need to Grow' in 2003.

Report *Service 2020 – Return on Service*, published by BDO and written by The *Economist* Intelligence Unit, 2014.

From Abraham Maslow's *Theory of Motivation and Personality*, first published in 1954.

Moments of Truth, attributed to the CEO of Scandinavian Airlines, Jan Carlzon.

From Social Media to Social CRM: Reinventing the Customer Relationship – a report published in 2011 by IBM Institute for Business Value.

———

The following exercises and tools were created by colleagues in Marketing Improvements Group. The company was purchased by Robson Rhodes in August 1999 and thereafter ceased to operate under its original name.

How Clients Buy – modified from the original, attributed to my colleague Anthony Culley.

BUYER MOTIVATIONS

BACPOD tool – attributed to my colleague Rob Fear.

CLIENT MAPPING TOOL

Features, Advantages, Benefits, Evidence exercise, modified by the author.

Index